The Host of Gethsemane

Eucharistic Hospitality in the Gethsemane Narratives

Discovering the Garden of Gethsemane as
an Invitation to More Fervent Prayer,
Obedience to the Will of God, and Deeper
Love of the Eucharist

Dr. Annabelle Moseley, Th.D.

⊛ENROUTE

Make the time

En Route Books and Media
5705 Rhodes Ave.
St. Louis, MO, 63109
Contact us at
contactus@enroutebooksandmedia.com

ISBN: 979-8-88870-334-2
E-book ASIN: B0DVSW3DZG
Library of Congress Control Number: 2025932039

Printed in the United States of America
1 3 5 7 9 10 8 6 4 2

A Word from the Author

Through the grace of God, the book you hold before you began as my Doctoral Dissertation, which, once accepted and defended, earned my Doctorate of Theology with a special concentration in the field of Eucharistic Theology. This book could be called an Academic Monograph, in that this is a rigorous study, deeply researched, about Gethsemane. But it is more. It is a labor not only of study, but of love—a defense of Jesus of Gethsemane in every sense of the word. There are very few books dedicated entirely to the subject of Gethsemane. As I researched, I became more struck by this reality and compelled to remedy this abandonment of Our Lord's Agony.

Throughout the long years of research, this thought kept me going…the hope that I would contribute to the study of Theology by putting together an in-depth book about the profound significance of Gethsemane. My hope is that ultimately the *study* of Gethsemane will lead others to a greater *love* of Jesus of Gethsemane. In the words of St. Thomas Aquinas, "love follows knowledge." What is before you is an invitation to draw near—ever-nearer—to the Host of Gethsemane. May you know Our Lord in Gethsemane better, that you may love Him more, and may you watch and pray with Him there, answering His invitation to keep Him company there.

Please keep in mind this was written as a Doctoral Dissertation, and so contains a Bibliography, footnotes, Abstract, Methodology, and other academic elements. The casual reader may wish to skip past such sections, and go right to Chapter One–or they may find themselves enjoying the full journey! May God bless you!

Abstract

The Host of Gethsemane: Eucharistic Hospitality in the Gethsemane Narratives

by Dr. Annabelle Moseley, Th.D.

In the Agony in the Garden described in the Gospels, Jesus's invitation to "stay here and keep watch with me" illuminates Him as the "Host/host" of Gethsemane. This role is displayed in several ways, in that "host" is simultaneously He who welcomes and receives others as guests to join Him in the garden; He the Eucharistic "Host," the Living Bread of the Last Supper just shared; He the "host life" on, in, and through which we live. Also, we, the host (or large number) of faithful souls in the Church, are individually called as guests through prayer, to enter the actual garden of Gethsemane by the grace of God who transcends time and space that we may keep our sorrowful Host/host company, sweetening his "cup of blessing which we bless" through staying awake (watching, adoring).

My goal in this study will be to show how an understanding of Jesus as Host/host in the scriptural accounts of the Garden of Gethsemane can contribute to the field of Eucharistic Theology, and from that, Eucharistic devotion. The importance of Eucharistic Adoration and receiving the Eucharist at the Sacrifice of the Mass will be established through a literary exegetical critique of the Agony in the Garden in the four Gospel accounts, and an examination of the many meanings of the word Host/host. This will show how, like the apostles, we, the faithful host (a large number of people) are invited personally by Jesus (the Host) to be His guests and keep Him company, in a true host-guest relationship (all elements of which will be explored). This dissertation will show the relevance of the Gethsemane narrative to

Eucharistic Theology and the ongoing invitation from Jesus as the Host/host, (in Gethsemane and in the Eucharist).

Contents

vi

Acknowledgements

Dr. Annabelle Moseley, Th.D.

This was written during the Eucharistic Revival, and completed in Summer 2024, a jubilee Anniversary (exactly 350 years from the Sacred Heart apparitions of Jesus to St. Margaret Mary requesting more devotion to the Eucharist and to the Garden of Gethsemane) and so the timing has felt providential. This project could not have happened without the support of my mentors, colleagues, friends, and family. First and foremost, I am abundantly grateful to my Dissertation Director, Fr. Dennis Billy, C.Ss.R. for his guidance with this project. I would like to extend sincere thanks to the members of my Dissertation Reading Committee, and with special thanks to Dr. Sebastian Mahfood, OP. I would like to offer my heartfelt thanks to my dear husband, Mark; and our adorable little boys, Johnny and Charlie. Without their tremendous understanding, patient support, and resounding encouragement, love and humor, it would have been impossible for me to complete my study. In a particular and special way I wish to thank my wonderful parents, Annabelle and Charles Rufino, for their unforgettable love, fervent prayers, wisdom, and support at every stage. Thank you, all, for helping me on my climb up the mountain and into the Garden.

I am grateful for the intercession and wisdom of the Communion of Saints, in particular the patrons saints of this project: St. Therese of Lisieux, Saints Peter, James, and John, Saints Martha and Mary, St. Veronica, Fra Angelico, St. Thomas Aquinas, St. Thomas More, St. Peter Julian Eymard, St. Margaret Mary Alacoque, St. Teresa of the Andes, St. Josemaria Escriva, Ven. Fulton Sheen, St. Manuel Gonzalez Garcia, Pope St. John Paul II, Pope Benedict XVI, and St. Padre Pio.

Dedication

To Jesus of Gethsemane

"...*We who have taken refuge might be strongly encouraged to hold fast to the hope that lies before us. This we have as an anchor of the soul, sure and firm, which reaches into the interior behind the veil, where Jesus has entered on our behalf as forerunner, becoming high priest forever according to the order of Melchizedek.*"

–Heb 6:10-20

Introduction

In the Agony in the Garden described in the Gospels, Jesus's invitation to "stay here and keep watch with me" illuminates Him as the "Host/host" of Gethsemane. This role is displayed in several ways, in that "host" is simultaneously He who welcomes and receives others as guests to join Him in the garden; He the Eucharistic "Host," the Living Bread of the Last Supper just shared; He the "host life" on, in, and through which we live. Also, we, the host (or large number) of faithful souls in the Church, are individually called as guests through prayer, to enter the actual garden of Gethsemane by the grace of God who transcends time and space that we may keep our sorrowful Host/host company, sweetening his "cup of blessing which we bless" through staying awake (watching, adoring).

This dissertation will show how an understanding of Jesus as Host/host in the scriptural accounts of the Garden of Gethsemane can contribute to the field of Eucharistic Theology, and from that, Eucharistic devotion. The importance of Eucharistic Adoration and sharing the Eucharistic Meal will be established through a literary exegetical critique of the Agony in the Garden in the four Gospel accounts and an examination of the varied meanings of the word Host/host. This will show how, like the apostles, we, the faithful host (large number of people) are invited personally by Jesus the Host, to be his guests and keep him company, in a true host-guest relationship (all elements of which will be explored). The dissertation will be important in its showing the relevance of the Gethsemane narrative for Eucharistic Theology and an ongoing invitation from Jesus the Host/host.

The topic is of great significance because, in the words of Pope Benedict XVI, "nowhere else in sacred Scripture do we gain so deep an insight into the inner mystery of Jesus as in the prayer on the Mount of Olives…"[1] and supporting this assertion, the Gethsemane narrative has been written about in great detail by pivotal scholars from the early church fathers to Pope Benedict XVI in recent years.[2]

Also, looking broadly, I have found that scholars consistently assert the importance of the Psalms sung at the close of the Last Supper, which show Jesus as the new David, the fulfillment of Old Testament prophecy. The Psalms continue as Jesus and the apostles leave supper and enter the Garden. Scholars agree that the Psalms sung were the "Little Hallel"[3] during dinner and then the "Great Hallel"[4] as they left. Praying these Psalms of Israel is an "element fundamental for understanding the figure of Jesus, but also for understanding the Psalms themselves, which in him could be said to acquire a new subject, a new mode of presence, and an extension beyond Israel into universality."[5] The psalms are "a verbal icon of Christ and of His church, a revelation into Revelation. 'In Psalms, say the Fathers, Christ Himself and his Church are praying, are crying and are speaking…'"[6]

The Psalms are a hinge prayer between the Old Testament and New Testament readings in our Eucharistic celebration in the Liturgy of the Word. The Psalms are an important part of our worship in Masses said throughout the world, sharing the depths of our responses

---

1. Benedict XVI, *Jesus of Nazareth* (New York: Rizzoli, 2009), 157.

2. David M. Stanley, *Jesus in Gethsemane: The Early Church Reflects on the Suffering of Jesus*, (New York: Paulist Press, 1980).

3. Ps 113 (New American Bible, Revised Edition / *The Catholic Study Bible,* Oxford University Press, 1990; all subsequent Bible citations are from this translation unless specifically noted).

4. Ps 114-118.

5. Benedict, *Jesus of Nazareth*, 146.

6. Vasile Mihoc, "The Messianic Prophecies of the Old Testament", in *Das Alte Testament als christliche Bibel in orthodoxer und westlicher Sicht*, Ivan Dimitrov, James D G Dunn, Karl-Wilhelm Niebuhr (eds), (Tübingen: Mohr Siebeck, 2004), 47.

to the Lord with early followers of Christ, and even in the prayers, hymns, and utterances of Jesus in Gethsemane.

St. Augustine writes this in his commentary on the Psalms:

Lord, I have cried to you, hear me. (Psalm 141:1) This is a prayer we can all say. This is not my prayer, but that of the whole Christ. Rather, it is said in the name of his body. When Christ was on earth he prayed in his human nature, and prayed to the Father in the name of his body, and when he prayed, drops of blood flowed from his whole body. So it is written in the Gospel: *Jesus prayed with earnest prayer, and sweated blood*. What is this blood streaming from his whole body but the martyrdom of the whole Church?"[7]

The bloody martyrdom of the Church and the Eucharist (our Host in Gethsemane) are connected. In the words of Bishop Abraham Mar Julios, "the mystery of the Eucharist, and the mystery of martyrdom, are intimately related."[8]

By connecting the work of such scholars I find solid backing for my assertion that the shedding of the blood in Gethsemane by Jesus, our Host, is Eucharistic. Further, in the lauded work, The Agony of Jesus, St. Padre Pio writes of the blood shed in Gethsemane, "I want to offer Thee to the Father. It is the Blood of His well-beloved Son, the God-Man, which ascends to His throne to pacify His justice, offended by our sins. He is superabundantly satisfied."[9] St. Padre Pio, a

---

7. Augustine, "Commentary on the Psalms", quoted in *The Liturgy of the Hours Vol 2,* (New York: Catholic Book Publishing Corp, 1976), Tuesday of the Second Week of Lent, 168-169.

8. Abraham Mar Julios, 2017, "Confession of Faith, Eucharist and Martyrdom", *Homilitic & Pastoral Review*, September 27, 2017, www.hprweb.com/2017/09/confession-of-faith-eucharist-and-martyrdom/.

9. Padre Pio, *The Agony of Jesus,* (North Carolina: Tan Books, 1992), 32.

consummate priest, instinctually desires to offer the blood of Jesus in Gethsemane as a sacrifice to the Father just as he would in a Mass.

Catholic Liturgy further supports my assertion that Gethsemane is a Eucharistic location into which we are invited by the Host. As described perfectly by The Most Reverend John O. Barres, Bishop of Rockville Centre, New York, On Holy Thursday:

> The Evening Mass of the Lord's Supper concludes in a unique way. Following the distribution of Holy Communion, the priest removes the Blessed Sacrament from the tabernacle, leaving one ciborium filled with consecrated hosts on the altar. Then, after saying the closing prayer of the Mass, the priest comes to the foot of the sanctuary, faces the altar and the Blessed Sacrament, and incenses it while kneeling. Then, with a humeral veil around his shoulders, he carries the Blessed Sacrament and leads the people in a procession to a place of repose. This is a reenactment of Our Lord's departure from the Cenacle at the conclusion of the Last Supper. He and His Apostles crossed the Kidron Valley and ascended the Mount of Olives, where the Lord asked them to stay awake with Him and pray. But they fell asleep...[10]

Then the priest processes with the Blessed Sacrament, and as Bishop Barres describes:

> ...it is a reenactment of the movement of Jesus and the band of Apostles that night following the Last Supper. The repository is a place near the church, and sometimes in

---

10. John O. Barres, "The Great Week: A Pilgrimage with the Lord in Holy Week: A Pastoral Letter from Bishop John O. Barres to the People of God of the Diocese of Rockville Centre", *The Long Island Catholic*, March 3, 2020.

another building or at a bit of a distance, where the Blessed Sacrament will be reposed for a time. The repository represents the Garden of Gethsemane. The people follow in procession, taking the part of the Apostles and disciples of the Lord. Upon arriving at the place of reposition, there is an altar erected where the Blessed Sacrament may be kept for the faithful to adore until midnight. This enables us to fulfill the request that the Lord made to the Apostles which they failed to accomplish: "Remain here and keep watch with me." (Mt 26:38)

…It is as if we ourselves are in Jerusalem two-thousand years ago, privileged to be with the Lord during these events that won our salvation. It also enables us to console Our Lord in the present for what He experienced in the past."[11]

Thus, the invitation to stay awake and pray with Christ our host, is still available to us.

I will consider the title of priest/high priest as it relates to Christ in the Garden, both in the subject of his prayer, and the posture of kneeling and laying prostrate before the Father. These are both markers of a Eucharistic theme as it relates to the Host and presiding priest/host of our liturgical celebrations and sacraments. In the Homily of the Most Reverend Placido Rodriguez at the Holy Mass at the Garden of Gethsemane as part of the Hispanic Bishops' Pilgrimage to the Holy Land on January 22, 2018 he states, "we know that Jesus prayed at this Garden of Gethsemane. We can easily imagine Jesus fully prostrated on this holy monument, where drops of blood make

---

11. Barres, "The Great Week".

this monument an altar of God, uttering his 'priestly prayers' and truly being heard, piercing the Heavens."[12]

An annual tradition in the Holy Land, on July first, the Feast of the Most Precious Blood, is that red rose petals are scattered all across the rock which is said to be the one upon which Jesus prostrated himself in prayer, the one upon which he cried tears of blood. The Solemnity of the Most Precious Blood, an Extremely Eucharistic feast closely tied to Corpus Christi, is celebrated annually in Gethsemane where Jesus shed his blood:

> The Custos of the Holy Land, Fr. Francesco Patton, who celebrated the Eucharist, underlined the Franciscan aspect of this solemnity. "St. Francis mentions the Blood of Christ on numerous occasions," he said during his comment on the Gospel, "as though to remind us that the whole life of Jesus is given for love." The Custos, following in the steps of St Francis, underlined the close bond between the place of the celebration (Gethsemane) and two other places in Jerusalem: the Cenacle, where Jesus gave the sacrament of his body and his blood and Calvary where blood was shed for our salvation.[13]

Jesus suffered in the Garden for many people in the world, invoking the tradition of suffering encapsulated in the Psalms of the Old Testament and Old Testament laments.

St. Thomas More asserts in *De Tristitia Christi*:

---

12. Placido Rodriguez, "Homily Bishop Rodriguez Garden of Gethsemane 01 22 2018", *USCCB,* January 22, 2018, www.usccb.org/resources/homily-bishop-rodriguez-garden-gethsemane-01-22-2018/.

13. Giovanni Malaspina, "Gethsemane: the Most Precious Blood of Jesus," *Custodia Terrae Sanctae: Franciscans serving the Holy Land,* July 1, 2019, accessed September 2021, www.custodia.org/en/news/gethsemane-most-precious-blood-jesus/.

…as for those drops of blood which flowed like sweat from his whole body, even if they (the apostles) had later clearly seen the stain left on the ground, I think they would have drawn almost any number of conclusions without guessing the right one, since it was an unprecedented phenomenon for anyone to sweat blood…it seems most likely that (he spoke of these things)…after He rose from the dead and there could no longer be any doubt that He was God, His most loving mother and beloved disciples heard from his own most holy lips this detailed account, point by point, of His human suffering, the knowledge of which benefit both them and (through them) others who would come after them, and which no one could have recounted except Christ Himself.[14]

Pope Saint John Paul II's writings help to back up and give credence to my assertion of the Gethsemane Jesus as "Host/host." Although one is hard-pressed to find many writings describing the blood shed by Jesus in Gethsemane as Eucharistic in so many words, Pope Saint John Paul II leaves no doubt that the blood is Eucharistic by writing this in his Encyclical on the Eucharist, "Jesus leaves the Upper Room, descends with his disciples to the Kidron valley and goes to the Garden of Olives…Christ in prayer was filled with anguish so that 'his sweat became like drops of blood falling on the ground.'"[15] The blood which shortly before he had given to the Church as the drink of salvation in the sacrament of the Eucharist, began to be shed; its outpouring would then be completed on Golgotha to become the means of our redemption: "Christ…as high priest of the good things to come…entered once for all the Holy Place, taking not the blood of

---

14. Thomas More, "The Valencia Manuscript", in *Complete Works of St. Thomas More, Volume 14, Part I, De Tristitia Christi*, ed. Clarence H. Miller (Connecticut: Yale University Press, 1976), 191-193.

15. Lk 22:44.

goats and calves but his own blood, thus securing an eternal redemption (Heb 9:11-12)"[16]

The cup plays great significance in Jewish tradition going back to Melchizedek. And the Passover meal includes four cups of wine, each highly symbolic. In the Last Supper meal, Jesus declines the fourth cup. In Gethsemane, Jesus asks the Father that the cup pass from him if it's possible and then obediently submits to the Father's Will, purposing to drink it. Many scholars assert the importance of the four cups of wine in the Passover meal in connection to the Gethsemane narratives. The first cup was taken as part of the introductory rites, the Kiddish cup, the cup of salvation. The second cup was the Haggadah cup and it signifies and commemorates the Israelites' freedom from Egypt. The third cup that accompanies the eating of the meal, the 'Berakah' is the cup of redemption and blessing. At the Last Supper this cup was the cup of the new covenant. The fourth cup, the Hallel cup, the cup of praise and celebration, was not taken by Jesus.[17] Brant Pitre, quoting David Daub, includes this information:

> There is…in Matthew and Mark a reference also to the fourth and last cup of the Passover liturgy. It is contained in the words: "I will not drink henceforth of this fruit of the vine until I drink it new in my father's kingdom" or "in the kingdom of God." The meaning is that the fourth cup will not be taken, as would be the normal thing, at a subsequent stage of the service; it will be postponed till the kingdom is established…the notice that "when they had sung a hymn they went out into the mount of Olives" now acquires a fuller sense. The implication is that they go out…without

---

16. John Paul II, *On the Eucharist: Ecclesia de Eucharistia*, (Washington, D.C: USCCB, 2003), 3.

17. Brant Pitre, *Jesus and the Jewish Roots of the Eucharist*, (New York: Doubleday, 2011), 158-160.

drinking the fourth cup and probably also without reciting "the blessing of the song." This portion of the liturgy is postponed till the arrival of the actual, final Kingdom...[18]

Pitre continues to explain how astonishing this must have been to the Apostles:

In other words, when the Last Supper is viewed through Jewish eyes, *Jesus did not actually finish his last Passover meal.* This is extremely significant. Jesus not only altered the meal by focusing on his own body and blood rather than the flesh of the paschal lamb. He also seems to have deliberately left the Passover liturgy incomplete, by vowing not to drink of the 'fruit of the vine' and by leaving the Upper Room without doing so.

It is hard to overestimate just how puzzled the disciples must have been by such actions...Every other Jewish Passover they had ever attended would have ended with the celebratory drinking of the fourth cup, the *hallel* "cup of praise." But this Passover was cut short. This meal was different. Why did Jesus vow not to drink of the Passover wine until the coming of the kingdom of God? Why did he leave the Upper Room after singing the hymn?...In the Garden of Gethsemane, in the midst of his distress, Jesus prayed to the Father three times about the "cup" that he must drink....Jesus is praying to the Father about the fourth cup, the final cup of the Passover liturgy.[19]

_____

18. David Daub, *The New Testament and Rabbinic Judaism* (Peabody, Mass.: Hendrickson, 1995), 330-331, quoted from Pitre, *Jesus and the Jewish Roots of the Eucharist*, 162.

19. Pitre, *Jesus and the Jewish Roots of the Eucharist*, 164.

Jesus abstained from the fourth cup (the cup of consummation) until the moment just before he, the Paschal Lamb, would die. Pitre continues:

> According to John, Jesus not only accepted the wine of his execution, he explicitly *requested* a drink at the moment before his death:

> After this Jesus, knowing that all was now finished, said (to fulfill the Scriptures), "*I thirst.*" A bowl full of sour wine stood there; so they put a sponge full of wine on hyssop and held it to his mouth. *When Jesus had received the wine, he said, "It is finished"*; and he bowed his head and gave up his spirit (John 19:23-30).

> ...when we remember Jesus' vow at the Last Supper, and his prayer about drinking the "cup" in Gethsemane, then the meaning of Jesus' last word becomes clear. It means that Jesus did in fact drink the fourth cup of the Jewish Passover. It means he did in fact finish the Last Supper. But he did not do it in the Upper Room. He did it on the cross...at the very moment of his death."[20]

Therefore, I assert the Last Supper is still ongoing in the Garden of Gethsemane and that is just another reason that therein Jesus is the Host/host.

Scholars assert the importance of the garden as location for Gethsemane (as with Golgotha) to refer to and evoke Paradise and the Fall. Aquinas explains, "Alcuin wrote: Over the brook Cedron, i.e. of cedars. It is the genitive in the Greek. He goes over the brook, i.e.

---

20. Pitre, *Jesus and the Jewish Roots of the Eucharist*, 167-168.

drinks of the brook of His Passion. Where there was a garden, that the sin which was committed in a garden, He might blot out in a garden."[21] It is clear that "early Christians conceived of Gethsemane as analogous to the garden of Eden in the divine plan for human redemption. The sinful actions of the first Adam are contrasted with the prayerful obedience of the second Adam–Jesus Christ. Other Christians claim that Jesus' examples in Gethsemane gave rise to the custom of kneeling for prayer."[22] The importance of the location known as "The Mount of Olives" is clear through the significance of the word "olives," and the fact that there was an oil press on the mount. William Saunders explains:

> Throughout the Bible, various references indicate the importance of olive oil in daily life. Oil was used in cooking, particularly in the making of bread, that basic food substance for nourishment (e.g. Nm 11:7-9); as a fuel for lamps (e.g. Mt 25:1-9); and as a healing agent in medicine (e.g. Is 1:6 and Lk 10:34). Moreover, with oil the Jews anointed the head of a guest as a sign of welcome (e.g. Lk 7:46), beautified one's appearance (e.g. Ru 3:3), and prepared a body for burial (e.g. Mk 16:1). In religious practices, the Jews also used oil to dedicate a memorial stone in honor of God (e.g. Gn 28:18); to consecrate the meeting tent, the ark of the covenant, the table, the lampstand, the laver, the altar of incense and the altar of holocausts (e.g. Ex 31:26-29); and to offer sacrifices (e.g. Ex 29:40). The use of oil was clearly a part of the daily life

---

21. Thomas Aquinas, *Catena Aurea: Commentary on the Four Gospels vol. IV, St. John*, trans. John Henry Newman (London: Baronius Press, 2013), 546.

22. David Noel Freedman, *The Anchor Bible Dictionary, Vol. 2*, (New York: Doubleday, 1992), 997.

of the people...Given this heritage, the early Church adopted the use of olive oil for its sacramental rituals.[23]

I will explore all of the pertinent components and uses of olive oil in connection to the priestly role of Host/host in Gethsemane and how the olive press near which he prays is relevant as Jesus also is "crushed" in his spirit, and near which he draws us as well.

Scholars assert the importance of the way Jesus prays in Gethsemane as an exemplar for His Church to follow and as a demonstration of Christ's high priesthood:

> Significant...however, is the prayer of Jesus in Luke 12: 27-29. The prayer itself, "Father, save me from this hour" (v. 27) has been variously punctuated – as a hypothetical question (RSV, NIV) or as a petition (NEB)...In an attempt to demonstrate Christ's qualifications for the high priesthood, the author of Hebrews utilizes material reminiscent of the Gethsemane tradition. This connection is suggested generally by the observation that the Gethsemane story is the only account in our canonical Gospels that comes close to this portrayal of Jesus praying with "strong crying tears to the one who was able to save him."[24]

Scholars assert Gethsemane as the basis for the doctrine of the two wills of Jesus as developed by St. Maximus the Confessor. Harrison Ayre writes:

---

23. William Saunders, "The Use of Sacramental Oils", *Catholic Education Resource Center*, accessed September 2021, www.catholiceducation.org/en/culture/catholic-contributions/the-use-of-sacramental-oils.html.

24. Joel B. Green and Scot McKnight, *Dictionary of Jesus and the Gospels*, (Illinois: InterVarsity Press, 2013), 268.

…who, in meditating on the words of Jesus in the Garden of Gethsemane, notes where Jesus asks the Father to take his suffering from him. Yet, Jesus concludes, "But not what I will but what you will." Here St. Maximus notes the two wills at play and states that it is the moment where the Son most perfectly draws the human will into a complete union with the divine will. It is the moment where Jesus as both man and God takes what is ours and unites it ever more perfectly with God. It is a part of his action of redemption of our humanity.[25]

Scholars assert also the importance of Gethsemane as part of Christ's Passion. St. Leo the Great says that "the Passion is prolonged until the end of time."[26]

The philosopher Pascal meditates on the agony of Jesus, asserting, "Christ will be in agony until the end of the world. During this time, we must not sleep."[27]

Pascal continues this meditation from the perspective of Our Lord:

I was thinking of you in my agony: Those drops of blood I shed for you. Do you always want to cost me the blood of my humanity, without you shedding a tear? I am more of a friend to you than this or that one, because I have done more for you than they, and they would never

25. Harrison Ayre, 2023, "Christology 101: Christ's Two Wills", *Simply Catholic,* June 6, 2023, accessed April 2024, simplycatholic.com/christology-101-christs-two-wills/.

26. St. Leo the Great, "Sermo" 70, 5: PL 54, 383, quoted by Raniero Cantalamessa, "Meditation on the Passion", Sec 5, *Franciscan Penance Library*, n.d., accessed September 2020, www.franciscanpenancelibrary.com/meditation-on-the-passion/.

27. Blaise Pascal, Pensées n. 553 Br., quoted by Raniero Cantalamessa, "Meditation on the Passion", Sec 5.

suffer what I have suffered for you, they would never die for you in the moment of your infidelity and cruelties, as I have done and am willing to do in my chosen ones and in the Holy Sacrament.[28]

In terms of my thesis' assertion of Jesus as "host" in Gethsemane, I will build upon the words of Benedict XVI:

...At Gethsemane [Jesus] invites Peter, James and John to stay closer to him...although Jesus arrives "alone" at the place in which he was to stop and pray, he wants at least three disciples to be near him, to be in a closer relationship with him. This is a spatial closeness, a plea for solidarity at the moment in which he feels death approaching, but above all it is closeness in prayer, in a certain way to express harmony with him at the very moment when he is preparing to do the Father's will to the very end; and it is an invitation to every disciple to follow him on the Way of [the] Cross.[29]

Methodology

The disciplinary perspective for this dissertation is primarily Eucharistic Theology, and the primary method for researching this topic will be a Literary Critique rooted in the Catholic Tradition as elucidated in the document "The Interpretation of the Bible in the

---

28. Pascal, Pensées n. 553.

29. Benedict XVI, "The Prayer of Jesus in Gethsemane", in *The Prayer of Jesus*, (Washington, DC: United States Catholic Conference Inc–Libreria Editrice Vaticana, 2013), 63.

Church," as presented by the Pontifical Biblical Commission to Pope John Paul II in 1993.

One form of literary critique, according to the Pontifical Biblical Commission, is Tradition criticism. "Tradition criticism situates texts in the stream of tradition and attempts to describe the development of this tradition over the course of time."[30] Much of my work explains how Jesus in Gethsemane is the fulfillment of Old Testament prophecies regarding the New Covenant of the New Testament, and the Sacrifice of the Paschal Mystery. For, "the Bible is not a compilation of texts unrelated to each other; rather, it is a gathering together of a whole array of witnesses from one great tradition."[31] My work also shows how the New Testament Gethsemane pericopes are texts rooted in the streams of Eucharistic tradition, developed over the course of time, but anticipated in Gethsemane.

One scholarly approach based on Tradition is the Canonical Approach. This "aims to carry out the theological task of interpretation more successfully by beginning from within an explicit framework of faith: the Bible as a whole. To achieve this, it interprets each biblical text in the light of the canon of Scriptures, that is to say, of the Bible received as the norm of faith by a community of believers. It seeks to situate each text within the single plan of God…The procedures are often midrashic in nature…each individual book only becomes biblical in the light of the canon as a whole…But above all, the church reads the Old Testament in light of the paschal mystery…"[32] Further, the approach by the history of the influence of the text (*Wirkungsgeschichte*) will be employed, as this approach, "attempts to evaluate the importance of the role played by tradition in finding meaning in biblical texts."[33]

30. The Pontifical Biblical Commission, *The Interpretation of the Bible in the Church,* (Vatican City: Libreria Editrice Vaticana, 1993), 6.

31. The Pontifical Biblical Commission, *Interpretation of the Bible*, 11.

32. The Pontifical Biblical Commission, *Interpretation of the Bible*, 11-12.

33. The Pontifical Biblical Commission, *Interpretation of the Bible*, 13.

Part of the Methodology employed will be interpreting the meaning of inspired scripture, through the fuller sense. "The term *fuller sense (sensus plenior)*, which is relatively recent...is defined as a deeper meaning of the text, intended by God but not clearly expressed by the human author. Its existence in the biblical text comes to be known when one studies the text in light of other biblical texts which utilize it or in its relationship with the internal development of a revelation."[34] This methodology asserts that "the relationship between Scripture and the events which bring it to fulfillment is not one of simple material correspondence. On the contrary, there is mutual illumination and a progress that is a dialectic: what becomes clear is that Scripture reveals the meaning of events, and that events reveal the meaning of Scripture."[35] For example, "right from the start of his public ministry, Jesus adopted a personal and original stance different from the accepted interpretation of his age, that of the scribes and Pharisees...above all, in his attitude of welcome...(which) represented a most profound fidelity to the will of God expressed in Scripture."[36] This welcome is paramount to understanding the Host/host inviting His guests to Gethsemane.

The methodology employed herein will also make use of interpretation of the tradition of the Church, specifically the formation of the Canon which is inspired by the Holy Spirit. Within the Canon is Patristic Exegesis, which comes from the fathers of the Church. "Within the broader current of the great tradition, the particular contribution of patristic exegesis consists in this: to have drawn out from the totality of Scripture the basic orientations which shaped the doctrinal tradition of the church and to have provided a rich theological teaching for the instruction and spiritual sustenance of the faithful."[37]

---

34. The Pontifical Biblical Commission, *Interpretation of the Bible*, 24.
35. The Pontifical Biblical Commission, *Interpretation of the Bible*, 25.
36. The Pontifical Biblical Commission, *Interpretation of the Bible*, 25.
37. The Pontifical Biblical Commission, *Interpretation of the Bible*, 28.

Allegory also has an important place here. The church fathers' recourse to allegory "stems…from the conviction that the Bible, as God's book, was given by God to his people, the church. In principle, there is nothing in it which is to be set aside as out-of-date or completely lacking meaning. God is constantly speaking to his Christian people a message that is ever-relevant for their time."[38]

The task of exegesis in this work is summarized well in "The Interpretation of the Bible in the Church," as presented by the Pontifical Biblical Commission to Pope John Paul II in these words: "Although each book of the Bible was written with its own particular end in view and has its own specific meaning, it takes on a deeper meaning when it becomes part of the *canon* as a whole. The exegetical task includes therefore bringing out the truth of Augustine's dictum: *"Novum testamentum in Vetere latet, et in Novo Vetus patet"* (The New Testament lies hidden in the Old, and the Old becomes clear in the New")…Exegetes have also to explain the relationship that exists between the Bible and the *church*."[39]

The other methodology being used is use of the Bible in the Liturgy. "…It is above all through the liturgy that Christians come into contact with Scripture, particularly during the Sunday celebration of the Eucharist. In principle, the liturgy, and especially the sacramental liturgy, the high point of which is the eucharistic celebration, brings about the most perfect actualization of the Biblical texts, for the liturgy places the proclamation in the midst of the community of believers, gathered around Christ so as to draw near to God. Christ is then "present in his word, because it is he himself who speaks when sacred Scripture is read in the church."[40]

Along with use of the Bible in the Liturgy, "…the Liturgy of the Hours makes selections from the Book of Psalms to help the Christian community pray. Hymns and prayers are all filled with the

---

38. The Pontifical Biblical Commission, *Interpretation of the Bible*, 28.
39. The Pontifical Biblical Commission, *Interpretation of the Bible*, 31.
40. The Pontifical Biblical Commission, *Interpretation of the Bible*, 37.

language of the Bible and the symbolism it contains. How necessary it is, therefore, that participation in the liturgy be prepared for and accompanied by the practice of reading Scripture."[41]

My sources include Scripture (primarily the New American Bible Revised Edition,) biblical commentaries, sermons of the early Church Fathers, Aquinas's commentary on the four Gospels in the *Catena Aurea*, and papal writings, especially those of Benedict XVI. Pertinent Catholic art history has also been consulted on the subjects of Gethsemane, the Agony in the Garden, and the correlation between Jesus as host in the Garden and the Eucharistic Host. The primary academic research for this study has been conducted in seminary theological libraries, and through books, patristic sources, and academic journals.

While it is the practice of many scholars to begin analysis with the Gospel of Mark because "Mark was written first, and both Matt[sic] and Luke drew on it,"[42] I depart from that practice, and instead, begin with the Gospel of Matthew. It indeed must be remembered that the Gospel of Mark was written between "60-75, most likely between 68-73…by…Mark, the follower and 'interpreter' of Peter, usually identified as the John Mark of Acts, whose mother had a house in Jerusalem;"[43] whereas the Gospel of Matthew was written later, between "80-90, give or take a decade…by…Matthew, a tax-collector among the Twelve."[44]

It must be acknowledged that there is a two-source and a four-source hypothesis regarding where the Gospel writers sourced their material:

> The two-source hypothesis is predicated upon the following observations: Matthew and Luke used Mark, both for its

41. The Pontifical Biblical Commission, *Interpretation of the Bible*, 38.

42. Raymond E. Brown, *An Introduction to the New Testament: The Abridged Edition*, (New Haven, CT: Yale University Press, 2016), 38.

43. Brown, *An Introduction to the New Testament*, 45.

44. Brown, *An Introduction to the New Testament*, 59.

narrative material as well as for the basic structural outline of chronology of Jesus' life. Matthew and Luke use a second source, which is called Q (from German Quelle, "source"), not extant, for the sayings (logia) found in common in both of them. Thus, Mark and Q are the main components of Matthew and Luke. In both Matthew and Luke there is material that is peculiar to each of their Gospels; this material is probably drawn from some other sources, which may be designated M (material found only in Matthew's special source) and L (material found only in Luke's special source). This is known as the four-document hypothesis, which was elaborated in 1925 by B.H. Streeter, an English biblical scholar. The placement of Q material in Luke and Matthew disagrees at certain points according to the needs and theologies of the addressees of the gospels, but in Matthew the Marcan chronology is the basic scheme into which Q is put. Mark's order is kept, on the whole, by Matthew and Luke, but, where it differs, at least one agrees with Mark. After chapter 4 in Matthew and Luke, not a single passage from Q is in the same place. Q was a source written in Greek as was Mark, which can be demonstrated by word agreement.[45]

So as preeminent Scriptural scholar Raymond Brown asserts, Mark was written first. I acknowledge this sequence, yet this dissertation begins with Matthew, in the interests of the Gethsemane narratives.

"While modern Gospel courses give Mark the most attention among the Synoptics, Matt[sic] stood first in the great ancient biblical

---

45. H. Grady Davis, Frederick Fyvie Bruce, "The Synoptic Problem", *Encyclopaedia Britannica,* last modified February 9, 2023, accessed July 2023, www.britannica.com/topic/biblical-literature/The-Synoptic-problem.

codices, and its organization and clarity have historically given this Gospel priority as the Church's teaching instrument."[46] I, too, give Matthew priority in this study of the host of Gethsemane. Firstly, because we will discover how the Gethsemane narrative unfolds as it is read in order of placement in the Gospels. Secondly, because while both Matthew and Mark are very similar, Matthew's Gospel begins with the genealogy of Jesus, and within that framework, enables me to discuss the Matthean Gethsemane pericope, through the lens of the roots of the primordial Garden of Scripture.

An Account of How This Topic Will Contribute to the Body of Knowledge and Understanding in the Field, or My Original Contribution to Scholarship in this Area as a Whole

The contribution I will make to the field is captured in my thesis statement that Jesus is both Host and host of Gethsemane, and that the Agony in the Garden narrative is Eucharistic. My contribution will reveal the repeated mention of the cup in Gethsemane and the act of sweating blood in the Garden as inherently Eucharistic (thereby showing Jesus as "Host") and the act of personally inviting the apostles to stay and keep watch as inherently hospitable (like a "host"). The request "stay with me" shows God (our host) looking for companionship from us.

The Church highlights the Last Supper as the Institution of the Eucharist. My thesis will urge: the significance of the Eucharist at the Last Supper is not concluded in the Upper Room, therefore the reception of the Host is not concluded there either…it continues into Gethsemane just as the Host/host continues into Gethsemane.

Just as Jesus in the Cenacle "took a towel and tied it around his waist. Then he poured water into a basin and began to wash the disciples' feet and dry them with the towel around his waist,"[47] and was

---

46. Brown, *An Introduction to the New Testament*, 58.
47. Jn 13:4-5.

therefore the most incomparably hospitable host imaginable, Jesus continues hosting his apostles (and through them, us) in Gethsemane as he tells them, "Remain here and keep watch with me."[48] Oftentimes in Scripture, Jesus is depicted as retreating to pray alone:

> …That night too Jesus prepares for personal prayer. However, this time something new happens: it seems that he does not want to be left alone. Jesus would often withdraw from the crowd and from the disciples themselves "to a lonely place" (Mk 1:35) or he would go up "to the mountain," (cf. Mk 6:46) St. Mark says. Instead at Gethsemane he invites Peter, James, and John to stay closer to him. They are the disciples he called upon to be with him on the Mount of the Transfiguration (cf. Mk 9:2-13). This closeness of the three during his prayer in Gethsemane is important.[49]

For this night, instead of going on his own, he hosts them, inviting intimacy and companionship for those who would answer his call to watch and pray. "As a companionable gesture so that Jesus will not be alone. Matthew's addition of 'with me' turns the phrase in this direction and underlines Jesus' unity with his disciples."[50]

Psalm 116 includes this verse: "I will raise the cup of salvation," and thus the very songs (Psalms) Jesus and the apostles sing on the way to the garden foreshadow their destination, in which Jesus will say, "Shall I not drink the cup that the Father gave me?"[51]

---

48. Mt 26:38.

49. Benedict, *The Prayer of Jesus*, 62-63.

50. Raymond E. Brown, *The Death of the Messiah Volume One*, (New York: Doubleday, 1994), 156.

51. Jn 18:11.

In Psalm 117, one of the final verses is "Join in procession with leafy branches up to the horns of the altar."[52] Therefore, one can conclude that as they are singing this, they arrive among actual leafy branches, the trees of Gethsemane, and having climbed the Mount of Olives, they have made their way "up to the horns of the altar," in that place where olives are pressed and where the Host's sacrifice continues, pressed in between the Last Supper and the Passion. The Agony in the Garden is an important bridge between the Last Supper and the Cross, and thus, this moment of the Passion contains elements of the un-bloody sacrifice of the Last Supper (as the "cup" is referenced in Gethsemane,) and the bloody sacrifice of Calvary (as the literal bloody sweat is referenced in Gethsemane). There is a chalice at the Mass of the Last Supper. There is a chalice at Cavalry, which Jesus drinks when he said, "It is finished."[53] This is the cup that Jesus referred to when he said at the Lord's Supper, "Amen, I say to you, I shall not drink again the fruit of the vine until the day I drink it new in the kingdom of God."[54] Immediately after He says this, it is written: "Then, after singing a hymn, they went out to the Mount of Olives."[55] There in Gethsemane, Jesus will once again encounter the chalice, "Take this cup away from me, but not what I will but what you will."[56] Though His body culminates in suffering at Golgotha, His soul's apex of agony is in Gethsemane, where He sweats blood.

The singing of the Psalms, beginning at the Last Supper and continuing into the Garden, serves as a kind of bridge connecting the Last Supper to Gethsemane, and past to present. Benedict XVI explains:

---

52. Ps 118:27.
53. Jn 19:30.
54. Mk 14:25.
55. Mk 14:26.
56. Mk 14:36.

This process of appropriation and reinterpretation, which begins with Jesus' praying of the Psalms, is a typical illustration of the unity of the Two Testaments, as taught to us by Jesus. When he prays, he is completely in union with Israel, and yet he is Israel in a new way: the old Passover now appears as a great foreshadowing. The new Passover, though, is Jesus himself, and the true "liberation" is taking place now, through his love that embraces all mankind.[57]

And so there is an ongoing invitation from the Host/host, taking place now and offered to all mankind.

And just as the psalms the apostles sang at the Last Supper didn't stop in the Upper Room, but continued into the Garden until the exhortation, "Remain here and keep watch with me,"[58] the Institution of the Eucharist is not just about receiving the Host, it's about receiving the host. We are called not only to receive the Host at Mass, we are called to keep our host company, whether through Eucharistic Adoration, or in simple prayer such as the Holy Hours we pray in our own homes. We, the host of faithful are each individually called to be good guests. We learn through Gethsemane that our God wants company. He's lonely and depleted and he wants to be loved. He is both priest and victim, host and Host, inviting us to actively love him, to stay awake with Him. Gethsemane is key to our relationship with God, through our acceptance of and response to our Host/host. Just as we receive his blood at the Paschal Supper, we must eagerly receive his blood shed for us in Gethsemane as we stay awake and keep watch. Building on St. Leo the Great's assertion that "Christ will be in agony until the end of the world," and Blaise Pascal's statement that during this time "we must not sleep," it becomes clear that we are being perpetually invited by the host of Gethsemane to stay awake with him, a literal wake-up call.

---

57. Benedict, *Jesus of Nazareth*, 147.
58. Mt 26:38.

As my research on Liturgy encapsulated in the eloquent letter by Bishop Barres in his 2020 Holy Week Pastoral Letter reminds, every Holy Thursday the Eucharist (Host) is brought to a place representing Gethsemane for the faithful to spend time with and adore. So from this I base my assertion that the blood Jesus sheds in Gethsemane is Eucharistic blood, and points to Jesus in the garden as "Host." Not only did Jesus just finish transubstantiating and distributing the first-ever Communion in the Cenacle, not only do the sleeping apostles still have the Body and Blood of Christ within their bodies, but the Christ, the Lamb of God, has now officially started his Passion. Further, any drop of blood shed by our Saviour is the "Most Precious Blood" and especially after his official Institution of the Eucharist has happened, any drop of blood shed by him is Eucharistic. Padre Pio's writings affirm this:

> Divine Blood, spontaneously Thou flowest from the loving Heart of my Jesus; the flood of pain, the extreme bitterness, the steadfast perseverance which He sustains press Thee from that Heart, and sweating from His pores Thou dost flow to wash the earth!…Let me gather Thee up, Divine Blood, especially these first drops. I want to keep Thee in the chalice of my heart. It is the most convincing proof that love alone has drawn Thee from the veins of my Jesus! I want to purify myself with Thee, and all the places contaminated by sin. I want to offer Thee to the Father.[59]

In Chapters two, three, and four, I will explore the Gethsemane accounts in each of the Gospels of Sacred Scripture. First I will show how Jesus is the Host/host of Gethsemane in the Gospel of Matthew and Mark. Then, I will show how Jesus is the Host/host of Gethsemane in the Gospel of Luke/Acts. Finally, I will show how Jesus is the

---

59. Pio, *The Agony of Jesus*, 32.

Host/host of Gethsemane in the Gospel of John. The final chapter will be a summary and conclusion.

Chapter 1 The Host/host of Gethsemane

Introduction

In this chapter, I will prove the authenticity of the title of Jesus as the "Host/host" of Gethsemane, and the reality that Jesus of Gethsemane is our Eucharistic Lord. I will introduce the title of Jesus as "Host/host" of Gethsemane, and why and how it is appropriate to refer to Jesus in this manner. Jesus is the Eucharistic Host; the Living Bread of the Last Supper just shared and the sacrifice of Calvary still to come. He is truly the Sacrificial Lamb as He offers His Body, "the Host" to His apostles and this continues in Gethsemane.

I will show how the New Covenant which began at the Last Supper continues in Gethsemane as Jesus prays and bleeds and agonizes alone, and as His appeal for company from His guests is denied Him. Jesus' role of high priest, so evident at the Last Supper, continues into Gethsemane through the events that take place there. I will assert the significance of olives and consider the relevance of the name "Christ," which means "anointed," as our Eucharistic Lord is indeed the anointed one; and I will consider such words as "hostly," which means behaving in a hospitable way toward guests.

Jesus is the Host/host of Gethsemane and He welcomes guests to join Him there; to watch and pray. The proper response to the Host/host of Gethsemane is hospitality in return. In that way, the role of host is then transferred to the faithful, the large group of those called to keep watch and to pray with Jesus as we, the church, worship and offer hospitality. Indeed, we are the host of Gethsemane, the army of souls called as guests to enter Gethsemane, just as did Peter, James, and John. Jesus offers an invitation to each of us there.

How Jesus is the Host/host of the Garden of Gethsemane

Jesus's invitation to remain with Him and keep watch illuminates Him as the "Host/host" of Gethsemane. This role is displayed in several ways, in that "host" is simultaneously He who welcomes and receives others as guests to join Him in the garden; He the Eucharistic "Host," the Living Bread of the Last Supper just shared: He the "host life" on, in, and through which we live. And we, the host (large number) of faithful souls in the Church, are individually called as guests through prayer, transcending the *chronos* of earthly time and space to enter the actual garden of Gethsemane and by the grace of God that we may keep our sorrowful Host/host company. Our time in Gethsemane is time in the *kairos* sense of the word, where we are witness to the hour that has come for Jesus, "The hour has come for the Son of Man to be glorified,"[1] as the "kernel of wheat begins the descent to the ground"[2] and where we are called to serve Christ. "Whoever serves me must follow me, and where I am, my servant also will be. My Father will honor the one who serves me."[3] For in Gethsemane was the *kairos* of the eschatological time of salvation, the decisive moment, the hour which has come, where the Son fully accepts the will of the Father. It is our hour, too – our time with Christ to witness, and to serve.

---

1. Jn 12:23.
2. Jn 12:24.
3. Jn 12:26.

28

This chapter will give an overview of the word "Host/host" in its direct and implied scriptural references. Exegesis of the word "Host" will be explored with the Scriptural and Eucharistic definitions, dynamics, and implications of "host" and at times, the implicit Guest, especially the different meanings of the word "Host/host" in Scripture. The word "Host/host" has different meanings and all of them are meaningful for illuminating an important aspect of the Agony in the Garden.

"Host" is defined as "a victim of sacrifice, and therefore the consecrated Bread of the Eucharist considered as the sacrifice of the Body of Christ. The word is also used of the round wafers used for consecration. (Etym. Latin *hostia*, sacrificial offering.)"[4] Interestingly, in the same source, the definition of Hospitality is "the virtue of kindness and generosity toward guests. It is characterized by the spirit of welcome to visitors and strangers, and is one of the conditions for salvation, foretold by Christ: 'I was a stranger and you made me welcome.'"[5]

The definition of Host is "the Eucharistic bread. The term derives from the Latin *hostia*, 'victim,' thus recalling Christ as the Paschal Lamb sacrificed for all. *Hostia* was used as one of several names for the Eucharistic bread in the Middle Ages and remains untranslated in most languages today."[6]

4. John A. Hardon, *Modern Catholic Library*, (Garden City, New York: Doubleday & Company, 1980), 258.

5. Hardon, *Modern Catholic Library*, 258.

6. Robert P. McBrien, *The Harpercollins Encyclopedia of Catholicism*, (San Francisco, CA: HarperSanFrancisco, 1995), 640.

How Jesus of Gethsemane is the Eucharistic "Host," the Living Bread of the Last Supper just shared and the Sacrifice of Calvary still to Come

Jesus is the Eucharistic "Host," the Living Bread of the Last Supper just shared. The word "host" comes from the Latin word *hostia*, meaning "victim, or sacrifice."[7] But what does the root word *hostia* derive from? The etymology of the word hostia derives from *hostus*, which is defined, with stunning implications as pertains to this thesis, as "the yield of olives from a single pressing."[8]

Jesus of Gethsemane in His Agony is pressed. Each of the faithful who receives Him in the Eucharistic Host receives Our Lord as *Hostus*. Jesus was pressed in agony under the weight of our sins until He sweated blood. The Host is truly our victim *Hostia* and our *Hostus*, the yield of olives from a single pressing. Olive oil was used for anointing priests and kings, and to bring light. Olive oil is produced under pressure–the more pressure, the more oil. It brings joy to those who produce and consume it. One might call it grace under pressure. That is the fruit of adversity for those who toil for the love of God. "God, your God, has set you above your companions by anointing you with the oil of joy."[9]

Olive oil production involves three pressings. This was the case in the ancient world just as it remains true today. The first pressing, in

---

7. Charlton T. Lewis and Charles Short, *A Latin Dictionary*, (Oxford: Clarendon Press. 1879), from www.perseus.tufts.edu/hopper/text?doc=Perseus:text:1999.04.0059:entry=hostia.

8. Michiel de Vaan, *Etymological Dictionary of Latin and the other Italic Languages*, (Leiden, Boston: Brill, 2016), 292.

9. Ps 45:7.

the time of Christ, was for God: it was reserved for anointings in the Temple. No wonder, then that in the Eucharist we receive the *Hostus*, or that sacred yield of olives from a single pressing. The first pressing of olive oil is also known as extra-virgin olive oil: oil which has only been pressed once, the most perfect, the choicest oil that can be consumed.[10]

The three agonized pressings of Christ in Gethsemane reveal that Our Lord gave Himself for us in a way that would not only anoint and consecrate, but also a way that would become spiritual food and medicine for our souls; a way that would warm and enlighten.

"Clearly God, who carefully plans, intends that we grow in understanding by contemplating the multiple processes of pressing oil from olives. The crushing of olives into oil involves three sequential steps: harvesting, crushing into pulp and pressing. Generally, there are three pressings, each one producing a lower quality of oil. The first pressing produces oil for anointing and the Temple service; the second pressing produces oil used for food and medicine; the third pressing produces oil for heating and lighting. Jesus Christ's three prayers to the Father symbolize these three pressings."[11]

Now we must consider the etymology of Gethsemane, called the "place of the oil press", from the Aramaic *Gath Shemani*, meaning "oil press.[12]

As Pope Benedict says, "They went to a place called Gethsemane; and He said to His disciples, 'Sit here, while I pray'.

_____

10. Petar Dz, November 28, 2023, "How Many Times Can You Press Olives When Making Olive Oil?", Olive Knowledge, accessed July 2024, oliveknowledge.com/how-many-times-can-you-press-olives-when-making-olive-oil/.

11. Ted E. Bowling, Feb. 29, 2020, "sermonette: Garden of Gethsemane: The Oil Press", Bible Tools, accessed June 2024, oliveknowledge.com/how-many-times-can-you-press-olives-when-making-olive-oil/.

12. "Harvesting of the Olives at the Hermitage in Gethsemane", *Custodia Terrae Sanctae: Franciscans serving the Holy Land*, October 17, 2012, accessed September 2020, www.custodia.org/en/news/harvesting-olives-hermitage-gethsemane/.

Gerard Kroll comments as follows: 'At the time of Jesus, in this terrain on the slopes of the Mount of Olives, there was a farmstead with an olive press for crushing the olives...The farmstead was named Gethsemane on account of the olive press..."[13]

Therefore, Jesus in Gethsemane in His Agony, is pressed. Each of the faithful who receives Him in the Eucharistic Host, receives Our Lord as *Hostus*, "the yield of olives from a single pressing," who was pressed in Agony under the weight of our sins until he sweated His Precious Blood–the Eucharistic yield, beneath the olive trees, crushed under the olive press of His Agony. "He was pierced for our sins, crushed for our iniquity."[14] The olive is crushed beneath the olive press. Our Host of Gethsemane, is truly our *Hostus*, our yield of olives from a single pressing.

The significance of olives

James Jordan writes:

The Olive Tree is taken as a symbol of Israel, but it is quite a bit more specific than that. The Olive Tree is a symbol of the Temple of God, created by the Holy Spirit, and it is especially a symbol of the Holy of Holies...First, on the third day, we find fruit trees and grain trees created, and only these plants. The other plants had not been made before Adam was created (Genesis 2:5). Thus, the olive was one of the semi-sacramental plants, like wine (fruit) and bread (grain) made on the third day. Accordingly, the Israelite is always said to have a vineyard, a field, and an

_____

13. Benedict, *Jesus of Nazareth*, p. 148.
14. Isa 53:5.

olive yard (Ex. 23:11, Dt. 6:11; Josh. 24:13; etc.). These are to lie fallow in the sabbath year (Ex. 23:11). Gleaning laws are phrased in terms of these three (Dt. 23: 19-22). The curse is phrased in terms of these three (Dt. 28:38-40).[15]

Olive oil is specifically important to our understanding of the Host of Gethsemane who is Himself "the yield of olives from a single pressing." For "bread is associated with priesthood and the Word (the Son), wine with kingship and rule (the Father), and olive oil with anointing and presence (The Spirit). It is with this last that we are concerned. All the articles of the Tabernacle and Courtyard, as well as the priests, were anointed with olive oil (Ex. 30:2-33), signifying the impregnation of these items with the Spirit of God. Symbolically, the Tabernacle was an olive grove."[16]

Therefore, Jesus, the Host of Gethsemane is, as He prays there, set in the tableau of a kind of tabernacle, made up of the olive grove of Gethsemane. Indeed, it can truly be said that the Tabernacle in the Old Testament was an olive grove:

> Take the anointing oil and anoint the tabernacle and everything in it, consecrating it and all its furnishings, so that it will be sacred. Anoint the altar for burnt offerings and all its utensils, consecrating it, so that it will be most sacred. Likewise, anoint the basin with its stand, and thus consecrate it. Then bring Aaron and his sons to the entrance of the tent of meeting, and there wash them with water. Clothe Aaron with the sacred vestments and anoint him, thus consecrating him as my priest. Bring forward his sons

---

15. James B. Jordan, 1996, "Christ in the Holy of Holies: The Meaning of the Mount of Olives", *Theopolis Institute*, April 28, 1996, accessed September 2021, theopolisinstitute.com/the-meaning-of-the-mount-of-olives-2/.

16. Jordan, 1996, "Christ in the Holy of Holies".

also…As you have anointed their father, anoint them also as my priests. Thus, by being anointed, shall they receive a perpetual priesthood throughout all future generations.[17]

Our Eucharistic Lord, our perfect High Priest, who has just left the Last Supper where there was both the Institution of the Eucharist and the Institution of the Priesthood, is now in the Garden of Gethsemane, in the place of the Olive Press. Symbolically the tabernacle is the olive grove. Our Lord is teaching, through His Presence in the grove of olives, that His presence there is priestly and Eucharistic. The Book of Exodus describes the way the tabernacle is consecrated with olive oil. Our Eucharistic Lord is in the tabernacle of this olive grove in Gethsemane.

"…the Holy of Holies in the Temple was guarded by the olive. Two large cherubim of olive wood stood next to the Ark in the Temple, and the doors leading to the Holy of Holies were of olive wood. The doorposts of both the Holy of Holies and the Holy Place were of olive wood. Thus, the olive has a particular association with guarding God's holiness, and with the Holy of Holies."[18]

In the Psalms we read, "But I, like an olive tree flourishing in the house of God, I trust in God's mercy forever and ever."[19] Describing a faithful subject as an olive tree in the house of God further adds to the understanding of Jesus' invitation in the olive grove of Gethsemane to being one of a host welcoming us in to watch and pray with Him in the house of God. Considering the use of olives for anointing and the understanding that a tabernacle is symbolically an olive grove, it is clear that Jesus of Gethsemane is also the Eucharistic Host and welcoming host, and our response to the Host/host must always be welcome and hospitality in return, whether we receive Him

---

17. Ex 40:9-13.

18. Jordan, 1996, "Christ in the Holy of Holies".

19. Ps 52:10.

in Communion, adore Him in Exposition, or watch and pray with Him spiritually in Gethsemane.

"The olive was the first tree to grow after the Flood, signifying obviously the re-creation of the Kingdom of God as the first order of events after the Flood (Genesis 8:11). Note that it was a dove, signifying the Spirit, who delivered the olive branch to Noah."[20] Since the olive tree was the first tree to grow after the Flood and signified the re-creation of the Kingdom of God, how intensely significant it is indeed that the Agony in the Garden takes place in an olive grove, as the re-creation of the Kingdom of God is begun through the Paschal Mystery.

In the Book of Zechariah, there is a vision beheld by that prophet. "The prophet sees the two olive cherubim as two olive trees, feeding the oil of the Spirit into the lampstand of Israel's witness."[21] This vision is extremely significant vis-a-vis the Gethsemane narratives and the understanding of Our Lord in the Garden as our Eucharistic Host/host.

In fact, the first verse of Chapter four of the Book of Zechariah is significant to our understanding of Gethsemane, since it begins, "the angel who spoke with me returned and aroused me, like one awakened from sleep."[22] One cannot help but draw a parallel between a man asleep awakened by an angel, with the sleeping apostles whom Jesus had exhorted to stay awake in Gethsemane, which place was also visited by an angel. This parallel is especially worth highlighting due to the fact that this pericope from the Book of Zechariah focuses heavily on olive trees. Zerubbabel has a vision of a light coming from a golden candlestick and lamp (we cannot help but think of Christ, the Light of the World, and of the Sanctuary Lamp indicating the Real Presence), "And beside it are two olive trees, one on the right of the

---

20. Jordan, 1996, "Christ in the Holy of Holies".

21. Jordan, 1996, "Christ in the Holy of Holies".

22. Zec 4:1.

35

bowl and one to its left."[23] Zerubbabel asks what is the significance of the two olive trees. "Then he said, 'These are the two anointed ones who stand by the Lord of the whole earth.'"[24] The commentary beneath the passage states that the two anointed, or the "sons of oil," are the two anointed ones: Joshua the high priest and Zerubbabel the prince.[25]

The Book of Revelation stresses the importance of the olive trees, echoing the reference to Joshua and Zerubbabel as anointed witnesses of God. "These are the two olive trees and the two lampstands that stand before the Lord of the earth."[26] With these passages in mind, the olive trees of Gethsemane signify the anointing that comes from their oil (showing Jesus both as High Priest with the Last Supper just shared and Calvary in sight; and Jesus as Eucharist, shedding His Eucharistic Blood and surrounded by the tabernacle of the olive grove) but the trees also represent a reminder of being anointed witnesses. That is what each of us is called to be who spiritually watches and prays with Jesus in Gethsemane, who stays awake and does not sleep: we are each called to give witness. This is what Peter, James, and John were being asked to do and sadly, missed. We are each given the opportunity to stay awake as Gethsemane witnesses.

Further, Zerubbabel was told he would finish the building of the second temple. In Chapter Four of the Book of Zechariah, we read: "This is the word of the Lord to Zerubbabel: Not by might, and not by power, but by my spirit, says the Lord of hosts. Who are you, O great mountain? Before Zerubbabel you become a plain. He will bring forth the first stone...The hands of Zerubbabel have laid the foundations of

---

23. Zec 4:3.

24. Zec 4:14.

25. Commentary for Zec 4:14, "The Book of Zechariah", *The Catholic Study Bible*, "The Old Testament", 1162.

26. Rev 11:4.

this house, and his hands will finish it. Thus you shall know that the Lord of hosts has sent me to you."[27]

This pericope shows striking corollaries with the Gethsemane narratives...in which the Lord of hosts goes singing the *Hallel* as He processes to Gethsemane which includes the verse about the corner stone, "the stone that the builders rejected," and we come to the realization that with the olive trees as "witnesses," Jesus Christ is about to complete the third and final temple. Also, Gethsemane is a house of sorts...the foundations of which we are called to witness and we are also called to receive the Lord's hospitality in Gethsemane and to give Him our hospitality in return...spiritually in the Garden and physically in the Eucharist.

A brief digression is worth making here. Jacob, while he was in the wilderness, ten miles north of Jerusalem, went to sleep, resting his head on a rock. He was awakened suddenly to a vision of a ladder of angels going up and down, to and from earth to heaven. "When Jacob awoke from his sleep, he said, 'Truly, the Lord is in this place and I did not know it!' He was afraid and said: 'How awesome this place is! This is nothing else but the house of God, the gateway to heaven!' Early the next morning Jacob took the stone that he had put under his head, set it up as a sacred pillar, and poured oil on top of it."[28] A clear connection can be made between this account, the story of Zerubbabel, and the Gethsemane narratives. Clearly, Gethsemane is a "house of God." Jacob poured oil to consecrate the stone of this house of God. Jacob did this after awakening from sleep and in the presence of the angelic hosts. We must respond to the invitation of the host of Gethsemane to enter the house of God that is Gethsemane, and the rock of Gethsemane, and the olive trees and the oil of consecration that must leave us forever changed, forever ministering to Our Lord, God of Hosts.

---

27. Zec 4:6-9.
28. Gn 28:16-18.

Since Zerubbabel is told he will complete the temple, and he sees the vision of the olive trees, we are brought to mind what Jesus is doing, what He begins in Gethsemane with the witnesses of olive trees. "'Destroy this temple and in three days I will raise it up.' The Jews said, 'This temple has been under construction for forty-six years, and you will raise it up in three days?' But he was speaking about the temple of his body. Therefore, when he was raised from the dead, his disciples remembered that he had said this, and they came to believe the scripture and the word Jesus had spoken."[29]

Jesus is beginning the process of the third temple in Gethsemane. The destruction and resurrection of that third temple is nigh. The temple is Our Lord the Bridegroom and He will also leave us the New Jerusalem, the Catholic Church, the Bride. Gethsemane, with its olive trees as witnesses, is where Jesus is preparing for and beginning His Paschal Mystery.

Christ comes from the Greek, "Christos" meaning "anointed one." The anointed one, Christ, is surrounded by the olive trees for His Agony in the Garden; which takes place in an olive grove, as the re-creation of the Kingdom of God is begun through the Paschal Mystery. His suffering in the Mount of Olives creates a perfect chrism which anoints, in a special way, the priesthood, the sacraments, and also each believer who follows Him into Gethsemane.

Our Eucharistic Lord was pressed to the ground, prostrate in agony in the place of the olive press, and what a sacramental yield indeed.

"With this background, we can see that when Jesus moves to the Mount of Olives at the end of His ministry, He is moving into the garden-form of the Holy of Holies to complete His work."[30]

How ought each of the faithful respond to this Host? First it is to see that intrinsically inseparable from seeing Jesus of Gethsemane as Our Eucharistic Lord, it is important to view His hostly invitation

---

29. Jn 2:19-22.

30. Jordan, 1996, "Christ in the Holy of Holies".

and to understand our response should be to host Him (and others) in return.

"Hostly" is an adjective[31] which describes behavior befitting and typical of a good host, implying one who is hospitable and servile. It describes the generous and kind way a host treats guests. It is fascinating that the word "host," which in the English language can refer to the Eucharist, or to one who is taking care of guests, is contained in the English word "hostly." I assert that this word, "hostly," describes the duty of a Catholic: to be hospitable both to the Eucharist, in the loving manner in which we receive the Body of Christ; and also in the generous and loving way we take care of guests. In this way we are responding to the call of the Host/host of Gethsemane.

How Jesus is the "host" of Gethsemane who welcomes guests to join Him

Jesus is the "host" who welcomes and receives others as guests to join Him in the garden. For example, "He said to his disciples: Sit here while I go over there and pray."[32] This verse is also addressed to every one of the faithful, each of whom is called to be a disciple, a follower of Christ. "Sit here while I go over there and pray," is an invitation from Jesus the host of Gethsemane. Just as a host of a home gathering may tell his guest, "Do sit down while I hang up your coat," or "have a seat at the table while I go over there and get you a drink," Jesus is welcoming those He has personally invited to join Him in close proximity while He prays to the Father and prepares Himself for

---

31. Cambridge Dictionary, s.v. "hostly",
https://dictionary.cambridge.org/us/dictionary/english/hostly.

32. Mt 26:36.

His Passion. In each of the Gospels, Jesus gives some form of this invitation to His disciples, as will be examined in greater detail in succeeding chapters, thereby making Him the host of Gethsemane, inviting each of His followers to spend time with Him watching and praying, at His invitation. What will also be examined in greater detail in succeeding chapters is how, in each Gospel account, Our Lord in Gethsemane is Our Eucharistic Lord. Truly, in the Garden of Gethsemane Jesus, whose very name means "Yahweh saves,"[33] is both host and Host.

What is the Eucharist?

It is important to define our terms, especially the key terms within the title and thrust of this dissertation. Therefore, as I have defined such terms as "host" and even "Gethsemane," I must now define "Eucharist," even though it is a familiar word to many who will read this. Many who receive the Eucharist at Mass might yet be unable to define what the Eucharist is.

A form of the word "Eucharist" appears in the Bible, not in English Bibles, but in the original Greek version of the Gospels. Jesus uses "a version of the word while celebrating the Last Supper. 'Take this, and divide it among yourselves …And he took bread, and when he had given thanks [εὐχαριστήσας – eucharistēsas] he broke it and gave it to them.'"[34]

---

33. Got Questions Ministries, "What is the meaning of the name Jesus?", *Got Questions Ministries,* last updated June 26, 2023, accessed June 2024, www.gotquestions.org/meaning-name-Jesus.html.

34. Philip Kosloski, "Yes, a form of the word 'eucharist' is in the original Greek New Testament, and is used by Jesus at the Last Supper.", *Aleteia,* June 15 2022, accessed June 2024, aleteia.org/2022/06/15/is-the-word-eucharist-in-the-bible.

The word "Eucharist," as used in that above example of the Greek version of the Gospel means "thanksgiving."

There are many definitions and descriptions of the Eucharist, due to its depth and importance. The Eucharist is a sacrament and a sacrifice.[35]

"It is called...Communion...it is also frequently called the Viaticum by sacred writers...because it is spiritual food by which we are sustained in our pilgrimage through this life..."[36]

The Baltimore Catechism, in answering the question, "What is the Holy Eucharist?" states: "The Holy Eucharist is the Sacrament which contains the body and blood, soul and divinity, of our Lord Jesus Christ under the appearances of bread and wine."[37] And in the Catechism of the Catholic Church prepared following the Second Vatican Council, it is defined in this way: "The Eucharist is 'the source and summit of the Christian life.' The other sacraments, and indeed all ecclesiastical ministries and works of the apostolate, are bound up with the Eucharist and are oriented toward it. For in the blessed Eucharist is contained the whole spiritual good of the Church, namely Christ himself, our Pasch."[38]

St. Thomas Aquinas asserts:

This sacrament has a threefold significance. One with regard to the past, inasmuch as it is commemorative of our Lord's Passion, which was a true sacrifice...and in this respect it is called a Sacrifice. With regard to the present it has another meaning, namely, that of Ecclesiastical unity, in which men are aggregated through this Sacrament; and in this respect it is called Communion or Synaxis. For

---

35. Third Council of Baltimore, *The Baltimore Catechism,* 872.

36. *Catechism of the Council of Trent*, (London: Baronius Press, 2018), 198-199.

37. *The Baltimore Catechism,* 238.

38. *Catechism of the Catholic Church,* (Washington, DC: United States Catholic Conference Inc–Libreria Editrice Vaticana, 1994), 1324.

Damascene says…that it is called Communion because we communicate with Christ through it, both because we partake of His flesh and Godhead, and because we communicate with and are united to one another through it. With regard to the future it has a third meaning, inasmuch as this sacrament foreshadows the Divine fruition, which shall come to pass in heaven; and according to this it is called Viaticum, because it supplies the way of winning thither. And in this respect it is also called the Eucharist, that is, good grace, because the grace of God is life everlasting or because it really contains Christ, Who is full of grace.[39]

The proper response to the host of Gethsemane is hospitality in return.

How interesting that the etymology of the word "hospitality" comes from the Latin root *hospes*,[40] which is the same Latin root that the word "host" comes from when used as one who takes care of a guest. Host, defined as "Body of Christ," or Eucharist, comes from the Latin roots mentioned above: from *hostia*, meaning "victim, or sacrifice" which itself comes from *hostus*, from the Latin referring to "the yield of olives from a single pressing." So the Latin roots of "host" with regard to hospitality comes from the root *hospes*, while the Latin roots of "Host" with regard to Eucharist comes from the roots *hostia* and *hostus*. All these words have the beginning letters "hos" in

39. Thomas Aquinas, Summa Theologiae, trans. Fr. Laurence Shapcote, (Green Bay, Wisconsin: Aquinas Institute, Inc., 2021), III, q. 73, art. 4 resp.

40. de Vaan, *Etymological Dictionary of Latin*, 291.

common. In English, the root is the same for these words: one who welcomes a guest (host) is the same as the word for the Eucharist (Host) except for a change in upper or lower case. In Gethsemane, Jesus is both the host and the Host and his invitation is neglected by the three drowsing apostles. "My soul is sorrowful even to death. Remain here and keep watch with me,"[41] the King tells his disciples. This invitation is a high honor from any king, let alone the King of kings: to be welcomed near at a time when His Majesty is in need. The apostles are not ideal guests to the Host of Gethsemane. They fall asleep. And so, the invitation to watch and pray in Gethsemane, through the eternal word of Scripture, falls to each one of us no matter what generation in which we find ourselves. Our Eucharistic Lord should be welcomed and hosted in our hearts.

Jesus Himself gives the directives in Matthew 25:

> Then the king will say to those on his right, "Come, you who are blessed by my Father. Inherit the kingdom prepared for you from the foundation of the world. For I was hungry and you gave me food, I was thirsty and you gave me drink, a stranger and you welcomed me, naked and you clothed me, ill and you cared for me, in prison and you visited me." Then the righteous will answer him and say, "Lord, when did we see you hungry and feed you, or thirsty and give you drink? When did we see you a stranger and welcome you, or naked and clothe you? When did we see you ill or in prison, and visit you?" And the king will say to them in reply, "Amen, I say to you, whatever you did for one of these least brothers of mine, you did for me."[42]

We are meant to apply these directives of Jesus in the way we treat those we encounter in this life. In that sense, having a general

---

41. Mt 26:38.
42. Mt 25:34-40.

spirit of hospitality for all those whom we encounter is advisable. We must not merely welcome guests and strangers alike who visit our home but we must bring that spirit of homeliness to all whom we encounter even when we are not at home.

The language used in the liturgy of the Eucharist itself teaches us this rule. We use the words of the Roman centurion who did not feel worthy for Our Lord to visit his home, "Lord, I am not worthy that you should enter under my roof, but only say the word and my soul shall be healed,"[43] or in the Latin, *"Domine non sum dignus ut intres sub tectum meum; sed tantum dic verbo, et sanabitur anima mea."*

This very understanding of telling Our Lord that we are not worthy He should enter under each one of our roofs but "only say the word and my soul shall be healed" shows profound humility but also gives Our Lord welcome, a loving and humble acknowledgment that we know and trust that He can and will heal us. It gives a profound sense of humble welcome and hospitality to Christ, showing in the words "that you should enter under my roof," that each one of us, in a manner of speaking, embodies a house; or perhaps the image of the body as a tent would work better, since a tent is transportable. Notably, a tent is frequently an image of hospitality in Scripture. Hospitality is of vital importance in Scripture. "Do not neglect hospitality, for through it some have unknowingly entertained angels."[44]

The main housing structure in the Old Testament was that of the tent. That was the only physical "roof" many people had to offer. And interestingly, it was transportable. That is a good reminder for us when we pray the words of the centurion as described in this chapter, "Lord, I am not worthy that you should enter under my roof," because the roof of each of our bodies goes with us wherever we go, and along with it must go our hospitality. Hospitality was of utmost importance to the Israelite world. The Holman Illustrated Bible Dictionary describes hospitality as:

---

43. Mt 8:8.
44. Heb 13:2.

...to entertain or receive a stranger (sojourner) into one's home as an honored guest and to provide the guest with food, shelter, and protection. This was not merely an oriental custom or good manners but a sacred duty that everyone was expected to observe. Only the depraved would violate this obligation.

Hospitality probably grew out of the needs of nomadic life. Since public inns were rare, a traveler had to depend on the kindness of others and had a right to expect it. This practice was extended to every sojourner, even a runaway slave (Deut. 23:15-16) or one's archenemy.

The Pentateuch contains specific commands for the Israelites to love the strangers as themselves (Lev. 19:33-34; Deut. 10:18-19) and to look after their welfare (Deut. 24:17-22). The reason for practicing hospitality was that the Israelites themselves were once strangers in the land of Egypt.[45]

Abraham mastered this skill of hospitality, and of pertinence, he did so "by the terebinth, or oak, of Mamre." That is to say, he offered hospitality outside, in a treed area. He brought water to wash the feet of the Lord, and food to refresh and revive. God responded by promising that Sarah would have a son.[46] This loving response from God to the generosity Abraham had showed Him, illustrates a value intrinsic to the ancient world: hospitality should always go both ways.

---

45. Trent C Butler, Chad Brand, Charles Draper, Archie England eds., *Holman Illustrated Bible Dictionary*, (Nashville, TN: Holman Reference, 2003), 786-787.

46. Gn 18:1-14 [*New American Standard Bible*].

What a sound example this is for us in light of the Garden of Gethsemane.

This illustrates the fruits of hospitality, how waiting upon God and serving Him leads to blessings from on high. It also shows hospitality given to God beneath a tree, which certainly brings to mind Gethsemane. Knowing that the Garden of Gethsemane with its many olive trees is symbolic of a tabernacle, we are called to wait upon the Host of Gethsemane who has invited us to be with Him. We, in turn, are called to wait upon Him there, to show hospitality, as the apostles were directed to do with their wakeful presence and did not fulfill by falling asleep. We must have this hospitable spirit as we watch and pray in solidarity with the request of Our Lord in Gethsemane and thus every time we wait upon Him in the Eucharist. The response called for in the Garden of Gethsemane and indeed our response as we pray after receiving the Eucharist must resemble the demeanor of Abraham, "and I will bring a piece of bread, so that you may refresh yourselves; after that you may go on, since you have visited your servant."[47]

For we know that we do have food to give Our Lord, even in the straits of Gethsemane, where He is in His Agony; even in His Eucharistic Real Presence within each of us after we have received Him. Our Lord has taught us thus in Scripture.

After asking the Samaritan woman by Jacob's well for a drink and inspiring her conversion of heart (the significance of this pericope of the woman at the well will be discussed further in chapter Four of this work,) Jesus is approached by his apostles who had brought Him back food. "Meanwhile the disciples were urging Him, saying, 'Rabbi, eat *something*.' But He said to them, 'I have food to eat that you do not know about.' So the disciples were saying to one another, 'No one brought Him anything to eat, did he?' Jesus said to them, 'My food is to do the will of Him who sent Me, and to accomplish His work.'"[48]

---

47. Gn 18:5.
48. Jn 4:31-34.

And so, Our Eucharistic Lord in Gethsemane can and should be waited upon with the food each of us may best provide Him, which is to "do the will of the One who sent me." After all, in Gethsemane, Jesus prays to the Father, "not My will, but Yours be done."[49] He invited the three apostles into the Garden to do His will; to stay awake and watch and pray. They did not give Him the food of the Will there.

But through His invitation to each one of us, to watch and pray with Him, we can give Him the food of doing God's will. In the Eucharist, when we receive Him, we can wait upon Him within each of our souls by bringing Him our desire to do His will. That is like a good host bringing food for the guest. In this case, our guest is also our Host.

But perhaps the best image of all for bringing hospitality to Our Lord wherever we go and especially to Our Host of Gethsemane is that image of each of our bodies as a temple, the word St. Paul and the Catholic Church have settled upon.

If each of us declares that we are not worthy that Jesus should "enter under my roof," it is referring to the roof of the body, a poetic way of describing a reality St. Paul describes, "Or do you not know that your body is a temple of the Holy Spirit within you, whom you have from God, and that you are not your own? For you have been bought for a price: therefore glorify God in your body."[50]

The Church echoes this in the Catechism of the Catholic Church: "The human body shares in the dignity of 'the image of God': it is a human body precisely because it is animated by a spiritual soul, and it is the whole human person that is intended to become, in the body of Christ, a temple of the Spirit."[51]

And so, since our bodies are temples, they are movable houses or tents of welcome for the Lord. Therefore, our hospitality must extend beyond the borders of our own brick and mortar house where

---

49. Lk 22:42; Mk 14:36; Mt 26:39.
50. 1 Cor 6:19-20.
51. *CCC*, 364.

we receive guests. It must accompany the house of each of our bodies. Our reciprocal hospitality is critical in our approach to the hospitable invitation of the Host/host of Gethsemane.

Because He is Our Eucharistic Lord, our Bleeding Host in the Tabernacle of the olive grove, we must be hospitable to Him, as though we are making a spiritual communion. Because He is our host, He invites us to watch and pray with Him, to be there with Him in His Agony, which is a privilege. We must respond to this invitation by hosting Him, the same way we are called to be hospitable to any stranger we encounter in the world according to the directives of Matthew 25, and then some because it is the Lord. Jesus Himself is in agony. How should each soul respond? Not by falling asleep. We must keep Him company, as He has invited us to do in Gethsemane. The late nineteenth and early twentieth century author and priest Fr. Albert Tesniere puts it this way:

> "The "Master of Prayer" (Jesus) gave in the Garden the ideal model of every prayer. Though under different conditions, He continues this example in the Eucharist. Instituted to be the perfect and perpetual memorial of the Passion of the Saviour, the Eucharist carries down through the centuries the remembrance of the prayer and the Agony of Gethsemane.
>
> …But desirous to perpetuate as much of His Passion as is possible, He continues His prayer in the lowliness of a state of inertia, which abases Him before His Father even below that of Gethsemane.
>
> There [in Gethsemane], the pallor of His divine countenance, the Agony and the blood, without doubt, disfigured Him; but here (in the Eucharist)…He dwells

alone, abandoned by indifferent, ungrateful, or hostile men, an abandonment far more displeasing to Him than was the sleep of the Apostles; and there He will remain night and day until the consummation of ages.[52]

The beauty and humility of His becoming the very food we eat at the Mass, the bread of the Eucharist, in which we receive His Body, Blood, Soul, and Divinity, is so poignant in that He continues to humble Himself all the more:

> Every morning at the Consecration, He descends, perseveringly overcoming all repugnance, into the Gethsemane of the Sacrament, there to resume His prayer, in the humility of His attitude and the ardor of His desires for the redemption of the world and the coming of His kingdom.

> But remaining truly man in His Heart and affections, seeking a return of love from us, still feeling the need of our presence and fidelity, of our sympathy and compassion, in which He finds consolation for His past sufferings and present humiliations, He calls upon us, He supplicates us to keep Him company, to stay with Him, to unite with Him in prayer as much for His sake as for our own.[53]

Again He invites…and again He warns us to allow Him into our lives for our own happiness and true freedom:

---

52. Albert Tesniere, *The Eucharistic Heart of Jesus: Readings for the Month of June*, (New York: Fathers of the Blessed Sacrament, 1908), 144-146.

53. Tesniere, *The Eucharistic Heart of Jesus,* 146.

It was this desire that He earnestly expressed at the moment He instituted the Eucharist, when He said: "*Manete in me, manete in dilectione mea—Remain in me, remain in my love.*" He did this in a manner still more precise when He deigned to throw off the sacramental veils and reveal the mystery of His existence, the love and the needs of His Heart in the Eucharist.[54]

We give right and proper hospitality when we receive our Eucharistic Host of Gethsemane with the desire to stay with Him and keep Him true company. One way we can do this is through frequent examinations of conscience and Confession "Just as the Jews were to remove all leaven and to fast before receiving the Passover (Mishnah, Pesahim 10:1), so, too, Paul calls his Christian audience to cleanse their hearts before receiving the Eucharist, lest they 'profane the body and blood' of Christ their Passover and thereby 'eat and drink judgment against themselves.'"[55]

In his famous Rule, St. Benedict tells his monks, "All guests who present themselves are to be welcomed as Christ, for he himself will say: *I was a stranger and you welcomed me.*"[56] We must receive Jesus in Gethsemane the same way. The temple of each of our bodies must reflect welcome. Staying awake, watching and praying accomplishes this. We must be good hosts to Jesus, our guest. This is true when we receive Him in the Eucharist or sit with Him in Adoration. It is true when we keep Him company spiritually in Gethsemane and when we follow His directives to stay awake, watch, and pray.

Jesus, the guest, also becomes the host who receives an alienated world. The Old Testament allusions in the feeding of the

---

54. Tesniere, *The Eucharistic Heart of Jesus,* 146.

55. Pitre, *Jesus and the Jewish Roots of the Eucharist*, 176.

56. Benedict, "The Reception of Guests", from *The Rule of St. Benedict,* ed. Timothy Fry, (Collegeville, Minnesota: The Liturgical Press, 1982), 73.

5,000[57] reveal the identity of Jesus. Taking the role of host to the multitude, Jesus is portrayed as one like Yahweh, who fed the people in the wilderness;[58] as one like the prophets of Yahweh, who fed his disciples and had food left over;[59] and as one like the coming Davidic shepherd, who would care for his flock in the wilderness.[60] In the institution of the Lord's Supper, Jesus not only serves as host, washing the disciples' feet[61] and directing the meal, but becomes the spiritually sustaining "meal" itself.[62] Identifying himself with the symbolic elements of the Passover meal, Jesus associated his body with the bread of affliction that was offered to all who were hungry and needy, and he associated his blood with the third cup of wine, the cup of redemption. Moreover, by halting the meal before the traditional fourth cup, Jesus anticipates his role as eschatological host, when he will drink again at the messianic banquet celebrating the consummation of the kingdom of God.[63] In post-resurrection appearances, the disciples perceive the identity of Jesus when he takes the role of host.[64]

Indeed, the host of Gethsemane's invitation to us to watch and pray with Him is inexorably linked with Jesus of Gethsemane's status as the Eucharistic Host. Both the Host and the host require and warrant welcome.

Jesus is the "host life," on, in and through which we live. Jesus said to them:

> Truly, truly, I say to you, unless you eat the flesh of the Son
> of Man and drink His blood, you have no life in yourselves.

---

57. Mk 6:30-44.
58. Ex 16.
59. 2 Kings 4:42-44.
60. Ez 34:11-31.
61. Jn 13:3-5.
62. Mk 14:12-2; see also Jn 6:30-40; 1 Cor 10:16-17.
63. Isa 25:6; Mt 8:11; Lk 14:15; Rev 19:9.
64. Lk 24:13-35; Jn 21:1-14.

The one who eats My flesh and drinks My blood has eternal life, and I will raise him up on the last day. For My flesh is true food, and My blood is true drink. The one who eats My flesh and drinks My blood remains in Me, and I in him. Just as the living Father sent Me, and I live because of the Father, the one who eats Me, he also will live because of Me. This is the bread that came down out of heaven, not as the fathers ate and died; the one who eats this bread will live forever.[65]

The very words "The one who eats My flesh and drinks My blood has eternal life," describes a sacred version of a host whose very life allows a parasitic life to live. Jesus is the "host life" for each of us lowly disciples. We cannot live without Him. He is our host in every sense of the word. Just as a tick or a louse draws life from its host by eating of its blood, so much more do we draw life from our Holy Host. It is infinitely more beautiful and sacred to be sure, but we must never forget that we are just as lowly (if not more so) in comparison with Our Lord as a mere parasite is to a mere human, and yet He raises us up to call us not slaves but friends. A better example, (more fitting in proper beauty) of Our Lord as the host life on and in which we live is the medieval illustration of Christ as "The Pelican in Her Piety," impaling her own breast with her beak so that her nestlings might live, even unto her own death.[66]

---

65. Jn 6:54-59.

66. William Saunders, "The Symbolism of the Pelican", *Catholic Education Resource Center*, accessed September 2021, www.catholiceducation.org/en/culture/catholic-contributions/the-symbolism-of-the-pelican.html/.

How we are the "host of Gethsemane," called as guests to enter Gethsemane, too:

We, the host (large number) of faithful souls in the Church, are individually called as guests through prayer, to spiritually enter the actual garden of Gethsemane by the grace of God who transcends time and space that we may keep our sorrowful Host/host company. We are there at God's command and we obey.

"Host of Heaven" refers to:

> ...Army at God's command...or angels. "Host" is basically a military term connected with fighting or waging a war. The most frequent use of the word is to designate a group of men organized for war. In this sense, the Hebrew word often refers to a human army (Gen. 22:22, 32; Judg. 4:2,7, 9:29; 1 Sam. 12:9; 2 Sam. 3:23; Isa. 34:2; Jer. 51:3). The term can refer to an act of war, as in Num 1:3, 20; Deut. 24:5; and Josh. 22:12. An extended meaning of "hosts" is that it designates a length of time of hard service (Job 7:1; Isa. 40:2, Dan. 10: 1). The term is used in the Book of Numbers to refer to the service of the Levites in the sanctuary.[67]

We, the host of Gethsemane, the large number of faithful souls who draw near to watch and pray as requested, are an army at God's command in that we are part of the Church Militant,[68] present for "a length of time of hard service"[69] since we understand that we are consolers in His Agony. We are also in some sense servants of the

---

67. Butler et al., *Holman Illustrated Bible Dictionary*, 787.

sanctuary, since we are reminded of the Tabernacle of the olive grove of Gethsemane which holds Our Eucharistic Lord. We know that an angel ministers to Him in the Garden, and that an angel is one of the host of angelic armies at God's command. All of this resounds in us as we pray at Mass:

> And so, with Angels and Archangels, with Thrones and Dominions, and with all the hosts and Powers of heaven, we sing the hymn of your glory, as without end we acclaim:

> Holy, Holy, Holy Lord God of hosts. Heaven and earth are full of your glory. Hosanna in the highest. Blessed is he who comes in the name of the Lord. Hosanna in the highest.[70]

We say this, "Lord God of hosts," during the Liturgy of the Eucharist and He is this "Lord God of hosts" in Gethsemane. He is the Lord God of hosts, of angel armies and of troops of souls who with one voice acclaim, "Holy, holy, holy." He is the Lord of Eucharistic hosts, too. Gethsemane urges us to arise from our slumber. When Jacob arose from slumber he saw the ladder of angels between heaven and earth. In Gethsemane, we must rouse from slumber not only to witness the angel who comforts Jesus but in a sense, to "be an angel", according to colloquial expression, meaning, "behaving in a compassionate manner" to Our Lord.

---

68. Kurt Godfryd, 2023, "The Church Militant, Suffering, and Triumphant", *St Clement of Rome Catholic Church*, September 3, 2023, accessed October 2021, www.stclementromeo.org/the-church-militant-suffering-and-triumphant/.

69. Butler et al., *Holman Illustrated Bible Dictionary*, 787.

70. "A.9.a. Preface of Sundays in Ordinary Time I", *iBreviary*, n.d., accessed June 2024, www.ibreviary.com/m2/messale.php?s=prefazio&id=469.

This chapter gave an overview of the word "Host/host" in its direct and implied scriptural references. Exegesis of the word "Host" was explored within the Scriptural and Eucharistic definitions, dynamics, and implications of "host" and at times, the implicit Guest, especially the different meanings of the word "Host/host" in Scripture. The word "Host/host" has different meanings, and all of them are meaningful for illuminating an important aspect of the Agony in the Garden.

We, the host (large number) of faithful souls in the Church, are individually called as guests through prayer, to enter the actual garden of Gethsemane spiritually by the grace of God who transcends time and space that we may keep our sorrowful Host/host company.

What is Eucharistic Hospitality?

We have earlier defined "Eucharist." Now it is important to pause to define "Eucharistic Hospitality." "Eucharistic" is an adjective which means "giving thanks, pertaining to the Lord's Supper, Eucharist."[71]

We know that "hospitality" means, as defined earlier in the chapter, "the virtue of kindness and generosity toward guests. It is characterized by the spirit of welcome to visitors and strangers, and is one of the conditions for salvation, foretold by Christ: 'I was a stranger and you made me welcome'."[72] Christ in Gethsemane is the Host/host in both the sense that there He is the "Eucharistic" Lord (as this dissertation elucidates) and the host inviting us to watch and pray with Him. Thus, Eucharistic Hospitality is a spirit of generosity and welcome, towards the Eucharist, and to the Host/host of Gethsemane,

---

71. Wordnik, "Eucharistic", *Wordnik,* n.d., accessed May 2024, www.wordnik.com/words/eucharistic.

72. Hardon, *Modern Catholic Library,* 258.

who is our model in this, the apex of all that is loving, generous, and hospitable, even in His Agony.

Conclusion

In this chapter, I showed the authenticity of the title of Jesus as the "Host/host" of Gethsemane. I introduced the title of Jesus as "Host/host" of Gethsemane, and why and how it is appropriate to refer to Jesus in this manner. He is truly the Sacrificial Lamb as He offers His Body, "the Host" to His apostles and this continues in Gethsemane. I showed how the New Covenant which began at the Last Supper continues in Gethsemane as Jesus prays and bleeds and agonizes alone, and as His hostly appeal for company from His guests is denied Him. Jesus' role of high priest, so evident at the Last Supper, continues into Gethsemane through the events that take place there.

I asserted the significance of olives and considered the relevance of the name "Christ," which means "anointed," as our Eucharistic Lord is indeed the anointed one; and I considered such words as "hostly," which means behaving in a hospitable way toward guests. Jesus is the Host/host of Gethsemane and He welcomes guests to join Him there; to watch and pray. It has been made apparent that the proper response to the Host/host of Gethsemane is hospitality in return. In that way, the role of host is then transferred to the faithful, the large group of those called to keep watch and to pray with Jesus as we, the church, worship and offer hospitality. Indeed, we are the host of Gethsemane, the army of souls called as guests to enter Gethsemane, just as did Peter, James and John. Jesus offers an invitation to each of us there. In the forthcoming chapters, we will see how this invitation from our Eucharistic Lord in Gethsemane unfolds in each of the Gospel accounts of Gethsemane.

Chapter 2 The Host of Gethsemane in the Gospels of Matthew and Mark

Introduction

This chapter will be focused on the Agony in the Garden in the Synoptic Gospels of Matthew and Mark. There are similarities and differences. Matthew is a very similar narrative to that of Mark, as they are Synoptic, but there are some key differences that help emphasize the Host/host that Jesus is in Gethsemane. Each Gospel has a distinct lens and focus. Each Gospel brings forth salient points to consider vis-a-vis the Gethsemane narratives.

As you recall in our methodology within the introduction of this work, I acknowledge that it is the practice of many scholars to begin analysis with the Gospel of Mark because "Mark was written first, and both Matt[sic] and Luke drew on it,"[1] yet I depart from that practice, and instead, begin with the Gospel of Matthew. It indeed must be remembered that the Gospel of Mark was written between "60-75, most likely between 68-73…"[2] whereas the Gospel of Matthew was written later, between "80-90, give or take a decade…"[3] As preeminent Scriptural scholar Raymond Brown asserts, Mark was written first. I acknowledge this sequence, yet see the import of beginning with Matthew in the interests of the Gethsemane narratives.

"While modern Gospel courses give Mark the most attention among the Synoptics, Matt[sic] stood first in the great ancient biblical

---

1. Brown, *An Introduction to the New Testament*, 38.
2. Brown, *An Introduction to the New Testament*, 45.
3. Brown, *An Introduction to the New Testament*, 59.

codices, and its organization and clarity have historically given this Gospel priority as the Church's teaching instrument."[4] I, too, give Matthew priority in this study of the Host of Gethsemane. Firstly, because we will discover how the Gethsemane narrative unfolds as it is read in order of placement in the Gospels. Secondly, because while both Matthew and Mark are very similar, Matthew's Gospel begins with the genealogy of Jesus, and within that framework, enables me to discuss the Matthean Gethsemane pericope, through the lens of the roots of the primordial Garden of Scripture.

The writer of the Gospel of Matthew, "according to traditional second-century attribution, [was] Matthew, a tax-collector among the Twelve, wrote either the Gospel or a collection of the Lord's sayings in Aramaic."[5] Raymond E. Brown says that the author of Matthew, who is "detectable from [the] contents [was] a Greek-speaker, who knew Aramaic or Hebrew or both, and…drew on Mark and a collection of the sayings of the Lord (Q), as well as on other available traditions, oral or written. [He was] probably a Jewish Christian."[6] The theology of the Gospel of Matthew "should be viewed as an attempt to show how the Jewish tradition is best preserved in a Jewish-Christian context."[7]

Matthew's Gospel was evidently written in the Antioch region.[8]

The general message of Matthew is described by Raymond E. Brown, "The Matthean account of Jesus' public ministry lies between the infancy and passion/resurrection narratives. Thus, a new beginning, a new ending, and a carefully remodeled and enlarged presentation of

---

4. Brown, *An Introduction to the New Testament*, 58.

5. Brown, *An Introduction to the New Testament*, 59.

6. Brown, *An Introduction to the New Testament*, 59.

7. John R. Donahue and Daniel J Harrington, *Sacra Pagina: The Gospel of Matthew*, (Collegeville, MN: The Liturgical Press, 1991), 17.

8. Brown, *An Introduction to the New Testament*, 59.

Jesus' words and deeds during his ministry distinguish Matthew's Gospel."[9]

Matthew and Mark both note the site of the Agony as "a place called Gethsemane."[10] In Matthew's Gospel, Jesus tells the apostles "Sit here while I go *over there* and pray;"[11] while in Mark's Gospel, Jesus merely says, "Sit here while I pray."[12] Matthew writes that Jesus took Peter "and the two sons of Zebedee,"[13] while Mark names them: "Peter, James, and John."[14] Meanwhile, in the Gospel of Matthew, Jesus "began to feel sorrow and distress," whereas in Mark's, Jesus "began to be troubled and distressed." Both the Gospels of Matthew and Mark depict Jesus asking the Father to take the cup away from Him, if it is the Father's will. In Matthew, Jesus says it three times. Mark mentions Jesus says it twice, but is the only one who includes the detail "Abba," or "Papa," when Jesus calls out to the Father.[15] In both Matthew and Mark, Jesus tells the apostles to "remain here and keep watch."[16] Both Mark and Matthew specifically mention that Jesus addresses Peter and asks, "you could not keep watch [with me] for one hour?"[17] In Matthews's Gospel, Jesus "fell prostrate in prayer,"[18] while in Mark's, Jesus "advanced a little and fell to the ground."[19] Both Gospels include a word of explanation for the sleeping apostles. Matthew says they were sleeping because "they could not keep their

---

9. Brown, *An Introduction to the New Testament*, 58.

10. Mt 26:36; Mk 14:32.

11. Mt 26:36.

12. Mk 14:32.

13. Mt 26:37.

14. Mk 14:33.

15. Mk 14:36.

16. Mt 26:38; Mk 14:34.

17. Mt 26:40; Mk 14:37.

18. Mt 26:39.

19. Mk 14:35.

eyes open."[20] Mark says, "they could not keep their eyes open and did not know what to answer him."[21] When examining the two Gospels side-by-side it is important to remind that Mark's Gospel distinguishes itself in Gethsemane not only by the use of the word "Abba," but by uniquely mentioning, at the close of the Gethsemane narrative, the "young man followed him wearing nothing but a linen cloth about his body. They seized him, but he left the cloth behind and ran off naked."[22]

Meanwhile, the Gospel of Mark is "the second book of the New Testament and shortest account of the ministry of Jesus... According to early church tradition Mark recorded and arranged the 'memories' of Peter, thereby producing a Gospel based on apostolic witness. Although Mark was a common Roman name, the Gospel writer is probably John Mark. Mark became an important assistant for both Paul and Peter, preaching the Good News to Gentiles and preserving the Gospel message for later Christians. Mark wrote his Gospel for Gentile Christians. He explains Jewish customs in detail for the benefit of readers unfamiliar with Judaism."[23]

This chapter will examine the Host/host of Gethsemane through the lens of the Gospel of Matthew and the Gospel of Mark. Matthew is a very similar narrative to that of Mark but there are some key differences that help emphasize the Host/host that Jesus is in Gethsemane. Each Gospel brings forth salient points to consider vis-a-vis the Agony in the Garden of the Gethsemane narratives. Matthew's Gospel will be the first to be addressed.

---

20. Mt 26:43.

21. Lk 22:45.

22. Mk 14:51-52.

23. Butler et al., *Holman Illustrated Bible Dictionary*, 1077.

Matthew's Gospel Elucidates Jesus as the Fulfillment of the Scriptures

The focus on the Agony in the Garden in the Gospel of Matthew will be filtered through the lens of this Evangelist whose *raison d'etre* is stressing "a strongly Jewish flavor. Its special concerns are to place Jesus of Nazareth within the traditions of God's chosen people and to show how this same Jesus bursts the bonds of those traditions and brought them to fulfillment."[24]

St. Matthew is a fascinating evangelist. "St. Matthew, one of the twelve Apostles, who from being a publican, that is, a tax gatherer, was called by our Savior to the Apostleship: in that profession his name was Levi. He...wrote the Gospel...in Hebrew or Syro-Chaldaic which the Jews in Palestine spoke at that time. The original is not now extant; but as it was translated in the time of the Apostles into Greek, that version was of equal authority."[25]

The Gospel of Matthew, "should be read as one of several Jewish responses to the destruction of the Jerusalem Temple in A.D. 70. The Matthean community still existed within the framework of Judaism but in tension with other Jewish groups–especially the early rabbinic movement. Matthew's theological program should be viewed as an attempt to show how the Jewish tradition is best preserved in a Jewish-Christian context."[26] Matthew was seeking to mitigate the

---

24. Donahue and Harrington, *Gospel of Matthew*, 5.

25. Preamble to "The Holy Gospel of Jesus Christ according to St. Matthew", *Douay-Rheims Bible*, "The New Testament", 5.

26. Donahue and Harrington, *Gospel of Matthew*, 17.

"crisis posed by the events of A.D. 70 and rooted Jesus and his teaching in Jewish tradition."[27]

Indeed, in Matthew's Gospel, it is elucidated that Jesus is the fulfillment of the Scriptures, the promised Messiah. "…Matthew went back to the Scriptures to show a continuity between the ancient Jewish tradition and the Christian movement. The most obvious element in this program is the use of 'fulfillment' or 'formula' quotations in which an OT quotation is introduced by a phrase such as 'all this took place to fulfill what the Lord had spoken through the prophet.' In the infancy narrative the fulfillment quotations confirm the extraordinary nature of Jesus' birth (1:23) and his itinerary as a child (2:15, 18, 23). They also appear in connection with Jesus' ministry in Galilee (4:15-16), his healing activities (8:17), his role as God's Servant (12:18-21), use of parables (13:35), entrance into Jerusalem on Palm Sunday (21:5), arrest (26:56), and betrayal by Judas (27: 9-10). The point is that Jesus' life from start to finish was in perfect harmony with the Scriptures. Or to put it more in keeping with Matthew's outlook–the Scriptures are in perfect harmony with Jesus' life."[28]

The Gospel of Matthew begins with the genealogy of Jesus. This sets the tone for the entire Gospel, reflected again here in this verse: "Do not think that I have come to abolish the law or the prophets. I have come not to abolish but to fulfill."[29] The Gospel's emphasis on Christ as the fulfillment of the Scriptures reminds that rooted to the Garden of Gethsemane is a memory of the primordial garden of Scripture: Eden. The understanding of the Host/host of Gethsemane is made clearer when considering this connection to Eden.

---

27. Donahue and Harrington, *Gospel of Matthew*, 17.
28. Donahue and Harrington, *Gospel of Matthew*, 17.
29. Mt 5:17.

Gethsemane's Hostly Roots In Eden

Bearing in mind the Matthean importance of fulfillment of the Scriptures, and the importance of the garden in Scripture since time began, and the pivotal importance of watching and praying there, it is necessary here to recall that very first garden. One might argue that one of the most sorrowful moments in the Old Testament comes early in Genesis after Adam and Eve sinned against God by eating of the fruit of the Tree of the Knowledge of Good and Evil. These are the sorrowful verses: "When they heard the sound of the Lord God walking about in the garden at the breezy time of the day, the man and his wife hid themselves from the Lord God among the trees of the garden. The Lord God then called to the man and asked him: 'Where are you?' He answered, 'I heard you in the garden; but I was afraid, because I was naked, so I hid.'"[30] God Himself was drawing his Presence near to them, which in itself is a hostly invitation from the Creator to His creations, an invitation to be together. Nevertheless, Adam and Eve shrank from the host's approach. They were not gracious or hospitable in turn. It can be said that God was their host in the Garden of Eden from the first, inviting them to delight in everything, but giving only one rule for not only how to conduct oneself graciously as befits a good guest, but how to preserve one's life and stay safe in Eden: "The Lord God then took the man and settled him in the garden of Eden, to cultivate and care for it. The Lord God gave the man this order: You are free to eat from any of the trees of the garden except the tree of knowledge of good and evil. From that tree you shall not eat; when you eat from it you shall die."[31]

---

30. Gn 3:8-10.
31. Gn 2:15-17.

After their grave sin, Adam and Eve hide themselves from the face of the Lord God, and instead of begging forgiveness and praying for mercy with contrite hearts, they cover themselves in shame and cowardice. One might say that Adam and Eve behaved as though they were in a kind of dangerous sleep, not alert to God's commands, not allowing either their love for Him; their sorrow for doing wrong; or their trust in Him to wake them from the slumber of sin. In this way, the hiding of Adam and Eve in the Garden of Eden demonstrates a drowsiness, a spiritual torpor, which Peter, James and John echo in the Garden of Gethsemane: "The Lord God therefore banished him from the garden of Eden, to till the ground from which he had been taken."[32] God sent Adam out to literally become a gardener, and await redemption.[33]

In Gethsemane, upon finding them asleep, Jesus rouses Peter, James and John with these words, "So you could not keep watch with me for one hour? Watch and pray that you may not undergo the test. The spirit is willing, but the flesh is weak."[34]

One may wonder how differently things might have gone had Adam and Eve followed that very advice in that first garden, Eden; had they watched and prayed. If Adam had been *watching over* his wife, Eve, he might perhaps have thrown a rock at that original and most vitriolic of all garden pests, the serpent. If Eve had been praying,

---

32. Gn 3:22-23.

33. No wonder Mary Magdalene "thought He was the gardener" (Jn 20:15) at the Resurrection when Jesus, the New Adam, appeared to her. Adam was sent "to till the earth from which he was taken," (Gn 3:23) but the New Adam is the gardener who has tilled the earth into which he was sent with the blood, water, sweat, and tears of His Passion. As the new Adam, Jesus tills the earth particularly in His Agony, in each drop of bloody sweat that falls to the ground from "the sweat of thy face" (Gen 3:19). The Passion of Jesus begins in Gethsemane. In the Garden, Jesus Himself is the Tree of Life from which we will eat. From His death upon a tree, we will receive the Eucharist, the Bread of Life. More of this will be discussed in greater detail in succeeding chapters.

34. Mt 26:40-41.

that is keeping in conversation with; or thoughts of; God, she might have desisted from conversing with the infernal snake and rather called out to God for help. If Adam and Eve had watched and prayed in the Garden of Eden, they would have had all the necessary assistance not to undergo the test.

The sleeping Peter, James, and John in Gethsemane echo the poor guests of Eden who, sadly, and even to their own chagrin, lack reciprocal hospitality to their generous host. There in the Garden of Gethsemane is arguably one of the most sorrowful moments in the New Testament. It even mirrors, in some ways, the sadness of Eden, as once again God directly encounters the sin of those He loves just at the very moment He is seeking their company.

In between hours of agony in which He has taken the weight of the world upon His pure being, Jesus looks for the company of Peter, James, and John; and each time He finds them sleeping. This echoes Adam and Eve hiding themselves from the Face of God in fear. God's beloved creatures again hide themselves, so to speak; this time in a sleep of sorrow; even while God Himself enters the garden grotto to begin His Passion. The sleeping trio can inspire a sense of regret, a desire to wake them up. Nevertheless, rather than passing judgment on the sleeping saints, each of us may recognize that we frequently need to rouse ourselves from sleep, actual or symbolic, in order to respond to the invitation of our Host/host in Gethsemane.

Once again, God is left alone, seeking company and finding those He loves inaccessible to Him. While in Eden, Adam and Eve were hiding from God; in Gethsemane the trio give way to a sad sleep. In both cases, the humans choose their own worries, fears, and bodily impulses over the requests of God.

The Drowsiness Factor

The drowsiness factor (physical and/or spiritual) is an important component as we consider these garden pericopes. Drowsiness makes another appearance in the Gospel of Matthew in another way that has strong implications for the Host/host of Gethsemane. Once again, the growth of a garden is seen, in conflict with drowsiness. It is the Parable of the Sower of the Cockle. The need to watch and pray in this parable is tantamount to the call from Gethsemane:

> He proposed another parable to them. "The kingdom of heaven may be likened to a man who sowed good seed in his field. While everyone was asleep his enemy came and sowed weeds all through the wheat, and then went off. When the crop grew and bore fruit, the weeds appeared as well. The slaves of the householder came to him and said, 'Master, did you not sow good seed in your field? Where have the weeds come from?' He answered, 'An enemy has done this.' His slaves said to him, 'Do you want us to go and pull them up?' He replied, 'No, if you pull up the weeds you might uproot the wheat along with them. Let them grow together until harvest; then at harvest time I will say to the harvesters, "First collect the weeds and tie them in bundles for burning; but gather the wheat into my barn."'"[35]

---

35. Mt 13:24-30.

It is worth noting that in this Parable of the Sower of the Cockle, it was through the sleep of those who should have been awake, watching, that evil ran its course. And in the Garden of Gethsemane, where Our Lord in His Agony is pressed under the sins of those He has come to save, and where with each passing hour the presence of evil draws ever nearer as the time of His betrayal, imprisonment, and death draw nigh, how resonantly does the request of Jesus in Gethsemane now resound as he says, "Remain here and keep watch with me."[36] The word "watch" that Christ uses denotes vigilance like the Virgins waiting for the Bridegroom with oil ready, to be discussed later in this chapter; or the watchmen of the Psalms.

The Watchmen

In the Bible, there are watchmen who were "guards responsible for protecting towns and military installations from surprise enemy attacks and other potential dangers. Ancient Israelite cities often stationed watchmen on high walls or in watchtowers. Their job was to keep watch and warn the townspeople of impending threats. The Hebrew word translated 'watchman' means 'one who looks out,' 'one who spies,' or 'one who watches.' Sometimes watchmen were scouts who looked out for approaching friends as well as enemies."[37]

How much indeed the Garden Agony of Our Lord calls out for watchmen. The apostles could have been these watchmen, keeping watch for the impending threat approaching Jesus. They could have been vigilant companions for Him who was in such deep sorrow, and kept re-approaching them seeking their company; instead finding them

---

36. Mt 26:38.

37. Got Questions Ministries, "What are the watchmen in the Bible?", *Got Questions Ministries*, October 18, 2018, accessed October 2021, www.gotquestions.org/watchmen-in-the-Bible.html.

in slumber. And since everything God asks of us is ultimately for each one of our own soul's benefits, it is clear that their vigilant watching and praying in Gethsemane would have been enormously beneficial for the apostles themselves. Christ tells them to watch and pray "that you may not undergo the test. The spirit is willing, but the flesh is weak.."[38] How much stronger their weak flesh might have been had they taken His advice and been as watchmen in Gethsemane. Jesus is ever the most perfect host, knowing just what will most benefit those He has invited to be near Him. This call to vigilance is also a reminder of the benefits of Eucharistic Adoration. At the Exposition of the Blessed Sacrament, we are called to keep a vigil. At Adoration, we both "watch and pray" in the presence of the Host.

The role of the watchman is seen time and again in Scripture. There is an example of the watchman appearing in the passage of the same chapter that King David is obliged to flee to the Mount of Olives. The watchman is sometimes translated as "messenger," or "sentinel." The role is important, it is the one who watches over, who is alert and ready, scouting enemy and friend alike. "An informant came to David with the report, 'The Israelites have given their hearts to Absalom, and they are following him.'"[39] A few verses later, David responds by taking action. "As David went up the ascent of the Mount of Olives, he wept without ceasing. His head was covered, and he was walking barefoot. All those who were with him also had their heads covered and were weeping as they went."[40] As soon as he reached the top of the hill, "Ziba, the servant of Meribbaal, was there to meet him,"[41] to give him more news, and supply him with food. This alert and obedient servant also embodies the role of watchman.

Jesus is the Son of David on the Mount of Olives, and the role of the sleeping apostles was meant instead to be the role of watchmen.

---

38. Mt 26:41.
39. 2 Sam 15:13.
40. 2 Sam 15:30.
41. 2 Sam 16:1.

"Remain here and keep watch with me,"[42] Our Lord tells them. What food could Peter, James, and John have given Him? They could have given Him the food of doing God's will. "My food is to do the will of my Father," Jesus tells His apostles at the well of Jacob, after the conversation with the Samaritan woman. And indeed, who knows what great good the three sleeping apostles might have supplied if they had stayed awake to watch and pray. They might have seen Judas and the torches of the soldiers sooner, and been able to react with more strength. They might have given Christ better consolation as they waited. They might have had time to better prepare themselves. Everything Christ asks his followers is for their own good.

St. Thomas More explains this well when he writes of Gethsemane:

> And so among the other reasons why our Savior deigned to take upon Himself these feelings of human weakness, this one I have spoken is not unworthy of consideration—I mean that having made Himself weak for the sake of the weak, He might take care of other weak men by means of His own weakness. He had their welfare so much at heart that this whole process of His agony seems designed for nothing more clearly than to lay down a fighting technique and a battle code for the fainthearted soldier who needs to be swept along, as it were, into martyrdom.[43]

The apostles, if vigilant, might have all been able to remain stronger and to remain at the foot of the cross. We will never know the graces with which they might have been supplied, had they done the will of Jesus, had they prayed as He asked; had they kept watch with Him and for Him, in His Agony.

---

42. Mt 26:38.

43. Thomas More, *The Sadness of Christ*, (Oxford: Benediction Classics, 2008), 21.

Nevertheless, there is an example of graces supplied to those who kept watch over Jesus, and at a perhaps seemingly unlikely time which is exemplary of the tantamount importance of keeping watch over Jesus. It takes place at the Crucifixion, of all places.

Immediately after Jesus dies, and the earth quakes, Matthew's Gospel records, "The centurion and the men with him who were keeping watch over Jesus feared greatly when they saw the earthquake and all that was happening, and they said, 'Truly, this was the Son of God!'"[44] Therefore, it is made abundantly clear that those who were "watching Jesus" believed. They who were watching grew in faith; even the very centurion who had stood guard at the execution and pierced Christ's side.

There is a psalm known as the *De profundis*, which is prayed frequently in the Night Prayer, or Compline, of the Divine Office:

"My soul is waiting for the Lord, I count on His word. My soul is longing for the Lord more than watchman for daybreak. Let the watchman count on daybreak and Israel on the Lord."[45]

This is a sinner's prayer, leaning upon God's mercy. It is also a prayer of one who is vigilant, one who is keeping watch. It is a prayer which the apostles could have prayed in Gethsemane, and it is one for the host of faithful to pray when they spiritually enter Gethsemane. It is a reminder to keep vigil.

Peter, James, and John might have learned the lesson of vigilance, of keeping watch at the Transfiguration of Christ. The Transfiguration narrative immediately follows Peter's Confession about Jesus, when the Petrine Primacy is established. Peter said, "'You are the Messiah, the Son of the living God.' Jesus said to him in reply, 'Blessed are you, Simon son of Jonah. For flesh and blood has not revealed this to you, but my heavenly Father. And so I say to you, you are Peter, and upon this rock I will build my church, and the gates of

44. Mt 27:54.

45. Ps 130, from *The Liturgy of the Hours Vol 2*, Fourth Sunday Evening Prayer, 1488.

the netherworld shall not prevail against it.'"[46] It is important to note the word, "church."

As Elena Bosetti explains, "...We find the word 'Ekklesia,' assembly, 'Church'—a word that occurs nowhere else in the Gospels."[47] Jesus has referred not to a *temple* He will build, but His *Church*. This is something new. It will be built upon Peter, the first Pope. Peter will be present among the inner sanctum of the three special apostles, including James and John—at the Transfiguration as well as the Gethsemane vigil. These three closest friends of Christ would have special roles of leadership in the church: Peter, the first Pope; James the first of the apostles to be martyred; and John the Beloved was not only an evangelist who authored one of the Gospels but was also the only apostle to remain at Christ's side at the foot of the cross. Thomas More adds:

> Whereas Christ willed the other eight of His disciples to stay somewhat behind Him, Peter, John, and his brother James went further with Him...Peter for the fervor of his faith, John for his virginity, and his brother James, because he was the first of his apostles that should suffer martyrdom for his sake, did indeed far pass and surmount all the rest. And these three also...were privy to his glorious Transfiguration. He had called them before all others to so wonderful a sight, and they had been comforted with the clear light of His eternal glory...convenient was it, I say, that these three especially, more strong-hearted than the others, should be placed nearest about Him at the time of His painful pangs foregoing His bitter Passion.[48]

---

46. Mt 16:16-18.

47. Elena Bosetti, *Luke: The Song of God's Mercy*, (Boston: Pauline Books and Media, 2006), 106.

48. More, *The Sadness of Christ*, 21.

The Transfiguration's Connection to the Agonizing Host/host

In the account in which Jesus declares, "you are Peter, and upon this rock I will build my church,"[49] the image of the rock is prominent and deeply significant. It is noted that after six days Jesus takes Peter, James, and John up Mount Tabor, an elevation made of rock. The Transfiguration is an important passage to consider in the midst of contemplating The Agony in the Garden:

> And he was transfigured before them; his face shone like the sun and his clothes became white as light. And behold, Moses and Elijah appeared to them, conversing with him. Then Peter said to Jesus in reply, "Lord, it is good that we are here. If you wish, I will make three tents here, one for you, one for Moses, and one for Elijah." While he was still speaking, behold, a bright cloud cast a shadow over them, then from the cloud came a voice that said, "This is my beloved Son, with whom I am well pleased; listen to him." When the disciples heard this, they fell prostrate and were very much afraid. But Jesus came and touched them, saying, "Rise, and do not be afraid." And when the disciples raised their eyes, they saw no one else but Jesus alone.[50]

It is interesting to note that there are three occasions when the three apostles, Peter, James, and John, are singled out by Jesus for

49. Mt 16:18.
50. Mt 17:2-8.

their witness to an important event. There are three occasions in the Bible in which Jesus takes three of the apostles, Peter, James and John, aside from the rest. All of them are included in Matthew's Gospel:

> First, in Matthew 5, it is the raising of Jairus' daughter from death. Jesus had the three accompany Him into the room where her body lay and he restored her to life (vs. 37). Second, in Matthew 17, He had the three accompany Him to a mountaintop where he was transfigured. As He shined forth brighter than the sun, Moses and Elijah, long gone from this world, appeared and discussed matters with Him. The Final time was on the night before His crucifixion. He asked Peter, James, and John to accompany Him as He went to a secluded spot to pray for strength as He faced His hour of suffering.[51]

All three show Christ's power over death: his ability to bring the dead back to life; to show supremacy over Moses and Elijah, the deceased luminaries of the Old Testament; and to gain mastery over the agony in Gethsemane preceding Christ's sacrificial death.

There is much to consider in the passage of the Transfiguration vis-à-vis the Agony in the Garden and the Host/host of Gethsemane. It is notable that in the Catechism when the question is posed: "Who accompanied Our Lord to the Garden of Olives on the night of His Agony," the answer is given thus: "The Apostles Peter, James, and John, the same who had witnessed His transfiguration on the mount, accompanied Our Lord to the Garden of Olives, to watch and pray with Him on the night of His Agony."[52] In answering who accompanied Jesus to His Garden Agony, the Catechism reminds that it was the same three who were present for the transfiguration.

---

51. Jon W. Quinn, "Peter, James, and John," *The Front Page*, August 2016, accessed October 2021, bible.ca/ef/topical-peter-james-john.htm.

52. *The Baltimore Catechism,* 372.

The word "foreshadowing" is often used among scholars to explain what happens in literature or in life that, upon reflection, hints at what is to come.[53] Indeed, in some ways it is as though the Transfiguration foreshadows, anticipates, the Agony in the Garden: the three apostles Peter, James, and John chosen to witness something important upon a mount. The very word "foreshadows" evokes a cloudy presence and indeed the voice of God speaks out of a bright cloud in the Transfiguration, but indeed everything upon Mount Tabor is all brightness, all triumph. In that way the careful reader may be inclined to coin a new word in saying that the Fourth Luminous Mystery: The Transfiguration "forelightens" the First Sorrowful Mystery: The Agony in the Garden. The Transfiguration "forelightens" the Agony in the Garden, just as the account of "The Loss of the Child Jesus in the Temple" and subsequent finding of Him three days later in which Jesus tells Mary, "Why were you looking for me? Did you not know that I must be in my Father's house?"[54] actually "forelightens" the death of Jesus and the three days prior to the Resurrection.

If the sorrowful apostles present for the Agony in the Garden had reflected upon their recent experience upon Mount Tabor, in which those three had witnessed the bright splendor of God, they might have been able to better withstand Gethsemane. Surely, the luminous majesty of Tabor was meant to strengthen them for the sorrowful agony of Olivet. The Catechism states, "By the transfiguration of Our Lord, we mean the supernatural change in His appearance when He showed Himself to His apostles in great glory and brilliancy in which 'His face did shine as the sun and His garments became white as snow.'"[55] Surely, the Agony in the Garden is meant to be "forelightened" by The Transfiguration, as it says in the poem by Annabelle Moseley:

53. Mirriam-Webster Online, s.v. "foreshadowing," accessed April 2024, www.merriam-webster.com/dictionary/foreshadowing/.

54. Lk 2:49.

55. *The Baltimore Catechism,* 373.

We have been given this: the rose-gold glow
of morning on Mount Tabor, torments far below
us. What he wore dazzled like snow.
His face was lightning-splendid as a star.
At first we were stuck in a web of dreams—
woven in sleep by fear, but we awoke
to pristine air, to bright and bridge-like beams
of light anchored to heaven as God spoke.
How much we long to pitch our tents and stay
where everything is luminous and clear.
Our test comes when that vision fades away.
To let our souls transfigure from veneer
to real faith, we must try to stay awake—
for both the glory and the passion's sake.[56]

Nevertheless, the Agony is, in some ways, a sorrowful juxtaposition of the Transfiguration. Fr. Murphy-O'Connor writes, "If the Transfiguration—the moment when Jesus is mystically transformed in the presence of Moses and Elijah—presents Jesus at his highest, here we see him at his lowest. The radiant Lord who stood erect on a mountain peak now struggles for light in the desolation of night. The disciples who were so attentive at the Transfiguration and begged to prolong the golden moment, do not want to hear or see what is happening to Jesus here. These contrasting images bear reflection."[57] And reflecting upon these contrasting images has great implications for the theme of host and hospitality. Both passages describe three men

---

56. Annabelle Moseley, *Sacred Braille: The Rosary as Masterpiece through Art, Poetry, and Reflections*, (St. Louis, MO: En Route Media and Books, 2020), 85.

57. Jerome Murphy-O'Connor, 1998, "What Really Happened at Gethsemane?", *Bible Review*, accessed April 2024, library.biblicalarchaeology.org/article/what-really-happened-at-gethsemane/.

on a mountain with Jesus; both passages show the hospitality of Jesus; but only one shows an attempt at reciprocal hospitality given back by Peter, James, and John.

In the depiction of the Transfiguration, Peter says to Jesus, "Lord, it is good that we are here. If you wish, I will make three tents here, one for you, one for Moses, and one for Elijah."[58] Although Peter is misguided in placing too much importance upon Moses and Elijah when Christ Himself is present, the desire to make a shelter for Christ on the mountain is one that shows an attempt at grateful, reciprocal hospitality. Christ has brought them to that mount in order to witness a deeply significant event and Peter wishes to lavish Him with care in return. It would be appropriate for that same spirit of willingness to serve Christ to be brought to the mount of the Garden of Gethsemane, too. Considering the grove of olives already symbolizes a tabernacle for the Holy of Holies, and that our Eucharistic Lord is pressed upon the ground there, trampled under the weight of His Agony, it is all the more fitting to bring a spirit of hospitality to Gethsemane, where the Lamb of God is actually requesting our consolation, where His "soul is sorrowful even to death."[59] The same desire to serve that Peter displayed at the Transfiguration is called for in Gethsemane.

Vigilant disciples could offer to make Christ a shelter via their consolation, their watchfulness, and their prayers. As Tesniere writes:

> Nothing is more necessary to a sufferer than the constant and faithful presence of a sympathizing friend, who understands, enters into, and compassionates his pain. And so does Jesus look for someone who will console Him by sharing His sadness. He is about to descend into the arena, to begin, in accordance with the will of His Father, a combat of tears and supplications, to mitigate His rigor and obtain that He will be pleased to allow the chalice to pass!

58. Mt 17:4.
59. Mt 26:38.

His Heart revolts at the thought of all the treason, abandonment, and denials in store for Him, and He has to combat against that repugnance. He has to struggle with His own soul to make it yield voluntarily to a flood of opprobrium and ignominy, and even against His flesh itself when imposing upon it the most horrible sufferings. He feels all the horror of one that has to combat alone, for if He fails, who will raise Him up? Oppressed by the necessities of the human nature which He so freely assumed, Jesus implores the presence and assistance of those whom He has a right to think His friends, since He had so loved them. He makes known to them the need that He has of them: "Ah! Watch ye and pray with me, for my soul is sad unto death!"[60]

Therefore, just as Peter offered to build a shelter for Christ at the Transfiguration, we are called to build a shelter for Christ at the Agony in the Garden. After all, if the olive grove represents a tabernacle for Our Eucharistic Lord of Gethsemane, we must offer at least a spiritual shelter for Him there, with as much attention as though we had built a physical shelter. Jesus Himself tells us how: "Remain here and keep watch with me;"[61] and so, it is by our consolation, our hospitality, and our friendship that we can offer a spiritual shelter to the One who was so kind as to invite us into His Presence. In the words of Samuel Taylor Coleridge, "Friendship is a sheltering tree."[62] This quote reminds of the connection between giving friendship and giving shelter and best of all, calls to mind that Gethsemane is filled

---

60. Tesniere, *The Eucharistic Heart of Jesus*, 140-141.

61. Mt 26:38.

62. "Samuel Taylor Coleridge: 'Friendship is a sheltering tree.'" *Socratic Method*, November 2023, accessed April 2024, www.socratic-method.com/quote-meanings/samuel-taylor-coleridge-friendship-is-a-sheltering-tree.

with the presence of trees. The Host of Gethsemane invites those He loves to console Him beneath the sheltering trees of the Garden; our reciprocal friendship and consolation is the way we can return hospitality in loving response.

The Rock of Gethsemane

Reflecting upon the fact that Peter was named the Rock upon which Jesus would build His Church just prior to the Transfiguration account, and considering the Transfiguration as a passage in Scripture featuring the rock, not only because of the presence of Peter but also because of the rock of the mountain itself; it is important to note that not only in countless images throughout art history, but also physically present in the Church of the Agony in the Holy Land, it is indicated that Jesus leaned against a rock as He prayed in Gethsemane: "the Rock of the Agony where Jesus is said to have prayed in great anguish on the night before He died. Located indoors now, in the apse before the altar of the Church of the Agony, this rock is normally surrounded by people kneeling, prostrating, caressing the stone, crying,"[63] as they process through while on tour of the Holy Land.

This rock on display at The Church of the Agony is considered an important relic. "This prayer at the rock marked the first…shedding of the Savior's blood, the first time the earth tasted the bitterly wrung-out wine of heaven."[64] Interestingly, this boulder-sized rock upon which Jesus is said to have prayed in agony would have been, "about a stone's throw"[65] away from James, John, and Peter, named for the rock

---

63. Mike Mason, 2016, "The Rock of the Agony", May 23, 2016, www.mikemasonbooks.com/the-rock-of-the-agony-chapter-51-of-jesus-his-story-in-stone/, para. 4.

64. Mason, "The Rock of the Agony", para. 4.

65. Lk 22:41.

upon which Jesus would build His Church. If Jesus did indeed agonize upon the very rock that is consecrated and visited in the Church of the Agony in the Holy Land, then it is reasonable to also consider that rock a relic; not only because Jesus shed His bloody sweat upon it and leaned over it to pray, but because it is the physical depiction of the cornerstone of the Church itself, a rock relic of Christ's agonized prayers, and His Passion. The Rock of the Agony is also a physical reminder of someone Jesus doubtless would have prayed for in Gethsemane: the first pope, Peter, and, for that matter, all the generations of popes, bishops, and priests that would follow. When considering this Rock of the Agony, the words of Scripture resound, those same words Jesus likely sang in the Hallel Psalms as He made His way from the Upper Room of the Last Supper to Gethsemane: "The stone that the builders rejected has become the cornerstone; by the Lord has this been done, and it is wonderful in our eyes."[66]

Where was the Lord ever more rejected than He was in Gethsemane? Even at Calvary, He had His Blessed Mother, Mary Magdalene, and St. John the Beloved watching and praying with Him. But this is not so in Gethsemane. There, God's permissive will allowed Him to be totally alone, abandoned, rejected, and yet, it can be argued that in fact, "it is wonderful in our eyes," because God through Gethsemane has provided an eternal example to each of us as to how to respond when we are in a similar state of suffering, and at the same time, creates a space for each praying soul to have the ability to console a lonely Christ, and enter an earthly landscape to be truly alone with Jesus in a place where He asked for company.

The Church of the Agony in the Holy Land is brick-and-mortar proof that the Catholic Church did, actually, build a physical church around the site of the Agony in a way reminiscent of Peter's desire to build tabernacles on Mount Tabor. And so, Peter's words resound, even in Gethsemane, "Lord, it is good that we are here."[67] Spiritually,

---

66. Mt 21:42.
67. Mt 17:4.

79

it is very good for us to be in Gethsemane. We can visit, as Chapter Five will address, every time we visit the Eucharist in Adoration, and with every Holy Hour we pray. The Mount of Olives is an important destination for prayer, and for spending time with the Host/host of Gethsemane, an olive tree-laden, consecrated tabernacle within an olive tree-laden church.

The Church as an Olive Tree of the Host/host

Scripture even describes the church as an olive tree in St. Paul's Letter to the Romans, which discusses the grafting of the Gentiles into the church of God, the rejection of the Jews and their eventual restoration, and the wisdom of God in the entire story:

> But if some of the branches were broken off, and you, a wild olive shoot, were grafted in their place and have come to share in the rich root of the olive tree, do not boast against the branches. If you do boast, consider that you do not support the root; the root supports you. Indeed you will say, "Branches were broken off so that I might be grafted in." That is so. They were broken off because of unbelief, but you are there because of faith. So do not become haughty, but stand in awe. For if God did not spare the natural branches, [perhaps] he will not spare you either. See, then, the kindness and severity of God: severity toward those who fell, but God's kindness to you, provided you remain in his kindness; otherwise you too will be cut off. And they also, if they do not remain in unbelief, will be grafted in, for God is able to graft them in again. For if you were cut from what is by nature a wild olive tree, and

grafted, contrary to nature, into a cultivated one, how much more will they who belong to it by nature be grafted back into their own olive tree.

I do not want you to be unaware of this mystery, brothers, so that you will not become wise [in] your own estimation: a hardening has come upon Israel in part, until the full number of the Gentiles comes in, and thus all Israel will be saved…[68]

And so it is clear from this letter of St. Paul that it is right and fitting to describe the Church of Christ as an olive tree, which is deeply relevant to the call of and response to the Host of Gethsemane. Jordan explains:

…We can see that when Jesus moves to the Mount of Olives at the end of His ministry, He is moving into the garden-form of the Holy of Holies to complete His work. Let us now turn to the passages that mention this. In Matthew 21, Jesus is specifically said to move in His triumphal entry from the Mount of Olives to the Temple, where He judges the Temple. Part of what is being "fulfilled" here is God's fiery judgment of Nadab and Abihu from His throne in the Holy of Holies (Lev. 10:1-2) …In Matthew 23-24, Jesus departs from the Temple for the last time and moves to the Mount of Olives to pronounce judgment upon the Temple and Jerusalem. Again the Holy of Holies judges the Temple. In Matthew 26:30, we find that after celebrating the Passover and instituting the Lord's Supper, Jesus and His disciples went to the Mount of Olives. Then Jesus went to Gethsemane, which means

---

68. Rom 11:17-26.

Olive Press, to pray to God. Here we see the High Priest in the Holy of Holies. Here in the Mount of Olives, in the very Holy of Holies, Jesus was captured and arrested.[69]

The Olivet Discourse of the Host/host

In Chapter 24 of Matthew there is the great "Olivet Discourse" which begins, "As he was sitting on the Mount of Olives, the disciples approached him privately and said, 'Tell us, when will this happen, and what sign will there be of your coming, and of the end of the age?'"[70] This question was sparked because heretofore this point Jesus had shown the apostles the buildings of the temple and told them, "You see all these things, do you not? Amen, I say to you, there will not be left here a stone upon another stone that will not be thrown down."[71] Note the mention of "stone" once again. This eschatological preaching of Jesus weighs upon the apostles and they ask him about it as soon as they return to the Mount of Olives. Christ's responses make up what is now known as The Olivet Discourse.

The Olivet Discourse "is a sermon that Jesus preached from the Mount of Olives, just east of Jerusalem, three days before His crucifixion. The Olivet discourse is recorded in its most complete form in Matthew 24:1-25, and in more abbreviated forms in Mark 13 and Luke 21. Jesus preached this sermon to a select group of His disciples in response to their question about the destruction of the Temple and the end of the age (Matthew 24:1-3). Mark 13:3 says that Jesus'

---

69. Jordan, 1996, "Christ in the Holy of Holies".
70. Mt 24:3.
71. Mt 24:2.

audience consisted of only four men: Peter, James, John, and Andrew."[72] The Olivet Discourse further illustrates the eschatological importance of the Mount of Olives in general, and the Gethsemane narratives in particular, including the wise advice: "But the one who perseveres to the end will be saved."[73] What is Gethsemane if not a reminder of perseverance, even in the face of grave darkness and evil. This is the invitation of our Host/host.

This Olivet Discourse also includes this pivotal wisdom teaching of Christ: "Therefore, stay awake! For you do not know on which day your Lord will come. Be sure of this: if the master of the house had known the hour of night when the thief was coming, he would have stayed awake and not let his house be broken into. So too, you also must be prepared, for at an hour you do not expect, the Son of Man will come."[74] This echoes one of the main lessons of Gethsemane: to watch.

The Oil

How interesting and notable it is indeed that immediately following this Discourse comes the Parable of the Ten Virgins in Chapter 25 of Matthew. In this, the Chapter just prior to the Gethsemane narrative, Jesus teaches the Parable of the Ten Virgins, in which oil is of paramount importance:

> Then the kingdom of heaven will be like ten virgins who took their lamps and went out to meet the bridegroom. Five

---

72. Biblical Christianity, "The Olivet Discourse: Blueprint to the End Times.", *Biblical Christianity*, November 20, 2019, accessed March 2024, biblical-christianity.com/the-olivet-discourse-blueprint-to-the-end-times.

73. Mt 24:13.

74. Mt 24:42-44.

of them were foolish and five were wise. The foolish ones, when taking their lamps, brought no oil with them, but the wise brought flasks of oil with their lamps. Since the bridegroom was long delayed, they all became drowsy and fell asleep. At midnight, there was a cry, "Behold, the bridegroom! Come out to meet him!" Then all those virgins got up and trimmed their lamps. The foolish ones said to the wise, "Give us some of your oil, for our lamps are going out." But the wise ones replied, "No, for there may not be enough for us and you. Go instead to the merchants and buy some for yourselves.'"While they went off to buy it, the bridegroom came and those who were ready went into the wedding feast with him. Then the door was locked. Afterwards the other virgins came and said, "Lord, Lord, open the door for us!" But he said in reply, "Amen, I say to you, I do not know you."[75]

This is clearly a parable about spiritual preparation, and the importance of watching and keeping vigil. Oil is the product of olive trees, and in a similar way, spiritual preparation is the product of time spent watching and praying with the Host/host of Gethsemane.

It is in Matthew 25 that The Parable of the Ten Virgins folds into the Parable of the Talents, in which Our Lord tells the victor one of the two possible responses Our Lord speaks of giving to the soul at the end of life: "Well done, my good and faithful servant. Since you were faithful in small matters, I will give you great responsibilities. Come, share your master's joy."[76] And just a bit further in Matthew 25, in the Parable of the Sheep and the Goats, the king tells those who were on his left, "Depart from me, you accursed, into the eternal fire prepared for the devil and his angels. For I was hungry and you gave

---

75. Mt 25:1-12.
76. Mt 25:23.

me no food, I was thirsty and you gave me no drink, a stranger and you gave me no welcome, naked and you gave me no clothing, ill and in prison, and you did not care for me…Amen, I say to you, what you did not do for one of these least ones, you did not do for me."[77]

Right after this dramatic conclusion of Chapter 25 which concludes, "And these will go off to eternal punishment, but the righteous to eternal life,"[78] Matthew's Chapter 26 begins with the account of the woman with the alabaster box of ointment. She encapsulates the embodiment of the wise young woman who had her oil ready for the Bridegroom and the fulfillment of the "sheep" who ministered to Jesus when He was in the "prison" of the impending agony of His approaching death.

Recalling the Matthean *raison d'etre* of teaching that Jesus is the fulfillment of the Scriptures, it is important to realize how the Mount of Olives, the location of the Gethsemane narratives, has deep and far-reaching connections to Old Testament people and prophecies, with strong implications for the Host/host of Gethsemane.

"The Mount of Olives is the tallest of three peaks on a mountain ridge that runs across the Kidron Valley, east of the Old City of Jerusalem."[79] It is interesting to note that it is east of Jerusalem. Jewish temples and altars traditionally had an eastern orientation, toward the sunrise. For example, the temple in Jerusalem faced east.[80] Catholic cathedrals and churches have traditionally often been built facing east also, symbolically connecting to the resurrection of Christ which happened early in the morning.[81] Eden is east of Jerusalem and so it works well with the symbolism of Gethsemane as an altar of sacrifice for the Host of Gethsemane. "At its peak, Mount Olivet (as it

---

77. Mt 25:35-45.

78. Mt 25:46.

79. Randy Southern, Christopher D. Hudson, and Selena Sarns, *Sacred Places of the Bible*, (New York: Time Home Entertainment, 2013), 60.

80. Steve Rudd, n.d. "East orientation of Jewish temples and altars", *The Interactive Bible,* accessed April 2024, bible.ca/archeology/bible-archeology-jerusalem-temple-mount-east-orientation-jewish-temples-altars.htm.

is also known) rises about 230 feet above the Temple Mount in Jerusalem. The mountain is named for the olive groves that were once plentiful on its slopes."[82]

The history of Mount Olivet, or the Mount of Olive's connection to Old Testament scripture, which through a Matthean lens is deeply relevant to the study of this Gospel, and to Christ's Agony in the Garden, "is first mentioned in Scripture in connection with a rebellion against King David that was initiated by David's son Absalom. Fearing for his life, David led his fighting men and members of his family out of Jerusalem and up the Mount of Olives (2 Samuel 15:13-37). At the top of the mountain he met a man named Hushai, who agreed to act as a spy for David."[83] The connection between David and Jesus on the Mount of Olives is profound. David was overcome with agony when he fled to the Mount of Olives, since his own son, Absalom, had betrayed him. "As David went up the ascent of the Mount of Olives, he wept without ceasing. His head was covered, and he was walking barefoot. All those who were with him also had their heads covered and were weeping as they went."[84] One of the psalms written by David reflects this agony: "Even my trusted friend, who ate my bread, has raised his heel against me."[85] How much indeed this image calls to mind Judas, who betrays Jesus immediately before the Garden of Gethsemane narrative. When the apostles ask Christ at the Last Supper which of them will betray Him, He replies: "He who has dipped his hand into the dish with me is the one who will betray me."[86] Both Absalom and Judas shared the bread of the table of the King. Both David and Christ have loved their betrayers as sons.

---

81. Chiara Dalessio, 2023, "Light, Worship, and Finding the Right Direction", *L'Italo Americano*, May 15, 2023, accessed April 2024, taloamericano.org/why-old-churches-face-east/.

82. Southern, Hudson, and Sarns, *Sacred Places of the Bible*, 60.

83. Southern, Hudson, and Sarns, *Sacred Places of the Bible*, 60.

84. 2 Samuel 15:30.

85. Ps 41:10.

86. Mt 26:23.

Christ's connection to David is essential to St. Matthew, who begins his Gospel with these words, "The book of the genealogy of Jesus Christ, the son of David, the son of Abraham…"[87]

Throughout the Gospels, Jesus is known as either the Nazarene or the Nazorean. There is a connection in the Gospel of Matthew between this title for Jesus and King David. The word more closely in line with Matthew's theological perspective is, "Nazorean," due to its etymological connotation of "one who is consecrated."[88] "In Matthew's eyes, Jesus is undoubtedly the *nazir*, the 'consecrated' one par excellence, the *Christos* whom he announces right from the first verses of his Gospel. But Jesus is also the *nezer*, the 'shoot' from David's root, the most beautiful 'flower' of Nazareth. And so Nazorean and Nazarene both contribute to illustrating the kind of Messiah Jesus incarnates"[89] in the Gospel of Matthew.

"He is the messianic flower-shoot who was born at Bethlehem, the birthplace of David, but who grew up in Nazareth, an unknown village of 'Galilee of the Gentiles.'"[90] The two titles express the paradox of Jesus the Messiah, who unites within Himself both the royal dignity of the 'son of David' and the humility of the 'God-with-us' who saves us from sin.

Speaking of the Mount of Olives, "the prophet Ezekial revealed the sacred nature of the mountain in one of his visions. 'After the Lord had finished speaking, the winged creatures spread their wings and flew into the air, and the wheels were beside them. The brightness of the Lord's glory above them left Jerusalem and stopped at a hill east of the city' (Ezekial 11:22-23). That hill was the Mount of Olives."[91]

---

87. Mt 1:1.

88. Elena Bosetti, *Matthew: The Journey Toward Hope*, (Boston: Pauline Books and Media, 2006), 53-54.

89. Bosetti, *Matthew: The Journey Toward Hope*, 53-54.

90. Mt 4:15.

91. Southern, Hudson, and Sarns, *Sacred Places of the Bible*, 60.

"The prophet Zechariah upped the ante with his apocalyptic vision of the Lord standing on the Mount of Olives and causing it to split in half from east to west. Zechariah foresaw that the wide valley created by the split would serve as an escape route for people fleeing the Lord's attack (Zechariah 14:4)."[92]

"Jesus offered one of His last extended teachings to followers on the Mount of Olives. In response to a question about how to recognize the time of His return, Jesus gave His disciples some insight into the future…As Jesus was sitting on the Mount of Olives, his disciples came to Him in private and asked, 'When will this happen? What will be the sign of your coming and of the end of the world?'"[93]

As one considers the invitation of the Host/host of Gethsemane, transcending time and space and welcoming each one of us, personally: "Remain here and keep watch with me,"[94] one may wonder if one can do better than Adam and Eve; or for that matter, Peter, James, and John did, succeeding where they failed. We can; because we have the great gift of the Resurrected Christ, the Master Gardener,[95] and His example of giving up His own will to do the Father's in Gethsemane, recorded in the Synoptic Gospels. So, too, we give up our own will for God's will.

The Hymn

It is notable that in the Gospel of Matthew, as in the Gospel of Mark, also, but only in those Gospels, Jesus and His apostles leave the Last Supper singing a hymn. The last words of the Gospel prior to the

---

92. Southern, Hudson, and Sarns, *Sacred Places of the Bible*, 60.
93. Southern, Hudson, and Sarns, *Sacred Places of the Bible*, 60.
94. Mt 26:38.
95. Jn 20:15.

hymn are these: "I tell you, from now on I shall not drink this fruit of the vine until the day when I drink it with you new in the kingdom of my Father."[96] And so He is plainly stating that the meal is not finished. Scott Hahn explains:

"The Passover meal was divided into four parts, or courses, and each was accompanied by a cup of red wine mixed with water…the meal's first course consisted of a special blessing (kiddush) spoken over the first cup of wine, followed by the serving of a dish of herbs. The second course included a recital of the Passover narrative, the questions and answers, and the 'Little Hallel' (Psalm 113), followed by the drinking of the second cup of wine."[97]

The Little Hallel Psalm that is referenced by Scott Hahn in his commentary on the second course of the Passover meal includes these words in the second and third verses, "Blessed be the name of the Lord both now and forever. From the rising of the sun to its setting let the name of the Lord be praised."[98] This psalm is frequently included in the prayers of the Liturgy of the Hours or Divine Office as part of morning or evening prayer. It is also a psalm that in and of itself explains the very point of praying the Liturgy of the Hours: "From the rising of the sun to its setting, the name of the Lord is to be praised." Of course, the Liturgy of the Hours also prays Night Prayer in the darkness, after the sunset. But this psalm shows a way to live out Scripture's assertion that we must "pray without ceasing"[99] This Little Hallel, with its reminder to praise the name of the Lord and its association with the Divine Office in which faithful pray the canonical hours, immediately precedes the Institution of the Eucharist which would have come at the third course of the Last Supper. Thus, the

---

96. Mt 26:29.

97. Scott Hahn, *The Fourth Cup: Unveiling the Mystery of the Last Supper and the Cross*, (New York: Image, 2018) 108-109.

98. Ps 113.

99. 1 Thes 5:17.

Little Hallel reminds of the Divine Office which includes canonical hours such as Lauds, Vespers, and Compline. Dr. Hahn details:

> The third course was the main meal, consisting of lamb and unleavened bread, after which was drunk the third cup of wine, known as the "cup of blessing."...David Daube notes that the cup Jesus pronounced to be the "blood of the covenant" (Mark 14:24) is clearly the third cup of the haggadah, which is known as the "blessing cup" because it was consumed with the prayer of thanksgiving at the main course. Saint Paul seems to confirm this cup as the third in his own discussion of the Lord's Supper: "The cup of blessing which we bless, is it not a participation in the blood of Christ?" (1 Corinthians 10:16)

> With the prayer over that cup, Jesus tells his disciples that he will "not drink again of the fruit of the vine until...I drink it new in the kingdom of God." David Daube observes: "The meaning is that the fourth cup will not be taken, as would be the normal thing, at a subsequent stage of the service; it will be postponed till the kingdom is fully established."

> In its immediate context, the fourth cup loomed large. It brought closure to the rites that renewed Israel's covenant with God. Its omission would be like a blank spot...the omission of the fourth cup, "the cup of consummation" would have been jarring. It would, indeed, change the disciples' sense of all that had gone before.[100]

---

100. Hahn, *The Fourth Cup*, 109-110.

Thus, what occurs after the fourth cup of wine is omitted in the Upper Room, in Gethsemane as well as Calvary, is Eucharistic. "When did Jesus partake of the fourth cup? At the hour of his death, when his sacrifice was consummated."[101]

But the third cup, the cup of blessing is, as Jesus at the Last Supper teaches and St. Paul confirms, "a participation in the blood of Christ." That cup of suffering we witness in Gethsemane, the cup that will not pass from Jesus but which is the will of God, attests to this participation and to this blood, literally shed in the Gethsemane narrative of St. Luke. Dr. Hahn explains:

"For Justin (Martyr), the Eucharist is the sacrifice that definitively fulfills the Old Testament prophecy of Malachi: 'For from the rising of the sun to its setting my name is great among the nations, and in every place incense is offered to my name, and a pure offering; for my name is great among the nations, says the Lord of hosts.' (Malachi 1:11) Justin comments: 'He then speaks of those Gentiles, namely us, who in every place offer sacrifices to him, i.e., the bread of the Eucharist, and also the cup of the Eucharist.'"[102]

In this passage by Justin Martyr, we see the use of "Lord of hosts," in the prophecy of Malachi, and it is described as being fulfilled in the Eucharist. Jesus, the Host of Gethsemane, is also the Lord of hosts: not only of angels or armies of faithful, but of the many Eucharistic hosts that in every place are offered. When Justin Martyr finds the Eucharist the fulfillment of the prophecy of Malachi, we once again see the words of Scripture "from the rising of the sun to its setting," echoed, and we are reminded of the Divine Office, and thus we are reminded also of the call from Gethsemane to continue to watch and pray and keep vigil with Christ even beyond the day and evening prayers…watching and praying during the night. We find this call anticipated time and again in the psalms (which are the very backbone of the Divine Office, Liturgy of the Hours, Breviary) such as

---

101. Hahn, *The Fourth Cup*, 181.
102. Hahn, *The Fourth Cup*, 135.

here, in the translation used in The Liturgy of the Hours, which makes it clear, the speaker of the Psalm will not sleep until the Lord is honored: "I will not enter the house where I live nor go to the bed where I rest. I will give no sleep to my eyes, to my eyelids I will give no slumber till I find a place for the Lord, a dwelling for the strong one of Jacob."[103] And in the Douay-Rheims the word "tabernacle" is used: "If I shall enter into the tabernacle of my house: if I shall go up into the bed where I lie…until I find out a place for the Lord, a tabernacle for the God of Jacob."[104] Also, this poetic verse is included: "…we have found it in the fields of the wood. We will go into his tabernacle: we will adore in the place where his feet stood."[105] Let us, therefore, go spiritually to Gethsemane where slumber is meant to be eschewed and watchful prayer extolled; where his tabernacle is amidst the fields of the garden, the wood of the olive trees, in the place where his feet stood. Dr. Hahn details the usage of the word "cup":

> Through the centuries of Roman persecution, the Fathers consistently spoke of martyrdom as a "cup." The cup of martyrdom, in fact, was seen as the same cup that Jesus offered. Saint Polycarp of Smyrna, a disciple of the Apostle John, thanked God that he "should have a part in the number of your martyrs, in the cup of your Christ"…In the middle of the following century—at a time of intense persecution—Saint Cyprian of Carthage frequently used the "cup" as a symbol for martyrdom. Those who confess Jesus Christ "willingly drink the cup of martyrdom," he wrote. It is by the cup of communion, he said elsewhere, that Christians were made "fit for the cup of martyrdom." Cyprian explained:

---

103. Ps 132, from *The Liturgy of the Hours Vol 3,* (New York: Catholic Book Publishing Corp, 1976), Thursday Evening Prayer, Week 3, 1078.

104. Ps 131:3-5 [*Douay-Rheims*], Ps 132:3-5 in other translations.

105. Ps 131:6-7 [*Douay-Rheims*]. Ps 132:6-7 in other translations.

"A severer and a fiercer fight is now threatening, for which the soldiers of Christ ought to prepare themselves with uncorrupted faith and robust courage, considering that they drink the cup of Christ's blood daily, for the reason that they themselves also may be able to shed their blood for Christ."[106]

Knowing that the sleeping apostles of Gethsemane would have to come face-to-face with martyrdom, it is no wonder that Jesus wished them to "watch and pray" as He Himself faced the "cup" that "[may not] pass without my drinking it."[107] As Scott Hahn reminds:

Jesus repeatedly spoke of his own death as his "cup." When James and John asked him for the privilege of becoming his prime ministers, he asked them in turn: Are you able to drink the cup that I drink, or to be baptized with the baptism with which I am baptized? When they answered that they could, he said to them that they would indeed drink his cup and undergo his baptism (Mark 10:38), presumably meaning that they would share his suffering. It is significant that he described his suffering twice in sacramental terms—as a "baptism" and as a "cup."[108]

The cup appears clearly in Gethsemane, our Host/host offering His guests the chance to learn how to drink of it, too, as they watch and pray:

In the upper room at the Last Supper, Jesus declared the third cup to contain his blood. A few hours later, in the Garden of Gethsemane, he begged in prayer that the cup of

---

106. Hahn, *The Fourth Cup*, 137-138.
107. Mt 26:42.
108. Hahn, *The Fourth Cup*, 138-139.

suffering might pass from him (Mark 14:36). And then, when Peter rose to defend him from his would-be executioners, Jesus said to Peter, "Put your sword into its sheath; shall I drink the cup which the Father has given me?" (John 18:11) The cup was martyrdom...[109]

"The culmination of the seder was the singing of the 'Great Hallel' (Psalms 114-118) and the drinking of the fourth cup of wine, often called "the cup of consummation."[110] In Matthew, the Great Hallel is indicated with these words: "Then, after singing a hymn, they went out to the Mount of Olives."[111] Considering the fact that the Eucharist was just instituted; that each of the apostles had just received Eucharist, and now with the species still present within them, as they walk behind Christ Himself, leading them to Gethsemane, it may be truthfully said that what is happening between the Upper Room and the Garden, is a Eucharistic Procession, indeed; the first ever and most poignant Eucharistic Procession ever to have existed. With these facts in mind: the Eucharist was just instituted, First Holy Communion was received and was still present within them as they walked. Jesus the Host led them as they sang the hymn. This Eucharistic Procession leads to Gethsemane, where the Host of Gethsemane will kneel and lie prostrate in prayer in His Garden Altar of Repose. There, the apostles are called to watch and pray with Him, just as the faithful do at Eucharistic Adoration, when the exposed Real Presence of Our Lord in the Eucharist makes clear the need to "watch" as well as "pray."

In Matthew, Jesus "...said to his disciples, 'Sit here while I go over there and pray.'"[112] and this use of "here" versus "there" shows a host arranging the placement, the literal seating of his guests. Matthew, unlike Mark, refers to James and John as "the two sons of Zebedee,"

---

109. Hahn, *The Fourth Cup*, 139.
110. Hahn, *The Fourth Cup*, 108-109.
111. Mt 26:30.
112. Mt 26:36.

94

which shows an intimacy to the presence of these "sons of thunder" and reminds that our Lord and host knows us deeply, even our lineage and ancestry is known by the one who invites us by name, who knows his guests' place in things. When Jesus invites us to "Remain here and keep watch," Matthew adds the words, "with me," which makes the invitation from our host all the more personal and direct and relational. Another noteworthy detail is that Jesus the host "advanced a little and fell prostrate in prayer,"[113] which not only emphasizes the great sorrow of the moment but also the priestliness of our victim host, in that he voluntarily and passionately lays his whole body down as part of the sacrifice he has begun.

Unlike Mark who uses the word "cup" only once in his narrative, Matthew uses the word twice, beginning with, "My Father, if it is possible, let this cup pass from me; yet, not as I will, but as you will,"[114] and culminating with "My Father, if it is not possible that this cup pass without my drinking it, your will be done!"[115] Finally, Matthew indicates that the cup was referred to a third time by stating, "He left them and withdrew again and prayed a third time, saying the same thing again."[116] The cup is a chalice image in Gethsemane that makes clear our Eucharistic Lord whose Passion has begun.

The Suffering Servant and the Angel of God's Will

"Such is the mystery of Christ's passion and death. He relieves others' suffering by embracing it, making it his own, and giving it new

---

113. Mt 26:39.
114. Mt 26:39.
115. Mt 26:42.
116. Mt 26:44.

meaning,"[117] Fr. Dennis Billy writes as he reflects upon some of the oldest Eucharistic prayers, attributed to Hippolytus (c.170-c.230). One prayer begins, "We give thanks to you, O God, through your beloved servant Jesus Christ, whom you have sent to us in the last times as Savior and Redeemer and Angel of your Will..."[118] and the reflection of the author upon this prayer notes, "Jesus is described as a Savior, a Redeemer, and an Angel, that is, a Messenger of God's will."[119]

This prayer calls to mind Gethsemane. The "beloved servant Jesus Christ" is never more of a servant than prostrate upon the ground of Gethsemane. It is arguable that in the Gospels Jesus is most associated with being an "Angel of God's will" in the Gethsemane narratives. "My Father, if it is possible, let this cup pass from me; yet, not as I will, but as you *will*."[120] As will be explored further in the next chapter that addresses the Gospel of Luke, Jesus is visited in the Garden of Gethsemane by an Angel. Therefore, a Messenger of God's will ministers to the High Priestly Messenger of God's will:

> After recalling the salvific significance of Jesus' passion and death, the presider then goes into the words of institution:

> When he was handed over to His voluntary suffering, that He might destroy death, and burst the bonds of the devil, and tread upon the nether world, and illumine the just, and fix the limit, and reveal the Resurrection, taking bread, He gave thanks to you, and said: Take, eat, this is my body, which will be broken for you.

---

117. Dennis Billy, *The Beauty of the Eucharist: Voices from the Church Fathers*, (Hyde Park, NY: New City Press, 2010), 101.

118. Billy, *The Beauty of the Eucharist*, 100.

119. Billy, *The Beauty of the Eucharist*, 100.

120. Mt 26:39.

Similarly also the cup, saying: This is my blood which is shed for you. When you do this, you are making a remembrance of me.[121]

The aforementioned words of institution state: "When he was handed over to His voluntary suffering." Jesus was undoubtedly "handed over" in Gethsemane when he is betrayed by one of his apostles with a kiss, and arrested. "Immediately he went over to Jesus and said, 'Hail, Rabbi!' and he kissed him. Jesus answered him, 'Friend, do what you have come for.' Then stepping forward they laid hands on Jesus and arrested him."[122] The verse even includes the words, "laid hands on Jesus and arrested him." And so the words of institution, "When he was handed over" echo Gethsemane.

Further, it is most abundantly clear in Gethsemane that His suffering is voluntary. "And behold, one of those who accompanied Jesus put his hand to his sword, drew it, and struck the high priest's servant, cutting off his ear. Then Jesus said to him, 'Put your sword back into its sheath, for all who take the sword will perish by the sword.'"[123]

A word about this sword: Remember that in Eden, a flaming sword was raised to keep guilty mankind out of the Garden and away from the Tree of Life. In Eden, angels guarded the entryway and "the fiery revolving sword east of the garden of Eden, to guard the way to the tree of life."[124] But in Gethsemane, Jesus the innocent Son of Man tells Peter not to defend Him, the Tree of Life, from the Passion that awaits. He specifically mandates that the sword be lowered and put away, as the soldiers grab Him, the Tree of Life, and the drama ensues that will admit man back into Paradise. Gethsemane follows The Last Supper (the Institution of the Eucharist) and precedes His Death. In

---

121. Billy, *The Beauty of the Eucharist*, 101.
122. Mt 26:49-50.
123. Mt 26:51-52.
124. Gn 3:24.

97

this garden, we encounter the same Tree of Life who will die for us at Calvary. We meet Agnus Dei, the very same Lamb we encounter at Mass and at Eucharistic Holy Hours.

The Lord of Hosts

The Matthean Gethsemane narrative continues: "'Do you think that I cannot call upon my Father and he will not provide me at this moment with more than twelve legions of angels? But then how would the scriptures be fulfilled which say that it must come to pass in this way?' At that hour Jesus said to the crowds, 'Have you come out as against a robber, with swords and clubs to seize me? Day after day I sat teaching in the temple area, yet you did not arrest me.'"[125]

Arguably no passage in Scripture shows more of Jesus "handed over to his voluntary suffering" than here in Gethsemane as depicted in Matthew's Gospel. Jesus makes clear that he could summon twelve legions of angels to free Him. These twelve legions of angels refers to the host of heaven:

> The phrase "LORD of hosts" is how many English versions of the Bible translate the Hebrew "*Yahweh Tsabaot.*" This name of God appears 261 times in the Old Testament. *Yahweh* is the name "I AM," showing God's self-existent, self-sufficient nature. God commands...the heavenly beings such as cherubim, seraphim, and other angels. Micaiah had a vision and said, "I saw the LORD sitting on his throne, and all the host of heaven standing beside him on His right hand and on his left." (1 Kings 22:19)... Surprisingly, the hosts God commands are not limited to

---

125. Mt 26:51-55.

celestial bodies and angelic beings, but also extend to human armies. When David confronted Goliath in battle, he said, "I come to you in the name of the LORD of hosts, the God of the armies of Israel" (1 Samuel 17:45).[126]

This verse, which in the Douay-Rheims Latin translation reads: "*ego autem venio ad te in nomine Domini exercituum, Dei agminum Israel*," also calls to mind the great prophet Elijah's words: "With zeal I have been zealous for the Lord God of hosts" (*Zelo zelatus sum pro Domine Deo exercituum*).[127]

At this moment in Gethsemane, as Jesus goes willingly to voluntary suffering, and makes clear that He could easily summon twelve legions of angels, we can almost hear the priest's voice resound in the words of the Eucharistic Prayer:

And so, with the Angels and all the Saints we declare your glory, as with one voice we acclaim:

Holy, Holy, Holy Lord God of hosts.
Heaven and earth are full of your glory.
Hosanna in the highest.
Blessed is he who comes in the name of the Lord.
Hosanna in the highest.[128]

Jesus, in this hour of "voluntary suffering" emphasizes that He is fulfilling the scriptures. He also makes the point that He was within

---

126. Compelling Truth, "What does it mean that God is the 'LORD of hosts'?", *Compelling Truth*, n.d., accessed March 2024, www.compellingtruth.org/Lord-of-hosts.html.

127. 3 Kings 19:14.

128. Frank O'Dea, "Eucharistic Prayer II", *Eucharist: The Basic Spirituality*, n.d, accessed March 2024, theeucharist.wordpress.com/index/appendix-of-eucharistic-prayers/eucharistic-prayer-ii/.

their grasp daily in the temple, and they never touched Him, which shows that it is only because it is His hour, in fulfillment of the will of the Father and according to Jesus' voluntary suffering, that they are able to apprehend Him. Thus, the Eucharistic prayer is describing Jesus, Our Eucharistic Lord, as He is in Gethsemane, our Host. He is also Our Lord God of Hosts.

The words of institution in the Eucharistic prayer of Hippolytus also include: "This is my blood which is shed for you." As the next chapter, which focuses on St. Luke, will discuss, Jesus sheds blood in Gethsemane. Gethsemane is a Eucharistic narrative and Jesus is truly our Host there. Fr Billy writes:

> In this section of Eucharistic prayer, the drama of the Redemption builds to its climax. The presider recalls not only what happened to Jesus (i.e. he was handed over), but also his interior mindset (i.e. he suffered voluntarily), and his main purpose for doing so (i.e. to destroy death). Jesus embraces death in order to destroy it. In destroying it, he breaks Satan's mortal hold over humanity and proclaims the power of divine love in the midst of the nether world. That power illumines the just, establishes the extent to which darkness can hold sway over the human heart, and reveals the Resurrection. Yet before any of this happened, he instituted the Eucharist for his followers to remember him by and through which they could proclaim all for which he lived and died. These words of institution link Jesus' Last Supper with his intimate friends very closely to his passion, death, and resurrection. The Eucharist cannot be separated from Jesus' Paschal Mystery—and vice versa. The same Jesus who died on the cross and rose from the

dead is present in the breaking of the bread and the sharing of the cup.[129]

Fr. Dennis Billy affirms "the Eucharist cannot be separated from Jesus' Paschal Mystery—and vice-versa." The Paschal Mystery is the suffering, death, and resurrection and ascension of Jesus. Therefore, as Christ suffered in Gethsemane, right after the Institution of the Eucharist and having willingly entered into His Passion, Jesus is the Host of Gethsemane.

Mark's Gospel Style and Motion

The Gospel of Mark is placed, according to early Christian tradition:

> ...in Rome preserving the words of Peter for Roman Christians shortly before the apostle's death (1 Pet. 5:13). According to tradition Peter was martyred in Rome during the Neronian persecution, which would place the date of Mark's Gospel about A.D. 64 to 68. Such a hostile environment motivated Mark to couch his account of the life of Jesus in terms that would comfort Christians suffering for their faith. The theme of persecution dominates the Gospel of Mark (Mark 10:30). Jesus' messianic suffering is emphasized to inspire Christians to follow the same path of servanthood.[130]

---

129. Billy, *The Beauty of the Eucharist*, 101-102.

130. Butler et al., *Holman Illustrated Bible Dictionary*, 1078.

The Gospel of Mark will be explored through the lens of this Evangelist whose *raison d'etre* is stressing "the humanity of Jesus and trust at the heart of discipleship…(and) service to others as the daily way of taking up Jesus' cup and cross."[131] Philip Van Linden writes:

> Of the four Gospel portraits, Mark's is by far the one that best reveals the human side of Jesus. While Mark's Jesus spends most of his time performing incredible acts of mercy, which reveal that he is God's Son, he is also depicted as a most human Lord. Only Mark preserves those details that bring out how sharp (1:25), deeply grieved and angry (3:5), or indignant (10:14) Jesus could be with those around him. Mark alone adds the touching detail to the story of Jesus' raising of the little girl from her death-bed: "she should be given something to eat" (5:43). Only Mark's Jesus looks at the rich man and loves him (10:21) before he challenges him to give up all to follow him…Mark reveals a Jesus who is at once the powerful Son of God and a most human person.[132]

Mark's Gospel shows Jesus challenging others to trust in Him, and this trust "leads to the cup and the cross. And in concrete, daily life, Jesus' cup and cross take the form of being 'the slave of all' and serving others rather than being served by them (10:44). Although Mark's Gospel does not give long lists of 'how to' serve God and others, its readers cannot avoid the model of Jesus in the Gospel of Mark as the suffering servant of all. They know that they must seize every opportunity to serve others in charity if they want to be his followers."[133] This kind of service is key to understanding the

---

131. Philip Van Linden, *The Gospel According to Mark*, (Collegeville, MN: The Liturgical Press, 1991), 8.

132. Van Linden, *The Gospel According to Mark*, 8.

133. Van Linden, *The Gospel According to Mark*, 9.

Host/host of Gethsemane and our proper response to Him there. The good host serves his guests and inspires them with his service. Jesus is the paragon of this Servant Host.

In Mark's Gospel, we see very clear examples of Jesus as "Host/host." Firstly, since the Agony in the Garden takes place in Gethsemane, which is on the Mount of Olives, and the apostles' journey to the Mount of Olives in Mark's Gospel is on the immediate heels of the Last Supper, the reality of Jesus as Eucharistic "Host" is immediately evident.

"Very characteristic of Mark's style is…the characteristic adverb *euthys* ("immediately," "right away") to join sections or describe transitions…This narrative style creates a sense of urgency in the narrative."[134] He is the first of the Gospel narratives, but as the shortest synoptic Gospel, much of what is contained in Mark is already present in the other synoptics. Therefore, most attention will be paid here to what is unique to Mark that is relevant to the Host/host of Gethsemane.

Of critical importance, the Garden of Gethsemane pericope in the Gospel of Mark is a key to the Gospel as a whole. Van Linden writes:

> It is in the garden of Gethsemane that the major themes of Mark's Gospel seem to come together. In his agony there, the human heart of Jesus is "troubled and distressed" (14:33). The one who has challenged his disciples to trust in God alone comes close to giving up himself: "Father… take this cup away from me." However, as his disciples sleep, Jesus continues his prayer in faith: "but not what I will but what you will" (14:36). Anyone can turn to the Gethsemane passage (14:32-42) and hear it all summed up: "Give yourself to the suffering Messiah. Trust as he did,

---

134. John R. Donahue and Daniel J Harrington, *Sacra Pagina: The Gospel of Mark*, (Collegeville, MN: The Liturgical Press, 2002), 17.

even though he would rather not have trusted. Join him in serving the needs of your brothers and sisters, even unto death."[135]

Just as the Gospel of Matthew as a whole is seeking to mitigate the aftershocks of the destruction of the Temple of Jerusalem, the Gospel of Mark reminds, "We heard him say, 'I will destroy this temple made with hands, and within three days I will build another not made with hands.'"[136] This temple refers to the Lord and His Spiritual Body, the Church. The Olivet Discourse in its most complete form in Mt 24:1-25 points to the fact that the Third Temple will be destroyed and raised in three days and flourish forever. In Mark's Gospel this eschatological reality is abbreviated in Chapter 13.

"As he was making his way out of the temple area one of his disciples said to him, 'Look, teacher, what stones and what buildings!' Jesus said to him, 'Do you see these great buildings? There will not be one stone left upon another that will not be thrown down.'"[137] How interesting these words are in light of our Host of Gethsemane who guides His apostles, having left the Last Supper, likely singing the Hallel psalms in hymns[138] that recall "the stone that the builders rejected has become the cornerstone." These words of the Psalmist were emphasized by Jesus during Holy Week after His entrance into Jerusalem with palms, and mere days before the Last Supper, in the temple when He was teaching. Jesus said, "Have you not read this scripture passage: 'The stone that the builders rejected has become the cornerstone; By the Lord has this been done, and it is wonderful in our eyes.'"[139] This was preached by Jesus in the temple during Holy Week,

135. Van Linden, *The Gospel According to Mark*, 9.

136. Mk 14:58.

137. Mk 13:1-2.

138. Jimmy Cox, 2020, "The Psalm Sang at the Last Supper", *AOK Music and Arts*, April 9, 2020, accessed March 2024, okmusicandarts.com/news/2020/4/9/the-psalm-sang-at-the-last-supper.

139. Mk 12:10.

so it had freshly been proclaimed even before the evening of the Last Supper. And so, "after singing a hymn, they went out to the Mount of Olives."[140]

The Bridge between the Upper Room and Gethsemane in Mark

For in Mark's Gospel, it is immediately after the account of the Institution of the Eucharist that the motion forward to Gethsemane takes place. These words are the catalyst: "This is my blood of the covenant, which will be shed for many. Amen, I say to you, I shall not drink again the fruit of the vine until the day when I drink it new in the kingdom of God;"[141] the apostles go "out to the Mount of Olives" (on the heels of singing a hymn to conclude the Last Supper.[142]) The blood of the covenant begins to be shed for many on the Mount of Olives, in Gethsemane, through the bloody sweat[143] Jesus endured just before the kiss of Judas, "at the time He was betrayed and entered willingly into His Passion,"[144] as Eucharistic Prayer II reminds us. This Eucharistic prayer, invoked at so many Masses is of course referring to the time Jesus "took bread and, giving thanks, broke it and gave it to his disciples"[145] at the Last Supper when Judas set out to begin his act of betrayal, but also connects the Eucharistic Lord to Gethsemane, where Jesus was in the midst of His Agonizing Passion and Judas brought his betrayal to culmination and completion.

---

140. Mk 14:26.
141. Mk 14:24-25.
142. Mk 14:26.
143. Verified in Lk 22:44.
144. O'Dea, "Eucharistic Prayer II".
145. O'Dea, "Eucharistic Prayer II".

There is, when carefully considered, a sense of the hymn bridging the action between the Upper Room and the Mount of Olives. The Eucharist remains in the body of the apostles as this bridge is journeyed from the high Upper Room to the heights of the olive mount. The closing hymn was likely Psalms 113-118, since they were the concluding psalms traditionally sung at Passover feasts. These psalms foreshadow the very words Jesus will speak in his prayers of Gethsemane.

The psalms sung include such verses as "I was caught by the cords of death; the snares of Sheol had seized me, I felt agony and dread,"[146] and "I kept faith, even when I said, 'I am greatly afflicted!' I said in my alarm, 'All men are liars!' How can I repay the Lord for all the great good done for me? I will raise the cup of salvation and call on the name of the Lord.'"[147] "In danger I called on the Lord; the Lord answered me and set me free. The Lord is with me; I am not afraid; what can mortals do against me? The Lord is with me as my helper; I shall look in triumph on my foes. Better to take refuge in the Lord than to put one's trust in mortals."[148] "The stone the builders rejected has become the cornerstone,"[149] and finally, "Join in procession with leafy branches up to the horns of the altar. You are my God, I give you thanks; my God, I offer you praise. Give thanks to the Lord, for he is good, his mercy endures forever."[150] There is a real host present in the way Jesus invited and led the apostles in song, even as he led them to the Mount of Olives. Seen in the light of this psalm, the "leafy branches" are the very trees of the Garden under which the apostles process. The "altar" they "process" to is the location of the Garden Agony, where the Lamb of God, is crushed as He lays prostrate under the weight of our sins, set in the tableau of olive trees representing an

---

146. Ps 116:3.
147. Ps 116:10-13.
148. Ps 118:5-8.
149. Ps 118:22.
150. Ps 118:27-29.

anointed tabernacle, under the canopy of which the Host of Gethsemane, our High Priest, having gone willingly into His agonizing Passion, supplicates for us to the Father.

Once at the Mount of Olives, he tells all the disciples with him, "Sit here while I pray,"[151] but takes with him Peter, James, and John, the three who had been with him at the Transfiguration to draw closer and go further. The act of taking them further with him is one of hosting them, as he invites them in an intimate gesture, to keep him company, even as he confides, "My soul is sorrowful even to death. Remain here and keep watch."[152] The great host invites the three to keep alert and prayerful in the garden into which he has welcomed them. How profound that Adam and Eve were cast out of the joyful Garden of Eden by God when they introduced sin and death; and now God invites man into this sorrowful garden as he prepares to vanquish sin and death. Through the host's invitation to the three to draw near, even through his admonition "Could you not keep watch for one hour?"[153] the host, or great number of faithful in Christendom are invited to enter, too. One way the Church allows us to enter this time and space is through Eucharistic Adoration, designed to keep watch for an hour. We can still be hosted in Gethsemane and we can strive to be wakeful guests. Mark has one reference to the "cup" when Jesus says, "Abba, Father, all things are possible to you. Take this cup away from me, but not what I will but what you will."[154] This Eucharistic and Paschal reference to the cup is a clear affirmation of Jesus-as-Host in Gethsemane.

Heightening the recognition of Jesus as Eucharistic Host in Gethsemane is also recognition of Jesus as High Priest there. Pope Benedict XVI explains this well:

---

151. Mk 14:32.
152. Mk 14:34.
153. Mk 14:37.
154. Mk 14:36.

After the invitation to stay with him to watch and pray which he addresses to the three, Jesus speaks to the Father "alone." Mark the Evangelist tells us that "going a little farther, he fell on the ground and prayed that, if it were possible, the hour might pass from him."(14:35) Jesus fell prostrate on the ground: a position of prayer that expresses obedience to the Father and abandonment in him with complete trust. This gesture is repeated at the beginning of the celebration of the Passion, on Good Friday, as well as in monastic profession and in the ordination of deacons, priests and bishops in order to express, in prayer, corporally too, complete entrustment to God, trust in him. It is not only man's fear and anguish in the face of death, but is the devastation of the Son of God who perceives the terrible mass of evil that he must take upon himself to overcome it, to deprive it of power.[155]

Pope Benedict XVI reminds, therefore, that the very gesture taken by the priest at his ordination follows the example of Jesus in Gethsemane. So while the Institution of the Priesthood and Institution of the Eucharist occur at the Last Supper, the Eucharistic and Priestly narrative has not ended when the reader of Scripture reaches Gethsemane. On the contrary, the very gesture of Christ in the Garden is part of the Ordination Rites for the priesthood. How Eucharistic and priestly indeed is our Host of Gethsemane.

It is important to note, as the Gospels of Matthew and Mark are compared vis-a-vis the Gethsemane narratives, that each one adds slightly new information to the way Jesus falls down to pray in the Garden. In the Gospel of Matthew, Jesus falls "prostrate in prayer,"[156] which calls to mind, "Moses, making haste, bowed down prostrate

155. Benedict, "The Prayer of Jesus in Gethsemane", in *The Prayer of Jesus*, 64-65.

156. Mt 26:39.

unto the earth, and adoring said, 'If I have found grace in thy sight: O Lord, I beseech thee, that thou wilt go with us (for it is a stiffnecked people,) and take away our iniquities and sin, and possess us.' The Lord answered: 'I will make a covenant in the sight of all. I will do signs such as were never seen upon the earth,'"[157] and then God proceeds to reveal the ritual decalogue. At the Last Supper which has just proceeded His Garden Agony, it is written: "And likewise the cup after they had eaten, saying, 'This cup is the new covenant in my blood, which will be shed for you.'"[158] Therefore, it is evident in Matthew's Gospel that in the Agony in the Garden, Jesus is the fulfillment of the Scriptures, the Son of Man interceding for mankind in a way far greater than even Moses laying prostrate and begging for God to take away the sins of a stiff-necked people; and Jesus is the Son of God, making a covenant and doing the greatest signs ever beheld, through the Paschal Mystery.

In the Garden of Gethsemane, Jesus in His words and postures is the Eucharistic Host, sealing His New Covenant with the blood He sheds (as will be discussed in Chapter Three) and laying prostrate, face down as the sacrificial High Priest, and speaking of the chalice or cup He must drink.

"The New Covenant is our whole relationship with Jesus Christ. But it is focused in the Eucharist, just as Jesus focused it in the sharing of the Passover bread, which he said was his own body, and the Passover cup of wine, which he said was his own blood, 'shed for many.' In the biblical tradition, covenants were sealed in blood. So, too, was Jesus' New Covenant in the Eucharist."[159]

---

157. Ex 34:8-10 [*Douay-Rheims*].

158. Lk 22:20.

159. Marilyn Gustin, *How to Read and Pray the Passion Story*, (Liguori, MO: Liguori, 1993), 30.

The Host of Gethsemane, Our Eucharistic Lord, accepts that He must drink the cup, the chalice, which He referred to at the Last Supper as the "new covenant," one He agonizes over upon Mount Olivet, one far greater than Moses was shown upon Mount Sinai.

The Douay-Rheims translation of the Agony in the Garden in Matthew's Gospel is "he fell upon his face,"[160] from the Latin vulgate, *"procidit in faciem suam,"* which evokes the Holy Face itself having a great level of participation in this Agony.

In the Gospel of Mark, however, Jesus falls "to the ground."[161] These two bits of information, when taken together, evokes the image of Christ's face upon the ground. This fact alone warrants the consoling hospitality of those Jesus invites into Gethsemane. Mark's Gospel also adds the word, "Abba," when Jesus calls to His Father:[162]

> Joachim Jeremias, in his book *The Parables of Jesus,* writes thus: "Jesus's use of the word *Abba* in addressing God is unparalleled in the whole of Jewish literature. The explanation of this fact is to be found in the statement of the fathers Chrysostom, Theodore, and Theodoret that *Abba* (as *jaba* is still used today in Arabic) was the word used by a young child to its father; it was an everyday family word, which no one had ventured to use in addressing God. Jesus did. He spoke to his heavenly Father in as childlike, trustful, and intimate a way as a little child to its father."[163]

---

160. Mt 26:39 [*Douay-Rheims*].

161. Mk 14:35.

162. Mt 14:36.

163. Joachim Jeremias, *The Parables of Jesus*, in William Barclay, *The Gospel of Matthew, volume 2*, (Philadelphia, PA: Westminster Press, 1976), 349.

Barclay continues, "We know how our children speak to us and what they call us who are fathers. That is the way in which Jesus spoke to God. Even when he did not fully understand, even when his one conviction was that God was urging him to a cross, he called *Abba*, as might a little child. Here indeed is trust, a trust which we must also have in that God whom Jesus taught us to know as Father."[164]

This poignant calling of what would have been a familiar word of boyhood, "Papa," makes returning Christ's hospitality in Gethsemane seems all the more vital.

Peter Singled Out

Three times in Mark chapter 14, Jesus moves apart from His disciples to pray, and returns to find them sleeping:

> The disciples serve as exemplars for the weakness of the flesh (14:38). Peter in particular is singled out for criticism (14:37). The one who earlier claimed he would never betray Jesus (14:29, 31) is not strong enough to "watch one hour" with him. The threefold proof of Peter's weakness ("Simon, are you sleeping?") prepares for his threefold denial of Jesus in 14:66-72. Nevertheless, even though Jesus has proof of his disciples' weakness and has prayed that they may not "enter into testing" (14:38), he still asks them in 14:42 to accompany him as he faces the mystery of the cross ("Get up. Let us go.")[165]

---

164. Barclay, *The Gospel of Matthew,* 349-350.

165. Donahue and Harrington, *Sacra Pagina: The Gospel of Mark*, 411.

Indeed, in Mark's Gospel, Jesus the victim host says, "Behold, the Son of Man is to be handed over to sinners. Get up, let us go. See, my betrayer is at hand."[166] The host invites his guests to arise and join him as he becomes the victim host.

The Young Man in the Garden

One of the most unique moments in the entire Gospel of Mark also happens to take place in the Markan Gethsemane narrative. It is the story of a young man in the Garden which none of the other Gospels record. "And they all left him and fled."[167] Truly, Gethsemane is the place where Jesus is not only betrayed by a traitor, but forsaken and abandoned even by his truest friends.

This is also the moment in Mark's Gospel that includes the unique Gethsemane account of the naked young man who loyally follows Jesus as the Roman soldiers take Christ away from the Garden: "Now a young man followed him wearing nothing but a linen cloth about his body. They seized him, but he left the cloth behind and ran off naked."[168]

Though scholars don't know for certain who exactly the young man is, some believe the young man with the linen cloth could be a young St. Mark the Evangelist himself. Whoever this young man was, this is a moment that does symbolize loyalty to Jesus when others turn away from Him. The cast-off linen cloth is a Scriptural allusion to the "Old Testament Joseph,"[169] and therefore a story of loyalty to one's master.

---

166. Mk 14:41-42.

167. Mk 14:50.

168. Mk 14:51-52.

169. Gn 39:11-12.

We must watch and pray that we stay loyal to Christ no matter what. We must be willing to run from temptation, stripped of worldly trappings, maintaining our innocence and faith. Remember that in Eden, when disloyalty reigned, the sinners covered themselves in shame, realizing they were naked. Here, now that Christ has come to set things right in His Passion, the naked young man is a model of loyalty, not needing to hide shame because he has none to hide.

Further, one may note there is a poignance and beauty in the fact that, as Jesus leaves the Garden to redeem us and invite us back to Paradise, the young man who remains faithful, runs out of the Garden naked and innocent. Contrast that with the exile from the Garden of Eden. In that garden, our loving God covers the nakedness of the sinful and ashamed Adam and Eve, as they tearfully run out of the Garden of Paradise and into their exile—clothed.

Elena Bosetti write about Gethsemane, "Jesus, betrayed by one of his most intimate friends, now finds himself in the hands of his enemies. All of his disciples have fled in panic. But a boy gives proof of his courage…The boy emerges from behind the olive trees, wrapped in a sheet, and they immediately seize him…Only Mark records this episode…On one hand, the youth resembles Jesus, since like the Master he was 'taken' (cf. Mk 14:44-45, 51)…"[170] The author continues in speculation that perhaps this young man in white could be the same youth in a white robe at the end of Mark's Gospel:

> On the morning after the Sabbath, when the women go to the tomb with the intention of anointing the body of their beloved Master with aromatic perfume, they find inside "a youth" (neaniskos, the same word used in Mk 14:51) dressed in a white robe. "Don't be alarmed," he says, "you are looking for Jesus the Nazarene who was crucified; he is risen, he is not here." (16:5-6) Only Mark speaks of a

---

170. Elena Bosetti, *Mark: The Risk of Believing*, (Boston: Pauline Books and Media, 2006), 3-4.

neaniskos inside the tomb—thus creating a link—at least a literary one, with the youth at Gethsemane.

These two young men, the one at Gethsemane and the one on Easter morning, reclothe themselves in symbolic meaning. Each represents us. In the background of the Gospel, we catch sight of a third "youth," the catechumen, who with the rite of Baptism takes off the old man and is reclothed with the new (cf Rm 6:3-11; Eph 4:22-24; 1 Pt 2:1-3). The believer also has to be ready to follow the Lord at the cost of his or her life. That is why the catechumen was asked to remove his garment before descending into the baptismal bath. And after the baptism, the newly baptized received a white robe…[171]

The Willing Martyr and the Loyal Guest

Dwelling on this unique young man of Mark's Gospel reminds of the host of Gethsemane as it shows his eagerness to be a guest among Jesus and the apostles and eagerness to remain loyal to Host. The white robe and nakedness, symbols of innocence in the Garden, speak to the kind of the good-intentioned guests the Host seeks.

St. Thomas More had much to say about this young naked man of Mark's Gethsemane narrative. More authored The Sadness of Christ, *De Tristitia Christi*, while in prison awaiting his own martyrdom. This reality of More's own abandonment and sorrow makes his writings on Gethsemane all the more powerful:

---

171. Bosetti, *Mark: The Risk of Believing*, 4-5.

I have sometimes asked myself this question: when Christ left off praying and returned to the apostles, only to find them sleeping, did He go to both groups or only to those He had brought farther along and placed nearest to Him? But when I consider these words of the Evangelist, "all of them abandoned Him and fled" I no longer have any doubt that it was all of them that fell asleep. While they should have been staying awake and praying that they might not enter into temptation (as Christ so often told them to do) instead they were sleeping and thus gave the tempter an opportunity to weaken their wills with thoughtless drowsiness and make them far more inclined to fight or flee than to bear all with patience.[172]

St. Thomas More reflects on the contrast of the naked young man. "Just who this young man was has never been determined with certainty…"[173] and he continues:

Here, then, is how I would imagine it. This young man, who had previously been excited by Christ's fame, and who now saw Him in person as He was bringing in food to Christ and His disciples reclining at table was touched by a secret breath of the spirit and felt the moving force of charity. Then, impelled to pursue a life of true devotion, he followed Christ when He left after dinner and continued to follow Him, at a little distance, perhaps, from the apostles but still with them. And he sat down and got up again together with them until finally, when the mob came, he lost himself in the crowd. Furthermore, when all the

172. Thomas More, 'The Valencia Manuscript", in *Complete Works of St. Thomas More, Volume 14, Part I, De Tristitia Christi*, ed. Clarence H. Miller (Connecticut: Yale University Press, 1976), 561-563.

173. More, *Complete Works Vol 14*, 565.

apostles had escaped in terror from the hands of the sluggish soldiers, this young man dared to remain behind with all the more confidence because he knew that no one as yet was aware of the love he felt for Christ...so when they (the soldiers) finally noticed that the rest of Christ's band had fled and saw that this one had stayed behind and still dared to follow Christ, they quickly seized him.[174]

More speculates that when Jesus stopped the aggression toward the apostles, he gladly included this young man who'd joined the group of followers, not having even been summoned. Thus the host of Gethsemane has provided safety and a means of escape for all of his followers, even this young man.

Conclusion

This chapter focused on the Agony in the Garden in the Gospel of Matthew and in the Gospel of Mark. There are similarities and differences. Matthew is a very similar narrative to that of Mark but there are some key differences that help emphasize the Host/host that Jesus is in Gethsemane. Each Gospel has a distinct lens and focus. Each Gospel brings forth salient points to consider vis-a-vis the Gethsemane narratives.

In Matthew's Gethsemane narrative, Jesus is shown to be the fulfillment of the Scriptures. It is apparent in this Gospel that Gethsemane has roots in Eden. In Matthew's Gospel, we see how the drowsiness factor of those who should have been awake watching and praying impacts the situation, allowing evil to run its course. Thus, Matthew's Gethsemane narrative teaches that watchmen are needed.

---

174. More, *Complete Works Vol 14*, 577-583.

The Transfiguration's connection to the Agonizing Host of Gethsemane was explored, as was the images of the Rock of Gethsemane, the Olive Tree and the oil, each with deeply symbolic implications for Christ and His Church. This chapter illustrated how the Suffering Servant in Matthew's Gospel is also the Lord of Hosts.

This chapter has also elucidated how Mark's Gospel shows, with its own style and motion distinct from Matthew's, the bridge between the Upper Room of the Last Supper and the Gethsemane narrative. The Markan pericope's treatment of Peter was explored. The fascinating and unique character of the young man in Mark's Gethsemane was also discussed in depth.

To summarize the similarities and differences of how Gethsemane is discussed in these Gospels, both the Gospels of Matthew and Mark, the site of the Agony is noted as "a place called Gethsemane."[175] In Matthew's Gospel, Jesus tells the apostles "Sit here while I go *over there* and pray;"[176] while in Mark's, Jesus says, "Sit here while I pray."[177] Matthew tells us Jesus took Peter "and the two sons of Zebedee,"[178] while Mark names them: "Peter, James, and John."[179] Meanwhile, in Matthew's Gospel, Jesus "began to feel sorrow and distress," and in Mark's Gospel, Jesus "began to be troubled and distressed."

Both the Gospels of Matthew and Mark depict Jesus asking the Father to take the cup away from Him, if it is the Father's will. In Matthew, Jesus says it three times. Mark mentions Jesus says it twice, but is the only one who includes the detail "Abba," or "Papa," when Jesus calls out to the Father.[180] Both Matthew and Mark have Jesus tell

---

175. Mt 26:36; Mk 14:32.

176. Mt 26:36.

177. Mk 14:32.

178. Mt 26:37.

179. Mk 14:33.

180. Mk 14:36.

the apostles to "remain here and keep watch."[181] Both Mark and Matthew specifically mention that Jesus addresses Peter and asks, "you could not keep watch [with me] for one hour?"[182] In Matthew, Jesus "fell prostrate in prayer"[183] while in Mark, Jesus "advanced a little and fell to the ground."[184] Both Gospels include a word of explanation for the sleeping apostles. Matthew says they were sleeping because "they could not keep their eyes open."[185] Mark says, "they could not keep their eyes open and did not know what to answer him."[186] When examining the two Gospels side-by-side it is important to remind that Mark's Gospel distinguishes itself in Gethsemane not only by the use of the word "Abba," but by uniquely mentioning, at the close of the Gethsemane narrative, the "young man followed him wearing nothing but a linen cloth about his body. They seized him, but he left the cloth behind and ran off naked."[187]

The student of Gethsemane may be encouraged to retain this account of the young man, running off naked from Mark's Garden of Gethsemane, in sharp contrast to the way Adam and Eve, formerly naked and innocent; now clothed in their shame, were banished from the Garden of Eden, with an angel holding a flaming sword barring their re-entry. Since Our Lord, the Host/host of Gethsemane, has agonized in this new garden, there is now a sheathed sword and a man running out naked, an image of innocence instead of sin; a reminder that through Christ's Paschal Mystery, heaven will no longer be barred from the one who follows Christ purely. Mark is an author who shows immediate motion and action, and we hold fast to this message of his Gospel's naked young man. In spirit, we run with this man, as we enter

---

181. Mt 26:38; Mk 14:34.
182. Mt 26:40; Mk 14:37.
183. Mt 26:39.
184. Mk 14:35.
185. Mt 26:43.
186. Lk 22:45.
187. Mk 14:51-52.

118

Luke's Gethsemane narrative, where we will learn even more details of how Gethsemane begins the re-opening of what we lost in Eden; through such details as Christ's perseverance in prayer; the anointing of the priesthood in Gethsemane; and the very shedding of His Blood.

Chapter 3 The Host of Gethsemane in the Gospel of Luke

Introduction

This chapter will focus on the Agony in the Garden in the Gospel of Luke. The Gospel of Luke was most probably written in Rome for an audience of Gentile Christians who needed their faith strengthened. It can be dated to "85, give or take 5-10 years."[1] It is written by "Luke, a physician, the fellow worker and traveling companion of Paul…an educated Greek-speaker and skilled writer who knew the Jewish Scriptures in Greek, and who was not an eye-witness of Jesus' ministry. He drew on Mark and a collection of sayings of the Lord (Q), as well as some other available traditions, oral or written. [He was] probably not raised a Jew…"[2] The Gospel of Luke is considered to be written by a Gentile, which would make Luke the only non-Jewish author among the Gospel writers.

"This Gospel, the longest, is only half of the great Lucan writing. It was originally joined to Acts as part of a two-volume work that in length constitutes over one quarter"[3] of the New Testament. I will not be referencing Acts in this dissertation as there are no accounts of Gethsemane within that volume. Therefore, it is not of particular necessity to this dissertation to address Acts of the Apostles.

"Among the four evangelists only Luke writes a verse at the beginning explaining reflectively what he thinks he is about. There is

---

1. Brown, *An Introduction to the New Testament*, 76.

2. Brown, *An Introduction to the New Testament*, 76.

3. Brown, *An Introduction to the New Testament*, 75.

one long sentence in a style more formal than that found elsewhere in the Gospel. There are parallels in the prefaces of classical Greek historians and of Hellenistic medical and scientific treatises…Luke's theological goal [is written on behalf of]…the dedicatee, 'most excellent Theophilus.'"[4] Theophilus means "friend of God, or loved by God"[5] in Greek.

This chapter will be filtered through the lens of this Evangelist, Luke, whose *raison d'etre* comes from how he is occasionally referred to, as "the Evangelist of the Holy Spirit" and the "Evangelist of prayer."[6] This is affirmed by Bede who asserted: "Rightly does He lead the disciples, about to be instructed in the mysteries of His Body, to the mount of Olives, that He might signify that all who are baptized in His death should be comforted with the anointing of the Holy Spirit."[7] I would be remiss if I were not to underscore the presence of the Trinity in Gethsemane which Bede's quote affirms. For indeed, in the Garden Agony, Jesus, the Son of God and Second Person of the Trinity, prays to the Father, the First Person of the Trinity. The Third Person of the Trinity is present in Gethsemane's oil from the olive press, the comforting anointing of the Holy Spirit.

The overarching Lukan theme of prayer is confirmed in this Lukan Gethsemane narrative in which great emphasis is placed upon the prayer of Christ in the Garden, with details the other evangelists do not include, worded in a way that emphasizes the importance of prayer

———————

4. Brown, *An Introduction to the New Testament*, 75.

5. Bible Info, "Who is Theophilus in the Bible books of Luke and Acts?", *Bible Info*, n.d., accessed July 2024, www.bibleinfo.com.

6. Jerome Kodell, *The Gospel According to Luke*, (Collegeville, MN: The Liturgical Press; 1991), 10.

7. Thomas Aquinas, *Catena Aurea: Commentary on the Four Gospels vol. III, St. Luke*, trans. John Henry Newman (London: Baronius Press, 2022), 720.

such as: "He was in such agony and he prayed so fervently,"[8] or, "being in agony, he prayed the longer."[9]

St. Luke's Gospel uniquely emphasizes Christ's perseverance in prayer by articulating that His Agony necessitated more time spent, until He was ready, and thus is a lesson for all who pray. St. Luke uniquely mentions the presence of an angel. Of great import, St. Luke is the only Evangelist to include the detail of Jesus sweating blood. Luke's Gospel is "interested in portraying this scene as a cosmic battle,"[10] and his Gospel and commentaries upon it will be an important study for this thesis, as the shedding of Jesus' blood in the Garden is a vital consideration that points to Him as the Eucharistic Host of Gethsemane. These three unique Lukan details: Jesus praying "the longer;" the ministering angel; and the shedding of blood will each be addressed vis-a-vis Jesus as the Host/host of Gethsemane.

The Evangelist of Hospitality

Of pivotal importance, the hospitality emphasized in Luke will be closely considered in light of this study. I assert that St. Luke could be called "The Evangelist of Hospitality," due to his unique Gospel, which is the only one to include The Good Samaritan, and also emphasizes the House at Bethany, in which Saints Martha and Mary show great hospitality to Jesus. There also many themes of hospitality throughout Luke's Gospel. Also in Luke, there is the famous "Road to Emmaus" pericope in which hospitality is a key element, and the lens in which that narrative is read; the same hospitality Jesus is offering and seeking in Gethsemane:

---

8. Lk 22:44.

9. Lk 22:43 [*Douay-Rheims*].

10. Green and McKnight, *Dictionary of Jesus and the Gospels*, 266.

And he went into the house of the Pharisee, and sat down to meat. And behold a woman that was in the city, a sinner, when she knew that he sat at meat in the Pharisee's house, brought an alabaster box of ointment; And standing behind at his feet, she began to wash his feet, with tears, and wiped them with the hairs of her head, and kissed his feet, and anointed them with the ointment...And turning to the woman, he said unto Simon: Dost thou see this woman? I entered into thy house, thou gavest me no water for my feet; but she with tears hath washed my feet, and with her hairs hath wiped them. Thou gavest me no kiss; but she, since she came in, hath not ceased to kiss my feet. My head with oil thou didst not anoint; but she with ointment hath anointed my feet. Wherefore I say to thee: Many sins are forgiven her, because she hath loved much.[11]

While I acknowledge that Jesus proclaimed "The Son of Man did not come to be served but to serve,"[12] nevertheless, it is clear in the above passage that Jesus notices and cares about the hospitality he receives from others. Furthermore, in response to the question, "Why did God make you?" the Baltimore Catechism answers, "God made me to know Him, to love Him, and to serve Him in this world, and to be happy with Him in the next."[13] And so, since Jesus is God, the Second Person of the Trinity, we are made to serve Him, and indeed, if we are to follow His example, we must.

"He was told, 'Your mother and your brothers are standing outside and they wish to see you.' He said to them in reply, 'My

---

11. Lk 7:36-47.

12. Mt 20:28.

13. *The Baltimore Catechism,* 6.

mother and my brothers are those who hear the word of God and act on it.'"[14]

The Son of Man Has Nowhere to Lay His Head

"As they were proceeding on their journey someone said to him, 'I will follow you wherever you go.' Jesus answered him, 'Foxes have dens and birds of the sky have nests, but the Son of Man has nowhere to rest his head.'"[15]

This verse, asserting that the animals of creation having their own places to rest but the Son of Man, the Second Person of the Trinity, does not have the same, is poignant. Its words resound through Scripture as a reminder of how little hospitality Jesus received, and when considered in Gethsemane, it is as though a challenge is posed to the host of faithful visiting Gethsemane in prayer, and further, visiting with the Eucharistic Lord. Does Christ have a place to rest His head in Gethsemane, or when one receives Him in the Eucharist? The answer is the same in both cases: He has a place to rest His head if He is offered the heart of His faithful servant. "Faithful friends are a sturdy shelter."[16] These words of Sirach teach that a shelter, a place to rest one's head, can be offered through friendship. Hospitality is more than just welcoming someone to a structure with a roof and four walls. It is the movable tent of how we humbly welcome Him to enter under the roof of each of our very selves, as we do at Holy Communion, as was discussed in more detail in Chapter One. Jesus deserves to be built this kind of house in Gethsemane, and each time one receives Him in the

---

14. Lk 8:20-21.

15. Lk 9:57-58.

16. Sir 6:14.

Eucharist. Faithful friends are a sturdy shelter, when they stay awake with a friend in need. As we learn in the Gospel of Luke:

> Into whatever house you enter, first say, "Peace to this household." If a peaceful person lives there, your peace will rest on him; but if not, it will return to you. Stay in the same house and eat and drink what is offered to you, for the laborer deserves his payment. Do not move about from one house to another. Whatever town you enter and they welcome you, eat what is set before you, cure the sick in it and say to them, "The kingdom of God is at hand for you." Whatever town you enter and they do not receive you, go out into the streets and say, "The dust of your town that clings to our feet, even that we shake off against you." Yet know this: the kingdom of God is at hand.[17]

Luke's Good Samaritan and the Host/host of Gethsemane

A parable that is completely unique to Luke's Gospel is that of the Good Samaritan; and it has an important bearing on the theme of the Host/host. After Jesus is asked by a lawyer "who is my neighbor," Jesus tells the Parable of the Good Samaritan, about a man who fell among robbers that left him half dead. A priest and a Levite passed by the poor man:

> But a Samaritan traveler who came upon him was moved with compassion at the sight. He approached the victim,

---

17. Lk 10:5-11.

poured oil and wine over his wounds and bandaged them. Then he lifted him up on his own animal, took him to an inn and cared for him. The next day he took out two silver coins and gave them to the innkeeper with the instruction, "Take care of him. If you spend more than what I have given you, I shall repay you on my way back." Which of these three, in your opinion, was neighbor to the robbers' victim? He answered, "The one who treated him with mercy." Jesus said to him, "Go and do likewise."[18]

It is worth noting that the Samaritan is "moved with compassion" for this man half-dead. And yet, in the Gethsemane narrative, Jesus declares that his soul is sorrowful unto death. Therefore, it is clear that what is called for by the guests in Gethsemane is compassion. Further, the Samaritan pours "oil and wine" on tbe victim's wounds, and then brings him to an innkeeper (a "host"). In Gethsemane, Jesus, the Host/host who is the paragon of any possible Good Samaritan, is pouring the oil of His agony and wine of His bloody sweat into the wounds of a bruised humanity in this agonizing hour of His Paschal Mystery. The guests of Gethsemane, the host of the faithful called to enter in prayer where Peter, James, and John fell asleep, are faced with the same option those three slumbered through: will we offer the pressed oil of Gethsemane, sanctified by Jesus, (as every good thing we ever have to offer comes to us from God) as a kind of salve for his bloody sweat in the Garden? "For indeed, Christ says: Go, and do thou in like manner." Let this, then, be done in Gethsemane: may the faithful be Good Samaritans there.

Luke constructs the second half of Chapter 10 in a cohesive and thematic structure. Immediately after the conclusion of the story of the Good Samaritan, in the very next verse which follows,"Go, and do

---

18. Lk 10:25-37.

likewise," it is written: "As they continued their journey he entered a village where a woman whose name was Martha welcomed him."[19]

Martha and Mary: Two Prototypes of "Watching" and "Praying"

Martha "received" Him; just as the faithful "receive" Holy Communion. Martha has opened her home to Him, the same Christ who in just the previous chapter declared that He has nowhere to rest His head. This is of great significance, and this perhaps overlooked part of the story reveals that it was Martha, not Mary, who initiated the hospitality, and who first received Him. This is the kind of hospitable initiative that the Host of Gethsemane deserves to be given by the faithful in the Garden.

When viewed from the perspective of the Host/host of Gethsemane, the rest of the Martha and Mary story is equally relevant. Martha is anxious about serving Jesus, and becomes angry that Mary is not helping her serve. "She had a sister named Mary [who] sat beside the Lord at his feet listening to him speak."[20] Jesus told Martha, "Mary has chosen the better part and it will not be taken from her."[21] It is notable that Mary did not leave Christ's side. Martha was directly serving Jesus, but she did so not only with a grumbling heart; she did so *at a distance*. Christ asks for loving company, a heart of friendship and consolation, which is actually a place He *can* rest His Head. Mary, settled at the Lord's feet, could not be pulled away, even under the worldly pressures of being called to help family, which can be a distraction for so many. Jesus asks for company in Gethsemane to

---

19. Lk 10:38.
20. Lk 10:39.
21. Lk 10:42.

watch and pray with Him, near Him, and not to be distracted by sorrow, anxiety, or slumber.

In the verse immediately following Luke's recount of Mary choosing the better part, Jesus teaches the Our Father. "He was praying in a certain place, and when he had finished, one of his disciples said to him, 'Lord, teach us to pray just as John taught his disciples.' He said to them, 'When you pray, say: Father, hallowed be your name, your kingdom come. Give us each day our daily bread and forgive us our sins for we ourselves forgive everyone in debt to us, and do not subject us to the final test.'"[22]

It is no accident that the prayer par excellence is taught right after Mary sits at Christ's feet and listens to Him speak in her home at Bethany. It is no accident that Luke's placement of the Martha and Mary story is exactly between the Parable of the Good Samaritan and the teaching of the Our Father. Martha, the first character in the Bethany story, embodies the vigilant watching of a Good Samaritan. The lesson of Mary listening to Jesus preach closes the end of the Bethany account and fittingly precedes the teaching of the Our Father. The Our Father is the ultimate prayer; and Mary is the embodiment of the faithful one who prays.

In his masterpiece, "Agony in the Garden,"[23] (see Figure 1) Fra Angelico, the holy Dominican Friar also known as Guido di Pietro or Blessed John of Fiesole, the Patron Saint of Artists, juxtaposes the three fast-asleep apostles: Peter, James, and John, reclining sleepily in the garden. Meanwhile, Martha and Mary, who are staying awake, are watching and praying in their Bethany house. It appears in the painting as though St. Peter's elbow is leaning upon the stone wall of the sisters' house.

---

22. Lk 11:1-4.

23. Fra Angelico, "Christ in Garden of Gethsemane", fresco, 1450, Museum of San Marco, accessed April 2024, at useum.org/artwork/Christ-in-Garden-of-Gethsemane-Fra-Angelico-1450.

Figure 1. Fra Angelico, Christ in Garden of Gethsemane, ca. 1450, oil on canvas.

Of course the sisters were not actually physically present in Gethsemane. But Fra Angelico recognizes, and depicts, the reality that anyone may arrive in the Garden of Gethsemane to keep vigil with Christ, through their prayers. God, who is beyond time and space, is omnipotent, omniscient, and omnipresent; therefore He will recognize the presence of anyone who spiritually enters Gethsemane in watchful prayer, which is an act of reciprocal hospitality, one even the apostles did not give Him.

In the mind's eye, as the viewer gazes upon Fra Angelico's painted Bethany house, one can insert one's own house in its stead, open to receive the Lord, to console Him there in Gethsemane, on the Mount of Olives, with the same kind of loving hospitality He received in the house at Bethany.

It is plausible that Martha and Mary, being such close friends of Jesus, would have some knowledge of where their Master was that night and what He was preparing for in Gethsemane. Scripture reveals that He had told them that the fragrant oil with which Mary anointed Him was preparing Him for His death (to be discussed further in the next chapter devoted to John's Gospel). Just as the sisters cooked for him and anointed Him mere days before His Passion began, it would be plausible that they'd characteristically continue to do what they could for Him as He entered the garden; that is to say, be willing to keep vigil for Him.

In a brilliant artistic maneuver, Fra Angelico painted the devoted sisters of Bethany following the request of Jesus: watching and praying, keeping vigil. The prototypical "watchman," one who embodies watching; alert work; and action, is St. Martha. The prototypical contemplative, who embodies rest, contemplation, and prayer is St. Mary of Bethany. In Fra Angelico's time, the Bethany sisters were indeed known as the two prototypes of the *vitae contemplativa* (the contemplative life, as exemplified by Mary) and the *vitae activa* (the active life, as exemplified by Martha).

In the painting, Mary is engaged in contemplative *lectio divina*, with the Bible open on her lap as she contemplates and listens to God's Word. Martha, her hands folded, actively prays, talking to God. Each cares for the garden of her soul by watching and praying as Jesus asks in Gethsemane, and thus, inviting God in. Both sisters are very much awake.

Fra Angelico was awake, in the eschatological sense of the word. He knew the destiny of mankind was meant to know God, love God, and serve God,[24] and he wasted no time in going to work, using his God-given talent to love and serve, literally watching and praying as he worked. "Angelico was a tireless worker and finished a great number of paintings in his lifetime, but, thinking it would somehow be against God's will, he never retouched or reworked any of them. He always prayed when he painted, and he would say, 'To paint the things of Christ, one must live with Christ.'"[25] Thus, Fra Angelico is an exemplar: he chooses the better part and prays like Mary, but he also

---

24. *CCC*, 1721.

joins that prayer to the work of his hands, like Martha. Due to this, his labor becomes a thing of great beauty. The fruit of his prayerful work, his painting, is a reminder for all, throughout the generations, to stay awake with Christ in Gethsemane. It is a colloquial expression to state when one can't be present at a friend's side: "I'll be with you in spirit." It is interesting to ponder who was with Jesus "in spirit" as He suffered in Gethsemane. The Blessed Mother surely was. Perhaps, as Fra Angelico envisions, Martha and Mary of Bethany were, too. In any case, each and any of the faithful may enter Gethsemane, spiritually, with each Holy Hour that is prayed. There will be more details on this subject in Chapter Five.

In the Garden of Gethsemane, Jesus, the ever-attentive host, teaches us to watch. Like the Good Samaritan, He pours (with each drop of the blood He sweats) the pressed oil of healing balm into man's sores created by sin. In Gethsemane's garden, He also teaches us to pray, "Thy Will be done," the ultimate outcry of the Our Father. In Bethany, Jesus found disciples willing to do the Gethsemane work of watching and praying, of being an active, hospitable Good Samaritan, and a contemplative at the feet of Christ. These two prototypes of "watching" and "praying" live in Bethany, which is on that very same Mount of Olives upon which Gethsemane is located.

Bethany: House of Figs and Faith

"The name Bethany is translated by some to mean 'House of Figs,' as there are many fig trees and palms in the area."[26] Bethany,

---

25. Charles Shonk, excerpt from "A Pale Light", *Dominican Friars Foundation*, n.d., accessed May 2024, dominicanfriars.org/bl-john-fiesole-fra-angelico/.

26. Holy Land Site, "Bethany, Tomb of Lazarus", *Holy Land Site*, n.d., accessed April 2024, www.holylandsite.com/bethany-tomb-of-lazarus.

"House of Figs" is located on the Mount of Olives, where Gethsemane, "the Place of the Olive Press," is also located. The two areas are proximate to each other.

How important the House of Bethany is to the discussion of the Host/host of Gethsemane. "Known primarily in the Gospels as the home of Mary, Martha, and Lazarus, ancient Bethany occupied an important place in the life of Jesus. Jesus often found Himself staying in Bethany at the home of His closest friends as He ministered in Jerusalem. Located on the Mount of Olives...the road between Bethany and Jerusalem provided a ready avenue for travel across Olivet with the journey taking about 55 minutes to walk."[27]

Bethany is the location in which Jesus found welcome, rest, and nourishment offered to Him by Saint Martha. It is also where He was lavished with the prayerful adoration of Saint Mary. It is a poetic detail that the land of Bethany, where Christ received companionable consolation; touches the land of Gethsemane, where Christ was agonizingly alone.

"Some translate the meaning of Bethany as 'house of misery,' believing that Bethany was a designated place for those with contagious diseases."[28] Indeed, every house has its share of affliction. Focusing on the translation "House of Figs," one may consider that figs were used in the teachings of Christ to represent faith. For example, Christ uses the barren fig tree to teach His followers about tending their faith:

> And he told them this parable: There once was a person who had a fig tree planted in his orchard, and when he came in search of fruit on it but found none, he said to the gardener, "For three years now I have come in search of fruit on this fig tree but have found none. [So] cut it down. Why should it exhaust the soil?" He said to him in reply,

---

27. Butler et al., *Holman Illustrated Bible Dictionary*, 189.
28. Holy Land Site, "Bethany, Tomb of Lazarus".

"Sir, leave it for this year also, and I shall cultivate the ground around it and fertilize it; it may bear fruit in the future. If not you can cut it down."[29]

Christ seeks faith in Gethsemane, among those who watch and pray with Him. Three times He comes to wake not only Peter, James, and John, but through them; each one of us.

Bethany, then, by its very name, symbolizes the faith Christ finds even in the midst of affliction. Every earthly house is one of affliction; is it also one of faith? That is the question. The house of affliction may be made sweeter when it is simultaneously a house of faith. Hospitality is a key component to staying awake to watch and pray; that is, being receptive to the Host/host's invitation and responding in kind as a good and attentive guest. May Gethsemane be a testing ground that finds each one faithful in the midst of affliction, as our Host has taught us by His peerless example. May each personal Gethsemane in the life of each of the faithful be grounded in a personal House of Bethany, and with faithful watchmen to help keep vigil. But whatever the situation, however dismal or lonely or without succor, may that personal Gethsemane be endured by keeping one's gaze fixed upon the one non-variable: the steadfast example of Jesus of Gethsemane, whose absence of wakeful friends in the Garden guarantees His ability to compassionate the most lonely among us; and guarantees the most lonely among us the opportunity to console God Himself, and therefore, cease to be lonely.

---

29. Lk 13:6-9.

Blessed Are the Servants Whom the Lord Shall Find Watching

In the Gospel of Luke, these words foreshadow, or as I prefer to say in the term I coined earlier, "forelighten" Gethsemane:

> For where your treasure is, there also will your heart be. Gird your loins and light your lamps and be like servants who await their master's return from a wedding, ready to open immediately when he comes and knocks. Blessed are those servants whom the master finds vigilant on his arrival. Amen, I say to you, he will gird himself, have them recline at table, and proceed to wait on them. And should he come in the second or third watch and find them prepared in this way, blessed are those servants. Be sure of this: if the master of the house had known the hour when the thief was coming, he would not have let his house be broken into. You also must be prepared, for at an hour you do not expect, the Son of Man will come.[30]

At the very least, I assert Gethsemane is the way Jesus lives out His teachings in this "where your treasure is" passage, by example. It is the place and time in which we see Jesus literally arrive a second and even a third time to His servants, whom He finds asleep. This teaching, I assert, makes Gethsemane a fitting garden in which to focus the hearts of the faithful; for therein is the Treasure: the Host/host who comes to check on those He has invited three times; who warns against the thief and teaches how to prevent being caught

---

30. Lk 12:34-40.

off guard; who offers the Garden as a school and a hospital: a location in which the soul may be trained and healed; simultaneously. Jesus is the treasure. He spends time in the Garden of Gethsemane; and He lingers there; so must we.

Blessed Are Those Called to the Supper of the Lamb

"One of his fellow guests on hearing this said to him, 'Blessed is the one who will dine in the kingdom of God.'"[31] This Chapter of Luke, known as "The Parable of the Great Feast," reminds of what occurs in Gethsemane. For Jesus responds to this fellow guest, "A man gave a great dinner to which he invited many. When the time for the dinner came, he dispatched his servant to say to those invited, 'Come, everything is now ready.' But one by one, they all began to excuse themselves…"[32] This leads to the host of the dinner inviting the poor and the blind, and those among the highways and hedgerows.

It is among hedgerows of a certain garden on the Mount of Olives that each one of the faithful is still invited, through the call of Gethsemane that continues to resound, an ongoing invitation across time and space through the living word of Scripture: "you could not keep watch with me for one hour?"[33] The Gethsemane narrative of Luke 22 shows Jesus inviting them to "Pray, that you may not undergo the test,"[34] and to vigilantly remain at His side during His Agony, which is an honor, a chance to serve the Suffering Servant. But did not Peter, James, and John "excuse themselves" as those invited in the

---

31. Lk 14:15.
32. Lk 14:16-18.
33. Mt 26:40.
34. Lk 22:40.

Lukan Parable of the Great Feast? Indeed, their excuse was the fatigue of sleep.

And yet, it is important to note that Luke 22 does not simply contain the narrative of the Garden of Gethsemane, but also includes the account of the Last Supper. This is similar to Matthew 26 and Mark 14. Thus, even Scripture itself elucidates the fact that Jesus is the Host of Gethsemane, the same Eucharistic Lord who presides over the first Mass in the Upper Room. A fascinating detail from the same chapter as Gethsemane in Luke 22 is a passage in which the role of the disciples is described. What Jesus says here reveals much about the Host/host of Gethsemane and His invited guests. "For who is greater: the one seated at table or the one who serves? Is it not the one seated at table? I am among you as the one who serves."[35] The Host of Gethsemane is the Great Servant. We who are called to Gethsemane to watch and pray with Him as His servant guests are meant to follow His perfect example.

In Revelation we read: "Blessed are those who have been called to the wedding feast of the Lamb,"[36] and this reminds of the Host/host relationship of Christ and His guests. These words are part of the Mass as the priest holds up the Eucharistic Host: "Blessed are those called to the supper of the Lamb." Edward Sri expounds on the significance of these words:

> …they underscore how the Eucharist is no ordinary meal, for they recall a climactic moment in the book of Revelation when Jesus comes to unite himself to his people in a great heavenly wedding feast. In this scene, Jesus Christ, the Lamb of God, is depicted as a bridegroom joining himself to his bride, the Church. An angel announces this loving union by saying, "Blessed are those who are invited to the marriage supper of the Lamb"

---

35. Lk 22:27.
36. Rev 19:9.

(Revelation 19:9). In the new translation, the priest at Mass more clearly echoes this angelic invitation to the heavenly wedding feast. When you hear these words in the liturgy, therefore, you should realize that you are, in a sense, receiving a wedding invitation! And at this great marriage feast, you are no ordinary guest. When you come down the aisle to receive Holy Communion, you come as the bride, as a member of the Church. And you come to be united with your divine Bridegroom who gives Himself to you in the most intimate way possible here on earth—in the Holy Eucharist. Here, we see how the Eucharist involves an intimate, loving communion with our Lord Jesus—one that is likened to the union shared between a husband and wife. Indeed, Holy Communion is a participation in that heavenly wedding supper of the Lamb, which celebrates the union of the divine bridegroom, Jesus, with his bride, the Church.[37]

In Gethsemane, the Paschal Lamb has begun to shed His Blood; the Eucharistic chalice of sacrifice which He must drink looms above Him; the High Priest prays for His guests. It is a continuation of the Last Supper which culminates at Calvary. We must watch and pray in adoration of the Eucharistic Host; we must not sleep at this Altar of Repose. The "hedgerows"[38] of Gethsemane is where we may be gathered by the Host/host to taste the food which many do not know; the food of doing the Father's will[39]. "The master then ordered the servant, 'Go out to the highways and hedgerows and make people

---

37. Edward Sri, "The Supper of the Lamb", *Catholic Education Resource Center*, October 28, 2011, accessed April 2024, www.catholiceducation.org/en/culture/catholic-contributions/the-supper-of-the-lamb.html.

38. Lk 14:23.

39. Jn 4:32-34.

come in that my home may be filled. For, I tell you, none of those men who were invited will taste my dinner.'"[40] For as we recall, those invited at first excused themselves and it was those among the highways and hedgerows who came to the Great Feast. Let us not allow the excuse of slumber to keep us from the taste of the food of doing the Father's will, to be discussed in more detail next chapter, which will focus on the Gospel of John.

The Prodigal Feast

The food of doing the Father's will leads to inclusion in the Host/host's banquet. The image of inviting others to His company is a prominent theme in the Gospel of Luke, or as I refer to it, the Gospel of Hospitality. Chapter 15 focuses on the Parable of the Prodigal Son, preceded in that very same chapter by the Parables of the Lost Coin and the Lost Sheep. This chapter of Luke, then, is an ongoing celebration of recovering what had been lost, and of the forgiveness of sin. About forgiveness, Fr. Francis P. Donnelly writes:

> Forgiveness which comes from the heart is the most consoling, and Jesus has put in rubrics all that can read the message of God's loving forgiveness. No better attestation of full forgiveness could you ask for. Your likeness to God which was disfigured by sin is restored and ennobled. The justice of the Redemption repairs the ravages of original sin and builds a grander edifice upon the ruin of Adam. "Happy fault," the Church dares to say, "which merited so excellent a Redeemer..." Jesus has prayed and has fasted for you, and shed tears of blood for you. He has given you

---

40. Lk 14:23-24.

a picture of Himself in the parable of the Prodigal's father. Forgiveness for Jesus means joy in Heaven and joy upon earth. Jesus through forgiveness and grace not only brings God to your soul, not only makes you partakers of divinity, not only gives you Heaven as your inheritance, but also makes you a child of God and clothes you in the finest raiment and sets you beside Him at the banquet of eternity. "This is my son who was dead, is come to life." "Yes, my God and my Savior, I am forgiven and have life again through thy Agony and through Thy death."[41]

It is through the Agony and Passion that we are forgiven and have life again: our invitation to join the Host/host of Gethsemane is an invitation to forgiveness of sin and the promise of everlasting life.

The Anointing of Jesus with Oil and The Olive Press of Gethsemane

Bede asserts, "Rightly does He lead the disciples, about to be instructed in the mysteries of His Body, to the Mount of Olives, that He might signify that all who are baptized in His death should be comforted with the *anointing* of the Holy Spirit."[42]

But before Jesus leads the apostles to the Mount of Olives to be anointed, a woman brought "an alabaster flask of ointment, she stood behind him at his feet weeping and began to bathe his feet with her tears. Then she wiped them with her hair, kissed them, and anointed

---

41. Francis P. Donnelly, *The Our Father in Gethsemane*, (New York: 1935, TAN Books), 86-87.

42. Aquinas, *Catena Aurea Vol III*, 720.

them with the ointment."[43] Christ's response to this was to declare to the host of the feast: "You did not anoint my head with oil, but she anointed my feet with ointment. So I tell you, her many sins have been forgiven; hence, she has shown great love."[44] Then He tells her, "Your faith has saved you; go in peace."[45]

The faith of each believer is the gift that saves them, through the love shown to Our Lord, and one such symbol of that love is an anointing with oil. Jesus anoints His followers through the oil of Gethsemane. Each of the faithful is called to anoint Him in return, like the woman with the alabaster flask, through the oil of watching and praying with Him, vigilantly in the Garden.

In Biblical times, oil poured out upon a guest was a sign of great hospitality. In the Catholic Church, oil is used to consecrate a church or altar; to consecrate the hands of a priest; to seal Confirmandi with the Holy Spirit.[46] Recalling Bede's words that Jesus leads the disciples to the Mount of Olives "that He might signify that all who are baptized in His death should be comforted with the anointing of the Holy Spirit," it is important to consider that when a priest receives the Sacrament of Holy Orders, his hands are anointed with chrism, holy oil:

> A *manutergium* (from the Latin manu and tergium = hand towel), is used to soak up the chrism oil after the bishop anoints a new priest's hands. Priestly hands are holy. The hands of the priest hold up the bread and wine when they are changed to the Body and Blood of Jesus Christ during the consecration of the Mass. Their hands also make the Sign of the Cross while absolving sins, anointing the sick

43. Lk 7:37-38.

44. Lk 7:46-47.

45. Lk 7:50.

46. Rhonda Miska, "What is chrism?", *U.S. Catholic*, June 29, 2016, accessed April 2024, uscatholic.org/articles/201606/what-is-chrism/.

and dying, baptizing, praying and serving their flocks in so many ways. During the anointing, the bishop prays: "The Lord Jesus Christ, whom the Father anointed with the Holy Spirit, empower, guard and preserve you, that you may sanctify the Christian people and offer sacrifice to God."[47]

The chrism is olive oil mixed with balsam.

Traditionally, the Chrism Mass of each diocese prepares the holy oils for the year: oil of the sick, oil of the catechumens, and chrism. The Chrism Mass is traditionally celebrated on Holy Thursday morning, although it can also be on an earlier day near Easter.[48] It is incredibly significant that Holy Thursday, the day Christ entered Gethsemane to endure His Agony, is the customary day of the Chrism Mass for each diocese. Traditionally, too, the chrism oils are received by each parish church at Holy Thursday evening Mass:

> Before consecrating the chrism, the bishop mixes the oil with balsam—a sweet, aromatic perfume used since ancient times, no doubt in connection to 2 Corinthians 2:15-16, where St. Paul refers to the fragrance of Christ that Christians must disperse everywhere they go. Then, before the prayer of consecration, the bishop breathes over the oil —indicative of the Holy Spirit's descent through invocation.

---

47. Patti Maguire Armstrong, "Holy Cloth for Mom", *National Catholic Register*, May 21, 2017, accessed March 2024, https://www.ncregister.com/features/holy-cloth-for-mom/.

48. "The Blessing of the Oils and the Consecration of the Chrism", *United States Conference of Catholic Bishops*, n.d., accessed May 2024, www.usccb.org/prayer-and-worship/sacraments-and-sacramentals/sacramentals-blessings/blessing-of-oils-and-consecration-of-chrism.

The verb "consecrate" is applied to the action of making holy the chrism and indicates its use to spiritually separate, sanctify and purify its recipients. While the oil of the sick and the oil of catechumens may, in emergency, be blessed by any priest, this is not the case with chrism. "Consecrate" indicates, then, that only a bishop may bless it.[49]

This oil of Chrism, blessed by the Bishop, is the very oil which anoints us at our Confirmation. It seals promises made by us, or our Godparents for us, at our Baptism. At Baptism, the oil of Chrism is traced on the crown of the child's head, and marks him as a Christian, an adopted child of God:

> Christ's holy name means "the anointed of the Lord."…
> And so the oil of chrism takes its very name from him and is the means by which Christians become sharers in his royal and prophetic priesthood. "We are called Christians because we are anointed with the oil of God," wrote St. Theophilus of Antioch in the second century.

There are two consecratory prayers optioned in the ritual, the first of which draws significant parallels between Christian use of this oil and similar biblical use of oil. The first prayer is one of thanksgiving for God's gifts given in the past, foreshadowing those given through anointing with this oil. In fact in the third-century Apostolic Tradition, it is referred to as the "oil of thanksgiving."[50]

---

49. Michael R. Heinlein, "A Closer Look at the Holy Oils", *Simply Catholic*, March 25, 2024, accessed May 2024, www.simplycatholic.com/a-closer-look-at-the-holy-oils/.

50. Heinlein, "A Closer Look at the Holy Oils".

The oil of Chrism given to us at our Confirmation is not only to mark us with an indelible sign of membership in the church, but also to strengthen us to live out that commitment. It imbues us with the gifts of the Holy Spirit; gifts that can assist us in our own Gardens of Gethsemane: wisdom, understanding, counsel, fortitude, knowledge, piety, and fear of the Lord:

> The strength Israel's kings needed in governing earthly affairs with divine guidance was symbolized in their Old Testament anointing (see 1 Sm 10, Samuel's anointing of Saul). The first of the consecratory prayers references King David twice—as he "sang of the life and joy that the oil would bring us in the sacraments," and it was through him that God prophesied that "Christ would be anointed with the oil of gladness beyond his fellow men." In history, a variety of Christian kings and emperors were anointed with sacred chrism by popes and bishops at their coronations.[51]

This oil of Chrism has such powerful significance in our faith going back to ancient tradition and continuing today in our church practices:

> In the case of Elisha, we learn of the biblical anointing of a prophet (see 1 Kgs 19:16). Recipients of sacred chrism will prophetically be "radiant with the goodness of life that has its source in (God)."

> Priests and bishops today are anointed with sacred chrism at their ordinations. An Old Testament source for this practice is found with Aaron, Moses' brother, whom he anointed a priest (see Ex 29:7 and Lv 8:12).

---

51. Heinlein, "A Closer Look at the Holy Oils".

"Let the splendor of holiness shine on the world from every place and thing signed with this oil," says the second of the consecratory prayers for chrism. Formerly, church bells were anointed on the inside with chrism and the oil of the sick on the outside. The ancient practice of using chrism to consecrate altars and churches remains in practice today.[52]

Oil, or chrism, is intrinsic to the very name of Christ Himself, and the Church, the Bride of Christ, is anointed also:

Using oil to dedicate things to God has Old Testament roots (for examples, see Gn 28:18 or Ex 30:25-29). Altars are set aside for sacrifice and early in Christianity the altar became representative of Christ himself, the perfect sacrifice. And so, since Christ's name means anointed one, it's most fitting that the altar—which is a symbol of the Anointed One par excellence—itself is anointed. In dedicating a church building, a church's walls are signed with chrism—since the building represents the anointed members of his Body, and, like us are called to be "holy, visible signs of the mystery of Christ and his Church." More on this is found in the Rite of Dedication of an Altar.[53]

I assert that the Sacrament of Holy Orders, instituted in the Upper Room at the Last Supper, continues in Gethsemane, as I also assert that all chrism, all sacred oil, has its roots in the oil of Gethsemane, pressed from the sacrifice Jesus gave in the literal "place of the olive press." The earth of Gethsemane Jesus lay prostrate upon, the ground he sweated blood on; what are they but the original site, consecrated by Christ, of the posture taken by each priest when he lays face down at his ordination. The rock in Gethsemane Jesus is

52. Heinlein, "A Closer Look at the Holy Oils".
53. Heinlein, "A Closer Look at the Holy Oils".

145

traditionally said to have leaned upon; would be as an altar, since the precious blood was shed in Gethsemane, and like an altar it would be consecrated with holy oil, the oil of Gethsemane formed under the press of Christ's heavy agony. I assert, too, that the oil of priesthood, the holy chrism that consecrates priestly hands, is spiritually marked with the oil of Gethsemane. Christ brought his three highest bishops into the Garden with Him right after their ordination in the Upper Room. The oil of His work in Gethsemane, the pressing He endured as He was "crushed for our iniquity"[54] anoints Peter, James, and John, even while they sleep. Christ is the anointed one. Anointed means "Sacred, dedicated to God, dabbed with holy oil."[55] Sacred means "set apart."[56] Gethsemane is, as a location, so intrinsically sacred, as it is a place set apart where Christ went to be alone, with His invited friends. There, in sacred, set-apart Gethsemane, I assert the holy oil of all holy oils was made by Christ, when He allowed Himself to be pressed upon the ground of the Garden of Olives, in Gethsemane, the "place of the olive press," under the weight of our sins, to the point of emanating a bloody sweat, his own sacred effluence in the Garden of Olives which surely was sweeter than balsam.

As described in Chapter Two of this work, Jesus was anointed at Bethany.[57] "She has done a good thing for me. The poor you will always have with you; but you will not always have me. In pouring this perfumed oil upon my body, she did it to prepare me for burial. Amen, I say to you, wherever this gospel is proclaimed in the whole world, what she has done will be spoken of, in memory of her."[58] And so, it is a loving woman who is allowed to anoint the Anointed One for His Burial. Thus, anyone, priest or religious, layman, or laywoman,

---

54. Is 53:5.

55. Dictionary.com, s.v. "anointed", www.dictionary.com/browse/anointed/.

56. Mirriam-Webster Online, s.v. "sacred," accessed April, 2024, www.merriam-webster.com/dictionary/sacred/.

57. Mt 26,Mk 14.

58. Mt 26:10-13.

may respond to the invitation of the Host/host of Gethsemane to anoint Him with our watchful prayers, our desire to do the Will of God, all the good fruit that comes from the oil press of Gethsemane. Anyone, too, may decide to become a Veronica of Gethsemane, wiping the Chrism of Gethsemane (which is the oil of agony, the bloody sweat endured under the weight of the olive press of sorrow) from the face of Christ. Every drop of the Passion is precious, every drop of blood; every bit of Gethsemane's chrism.

So, too, the chrism which anoints the hands of a new priest is precious. When wiped with a towel, a *maniturgium*, it cannot simply be discarded. Traditionally, this *maniturgium* is gifted to the mother of a priest. "Why the mother?...the mother of a priest is a special person. She nurtures his vocation from the very beginning just as the Blessed Virgin Mary nurtured her son, Our Lord Jesus Christ, from the very beginning...According to tradition, a new priest's mother is to safeguard the *maniturgium* she receives until the day she dies. Then, the cloth is placed in the hands of the priest's mother as she rests in the coffin. It is kind of a symbol saying 'you gave me life' and this is a symbol of my priesthood."[59]

During the ordination of a bishop, the bishop's head is anointed with Sacred Chrism, which is symbolic of the whole person being consecrated.[60] The connection between oil and priesthood is a deep one. The location of Gethsemane makes the place of the olive press and the Agony in the Garden, in a very real sense, the origin of all chrism; another reason Jesus is the Host of Gethsemane, High Priest and Sacrificial Lamb, His Blood shed for us. Before Jesus brought His apostles to Gethsemane, the place of the olive press, the woman with the alabaster flask anointed Him with oil in preparation for his death.

---

59. Jaimie Julia Winters, "Priests revive traditional gifts of cloth to mothers", *Jersey Catholic*, June 23, 2023, accessed May 2024, erseycatholic.org/priests-revive-traditional-gifts-of-cloth-to-mothers-1.

60. Karen Clifford, "Oils of Chrism—a sign of God's mercy", *Today's Catholic*, April 13, 2011, accessed May 2024, todayscatholic.org/oils-of-chrism-a-sign-of-gods-mercy/.

How fitting that the *maniturgium* is traditionally given to the mother of the priest, in preparation for her own death, when she is often the one who most tirelessly lavished him with the luster of faith, hope, and love and saw to it that he was anointed first with the oil of his baptism, when, like the Blessed Mother, she presented him as a newborn, as an offering to God.

A Stone's Cast: The Rock of Gethsemane

The stone referred to in Gethsemane, which is the place of the oil press, reminds of Jacob's dream at Bethel in which he saw the ladder of God's angels going from heaven to earth and vice-versa, as was previously discussed. "'Truly, the Lord is in this place and I did not know it!' He was afraid and said: 'How awesome this place is! This is nothing else but the house of God, the gateway to heaven!' Early the next morning Jacob took the stone that he had put under his head, set it up as a sacred pillar, and poured oil on top of it."[61] And so, Jacob consecrated this stone with oil, and recognized the holy spot as "an abode of God, a gateway to heaven." So much more, then, is Gethsemane, where Jesus Himself is physically present and sacrificing for us. Gethsemane is an abode of God, to which we are invited by the Host/host.

St. Augustine asserts, "He was torn from them about a stone's cast, as though He would typically remind them that to Him they should point the stone, that is, to Him bring the intention of the law which was written on the stone."[62] It is as though Augustine is reminding that Jesus is God who gave the ten commandments upon stone to Moses.

---

61. Gn 28:16-18.

62. Aquinas, *Catena Aurea Vol III*, 721.

148

Time spent with the Host/host under the olive trees of Gethsemane is a good foundation for our lives and yields good fruit:

> A good tree does not bear rotten fruit, nor does a rotten tree bear good fruit. For every tree is known by its own fruit. For people do not pick figs from thornbushes, nor do they gather grapes from brambles. A good person out of the store of goodness in his heart produces good, but an evil person out of a store of evil produces evil; for from the fullness of the heart the mouth speaks.

> Why do you call me, "Lord, Lord," but not do what I command? I will show you what someone is like who comes to me, listens to my words, and acts on them. That one is like a person building a house, who dug deeply and laid the foundation on rock; when the flood came, the river burst against that house but could not shake it because it had been well built.[63]

The house we must build is in Gethsemane, through our watching and praying among the olive trees that yield the fruit of strength, consolation, and hope, even after the pressing of sacrifice. The foundation of our house must be the cornerstone of Christ, where only "a stone's throw away" He has invited us to be part of the house He is building.

---

63. Lk 6:43-48.

Figure 2. Heinrich Hoffman,
"Christ in Gethsemane", 1890, oil
on canvas.

The image of Jesus kneeling before the rock of Gethsemane[64] (see Figure 2) resembles a priest at the altar at Mass, carrying our sacrifices on his back and bending in a deep genuflection before the altar. Gregory of Nyssa writes, "And thus He who bore our sicknesses and interceded for us, bent His knee in prayer, by reason of the man which He assumed, giving us an example, that we ought not to exalt ourselves at the time of prayer, but in all things be conformed to humility; *for God resisteth the proud, but giveth grace to the humble.*"[65]

---

64. Heinrich Hofmann, "Christ in Gethsemane", oil on canvas, 1890, Riverside Church, New York, accessed February 2024, at www.heinrichhofmann.net/christ-in-gethsemane.html.

65. Aquinas, *Catena Aurea Vol III*, 721.

The Host of Gethsemane Invites in Luke's Gospel

One moment in Luke's Agony passage that stands out is the first verse that reads, "Then going out he went, as was his custom, to the Mount of Olives, and the disciples followed him."[66] This reveals with the words "as was his custom," that he prayed there frequently. Scripture teaches us that Jesus usually prayed alone ("He would withdraw to deserted places to pray"[67]) and yet here he is, sharing the experience as the ideal host to his guests.

Pope Benedict XVI also confirms that Jesus is an inviting host seeking the companionship of His guests when he writes:

> Yet, although Jesus arrives "alone" at the place in which he was to stop and pray, he wants at least three disciples to be near him, to be in a closer relationship with him. This is a spatial closeness, a plea for solidarity at the moment in which he feels death approaching, but above all it is closeness in prayer, in a certain way to express harmony with him at the moment when he is preparing to do the Father's will to the very end; and it is an invitation to every disciple to follow him on the Way of Cross.[68]

Pope Benedict XVI reveals the host of Gethsemane offers an eternal invitation of hospitality from the Garden with the use of the phrases: "a plea for solidarity;" and "an invitation to every disciple."

---

66. Lk 22:39.

67. Lk 5:16.

68. Benedict, *The Prayer of Jesus*, 63.

151

Jesus is Ministered to by an Angel

Luke depicts Jesus being ministered to by an angel. "And to strengthen him an angel from heaven appeared to him."[69] As Fr. Francis Donnelly explains:

> The temptation in the Garden was more terrible than the temptations in the desert. The sensitive feelings of Jesus were lashed before His Body was scourged; His Heart bled before it was opened by the soldier's spear, and His Soul was crucified before He was nailed to the Cross on Calvary. Anticipation is sometimes more terrifying than the reality. In the desert the angel of comfort had to bring food alone; in the Agony the angel must staunch the flow of blood, dispel the black clouds of desolation, and comfort a soul sorrowful unto death.[70]

The presence of the Angel of Gethsemane also has powerful implications for our own lives that is a gift of the Host/host of Gethsemane watching over all those who console Him in His Agony. "The angelic visitation is firm assurance...that prayer shall be answered...weakness will be fortified...watchfulness increased and rewarded and...fortitude made like that to Jesus in His Agony."[71]

And so, "the fear of death and torments carries no stigma of guilt but rather is an affliction of the sort Christ came to suffer, not to escape...No matter how much the heart of the soldier is agitated and

---

69. Lk 22:43.

70. Donnelly, *The Our Father in Gethsemane*, 106-107.

71. Donnelly, *The Our Father in Gethsemane*, 107-108.

stricken by fear, if he still comes forward at the command of the general, goes on, fights, and defeats the enemy, he has no reason to fear that his former fear might lesson his reward in any way. As a matter of fact, he ought to receive even more praise because of it, since he had to overcome not only the enemy but also his own fear…"[72]

The words of St. Paul resound well here: "Therefore, since we have a great high priest who has passed through the heavens, Jesus, the Son of God, let us hold fast to our confession. For we do not have a high priest who is unable to sympathize with our weaknesses, but one who has similarly been tested in every way, yet without sin. So let us confidently approach the throne of grace to receive mercy and to find grace for timely help."[73] Fr. Francis Donnelly describes:

> Jesus experienced the horrors of sin without having the guilt of the slightest fault…beside original sin and venial sin the more heinous malice of mortal sin visited Jesus in the way God's justice demanded, and the willing love of the Redeemer accepted the visitation. Imagine, then, the sins of all the race of man from creation to the end of time, marshalling themselves in serried ranks and trampling into blood…their stainless Victim. Group, if you will, the armies of guilt under the standards of the seven deadly sins, study those sins in the history of man, note them at work in Christ's Passion, and if the vastness of the havoc appalls you, the glorious victory of Jesus will console and comfort you.[74]

---

72. More, *The Sadness of Christ*, 83-85.
73. Heb 4:14-16.
74. Donnelly, *The Our Father in Gethsemane*, 85.

Lukan Perseverance in Prayer

"And being in agony he prayed the longer."[75] Of this verse of Luke's Gospel, St. Ambrose writes:

Many are shocked at this place who turn the sorrows of the Saviour to an argument of inherent weakness from the beginning, rather than taken upon Him for the time. But I am so far from considering it a thing to be excused, that I never more admire His mercy and majesty; for He would have conferred less upon me had He not taken upon Him my feelings. For He took upon Him my sorrow, that upon me He might bestow His joy. With confidence therefore I name His sadness, because I preach His cross. He must needs have undergone affliction, that He might conquer. For they have no praise of fortitude whose wounds have produced stupor rather than pain. He wished therefore to instruct us how we should conquer death, and what is far greater, the anguish of coming death. Thou smartedst then, O Lord, not from thy own but my wounds; *for he was wounded for our transgressions.* And perhaps He is sad, because that after Adam's fall the passage by which we must depart from this world was such that death was necessary. Nor is it far from the truth that He was sad for His persecutors, who He knew would suffer punishment for their wicked sacrilege.[76]

---

75. Lk 22:44 [*Douay-Rheims*].
76. Aquinas, *Catena Aurea Vol III*, 724.

St. John Chrysostom asserts why Jesus prays the longer, returning to prayer for a second and third time. It "...comes of the feelings belonging to human frailty, through which He also feared death, thus giving assurance that He was truly made man. For in Scripture, when any thing is repeated a second and third time, that is the greatest proof of its truth and reality; as, for example, when Joseph says to Pharaoh, *And for that thou sawedst it twice, it is proof of the thing being established by God.*"[77]

Raban writes, "Or, the Lord prayed thrice, to teach us to pray for pardon of sins past, defence against present evil, and provision against future perils, and that we should address every prayer to Father, Son, and Holy Spirit, and that our spirit, soul, and body should be kept in safety."[78]

Remig writes, "...He prays thrice for the Apostles, and for Peter in particular, who was to deny Him thrice."[79] Indeed, when Peter's denial is foretold by Jesus with these words: "I tell you, Peter, before the cock crows this day, you will deny three times that you know me,"[80] Peter had just emphatically asserted that he was prepared for prison and death for Christ. Jesus tells him, "Simon, Simon, behold Satan has demanded to sift all of you like wheat, but I have prayed that your own faith may not fail; and once you have turned back, you must strengthen your brothers."[81] The three-time-denial is foreshadowed in the Garden of Gethsemane with the three calls from Jesus to awaken the apostles as seen in the Gospels of Matthew and Mark. But it is only in Luke 22 that we learn that Satan will sift the apostles like wheat. Here is great insight into why each of the faithful is called to stay awake, watching and praying in Gethsemane. The Host/host is inviting

---

77. Thomas Aquinas, *Catena Aurea: Commentary on the Four Gospels vol. I, St. Matthew*, trans. John Henry Newman (London: Baronius Press, 2022), 912.

78. Aquinas, *Catena Aurea Vol I*, 913.

79. Aquinas, *Catena Aurea Vol I*, 913.

80. Lk 22:34.

81. Lk 22:31-32.

us to be vigilant in the Garden so that we might end up as so much wheat rather than chaff. "His winnowing fan is in his hand to clear the threshing floor and to gather the wheat into his barn, but the chaff he will burn with unquenchable fire."[82] This assertion in the Gospel of Luke of Satan demanding to sift the apostles like wheat recalls the Parable of the Weeds Among the Wheat described in the Gospel of Matthew: "The kingdom of heaven may be likened to a man who sowed good seed in his field. While everyone was asleep his enemy came and sowed weeds all through the wheat, and then went off."[83] In this way, the Garden of Gethsemane is like unto the kingdom of heaven. We must stay awake and not fall asleep lest the enemy come and sow the weeds and sift the wheat.

The Blood Christ Sheds in Gethsemane. The Old Testament and Impending Martyrdom

"He was in such agony and prayed so fervently that his sweat became like drops of blood falling on the ground."[84] This is an example of the Eucharistic Host of Gethsemane as his sacrificial blood is poured out for us. It is also Eucharistic in the reconciliation it provides, as this passage with its drops of blood falling to the garden ground is like a ransom for Abel's blood which once cried out to God from the ground.[85]

Then Jesus said to them: "Why are you sleeping? Get up and pray that you may not undergo the test."[86] This message directly gives

---

82. Lk 3:17.
83. Mt 13:24-25.
84. Lk 22:44.
85. Gn 4:10.
86. Lk 22:46.

advice and counsel to the guests of Jesus, looking after their welfare and providing for them. More blood is mended than just Abel's blood crying for justice. The other mended blood happens when, upon Judas' betrayal, one of the apostles cuts off the ear of the high priest's servant and Jesus immediately mends it. In the garden where Jesus is host, he is the soul of courtesy to all.

Jesus in His Agony is also reminiscent of the suffering of Moses and Elijah, the two who appeared at the Transfiguration, that other scene in which Peter, James and John are uniquely invited to prayerfully watch. Benedict XVI makes this connection:

> Moses is dramatically aware of the trial he is undergoing while guiding the people through the desert and says to God: "I am not able to carry all this people alone, the burden is too heavy for me. If you will deal thus with me, rather kill me at once, kill me if I have found favor in your sight, that I may not see my wretchedness" (cf. Nm 11:14-15).

> Elijah too finds doing his duty to God and to his People difficult. The first book of Kings recounts: "He himself went a day's journey into the wilderness, and came and sat under a broom tree; and he asked that he might die, saying, 'It is enough; now, O Lord, take away my life; for I am no better than my fathers'" (19:4).[87]

---

87. Benedict, *The Prayer of Jesus*, 64.

In a way, Elijah's suffering closely resembles simultaneously Christ's Agony and also the slumber of the apostles. The Agony of Christ is foreshadowed through the angel ministering to Elijah and strengthening him. The continual sleep of the apostles in Gethsemane is foreshadowed by Elijah's drowsiness, but unlike the apostles he only sleeps twice, rather than the third time:

> He lay down and fell asleep under the broom tree, but then an angel touched him and ordered him to get up and eat. He looked and there at his head was a hearth cake and a jug of water. After he ate and drank, he lay down again, but the angel of the Lord came back a second time, touched him, and ordered, "Get up and eat, else the journey will be too long for you!" He got up, ate and drank; then strengthened by that food, he walked forty days and forty nights to the mountain of God, Horeb. There he came to a cave, where he took shelter. But the word of the Lord came to him, "Why are you here, Elijah?" He answered: "I have been most zealous for the Lord, the God of hosts, but the Israelites have forsaken your covenant, torn down your altars, and put your prophets to the sword. I alone am left, and they seek to take my life."[88]

The angel encouraged Elijah to "Get up and eat, else the journey will be too long for you!" Might this perhaps be part of what the angel reminded Jesus in the Garden; but what could He have eaten, since nothing of the kind is mentioned in Scripture? I assert we know one thing Jesus definitively ate in Gethsemane, which is the "food to eat of which you do not know."[89] Jesus, the host of Gethsemane also offers this same food to the guests He invites to join Him in the Garden: "My food is to do the will of the one who sent me and to

---

88. 1 Kings 19:4-10.
89. Jn 4:32.

finish his work."[90] Finally, in the same pericope in which Elijah is strengthened by the hearthcake, he soon encounters God not in the wind but in the whispering sound. Just prior to this encounter, Elijah is asked, "Why are you here?" and his answer could be the answer of Christ in Gethsemane, or the answer of any faithful soul who joins Him there: "I have been most zealous for the Lord, the God of hosts, but the Israelites have forsaken your covenant, torn down your altars, and put your prophets to the sword. I alone am left, and they seek to take my life." This motto: "*Zelo zelatus sum pro Domine Deo exercituum*"[91] is the motto of the Carmelites. Carmel means "Garden land" and the Carmelites are those who seek the Garden of God. Gethsemane, emblematic of the Garden of God, is truly a place in which to echo these words of Elijah as we watch and pray to the Lord, God of hosts; God of the hosts of strengthening angels; God of the hosts of the faithful.

Benedict writes, "What Jesus says to the three disciples whom he wants near him during his prayer at Gethsemane shows that he feels fear and anguish in that 'Hour,' experiencing his last profound loneliness precisely while God's plan is being brought about. Moreover, Jesus' fear and anguish sums up the full horror of man in the face of his own death, the certainty that it is inescapable and a perception of the burden of evil that touches our lives."[92]

Luke's Gospel is "interested in portraying this scene as a cosmic battle"[93] and his Gospel and commentaries upon it will be a vitally important study for this thesis as it is the only Gospel that describes the shedding of Jesus' blood in the Garden. Of course, Luke is the doctor and so he pays attention to this physical symptom, exhibiting "Luke's fondness for physical manifestations...

---

90. Jn 4:34.
91. 1 Kings 19:10.
92. Benedict, *The Prayer of Jesus*, 64.
93. Green and McKnight, *Dictionary of Jesus and the Gospels*, 266.

accompanying extramundane events."[94] "...A number of interpreters have understood Luke's presentation of this episode as a central element of Luke's portrayal of Jesus' passion as a martyrdom."[95]

St. Augustine writes this in his commentary on the Psalms:

Lord, I have cried to you, hear me. (Psalm 141:1) This is a prayer we can all say. This is not my prayer, but that of the whole Christ. Rather, it is said in the name of his body. When Christ was on earth he prayed in his human nature, and prayed to the Father in the name of his body, and when he prayed, drops of blood flowed from his whole body. So it is written in the Gospel: *Jesus prayed with earnest prayer, and sweated blood.* What is this blood streaming from his whole body but the martyrdom of the whole Church?[96]

As the New Adam, Jesus tills the earth of the garden in His Agony, in each drop of blood that falls to the ground from "the sweat of thy face."[97] The Passion of Jesus begins in Gethsemane. In the Garden, Jesus Himself is the New Tree of Life, from which we will eat, because from His death upon a tree, we will receive the Eucharist, the Bread of Life. In this Garden, Gethsemane, we encounter the same Tree of Life who will die for us at Calvary. We meet Agnus Dei, sacrificially bleeding.

When I say sacrificially bleeding, I mean that this bloodshed in Gethsemane is part of His Passion. It is so important to note that the Passion is not just the Crucifixion, but in fact includes the Agony in

---

94. Green and McKnight, *Dictionary of Jesus and the Gospels*, 266-267.

95. Green and McKnight, *Dictionary of Jesus and the Gospels*, 266.

96. Augustine, "Commentary on the Psalms", quoted in *The Liturgy of the Hours Vol 2* (New York, Catholic Book Publishing Corp, 1976), Tuesday of the Second Week of Lent, 168-169.

97. Gn 3:19.

the Garden. As the Baltimore Catechism asserts, "by Our Lord's Passion we mean His dreadful sufferings, from His agony in the garden to the moment of His death."[98] The Agony occurs immediately following the Last Supper (which is Eucharistic and part of the Passion), and just before the Cross (which is also Eucharistic). Therefore, Christ's blood in the Agony is Eucharistic: both Sacramental and sacrificial.

The Church teaches that a pious follower named Veronica, whose very name means literally, "true icon, or true image: *vera icona*" wiped Christ's face on the Via Dolorosa.[99] This act of love is venerated in the Sixth Station of the Cross. If it was lovingly apropos to wipe Christ's face on the Way of the Cross, it stands to reason that it is equally thus in the Garden of Gethsemane. This is another unspoken invitation of the Host/host of Gethsemane. Our Eucharistic Lord is sweating blood and suffering, and it is upon the faithful to offer reparation. The sleep of Peter, James, and John creates a spiritual opportunity for generations of faithful who heed the invitation of Gethsemane and decide to respond in reciprocal hospitality. This opportunity is to be the Veronica, the true image, of Gethsemane: to wipe His Holy Face through our prayers and our watchfulness.

Bede writes, "Let no one ascribe this sweat to natural weakness, nay, it is contrary to nature to sweat blood, but rather let him derive therefrom a declaration to us, that He was now obtaining the accomplishment of His Prayer, namely, that He might purge by His blood the faith of his disciples, still convicted of human frailty."[100]

Purging "by His blood the faith of his disciples, still convicted of human frailty," is one of the explanations for the Agony. According

---

98. *The Baltimore Catechism,* 369.

99. Jacob Stein, "The Historical Origins of Veronica's Veil: Inside the Cloth Relic of Jesus' Holy Face Wiped on Calvary", *EWTN Vatican*, March 25, 2024, accessed May 2024, www.ewtnvatican.com/articles/historical-origins-of-veronicas-veil-inside-the-cloth-relic-of-jesus-holy-face-wiped-on-calvary-2357.

100. Aquinas, *Catena Aurea Vol III*, 725.

to the Catechism of the Catholic Church, in answering the question of what caused Our Lord's Agony in the Garden, "It is believed Our Lord's agony in the garden was caused: (1) By His clear knowledge of all He was soon to endure; (2) By the sight of the many offenses committed against His Father by the sins of the whole world; (3) By His knowledge of men's ingratitude for the blessings of redemption."[101]

Fr. Josef Staudinger writes about this heroic struggle:

He realizes that the will of the Father is that He should die. From eternity He had lovingly submitted Himself to this will for man's salvation. The will of the Father, with which His own will is fully united, shines out even now as a kindly star above the sombre darkness that blankets his soul. He clings fixedly to it, making gradual headway against the fear of death in a heroic struggle within the human nature he had assumed. In this struggle, two opposing currents meet: in the soul, the will to die; in the flesh, the will to live. A fearful combat ensues which causes the blood vessels in His sacred body to dilate and contract in turn. The blood rushes, as in the heat of fever, through His veins, forcing its way through the opened pores, and is visible on his forehead in small thick drops till, increasing in volume, it falls to the ground, as St. Luke reports. Christ sweated blood! This passage of the Gospel during the early centuries of Christianity was sometimes suppressed in public reading and was actually expunged from some manuscripts. Nevertheless, despite the offense it occasioned, it must be regarded as genuine: Christ did in fact sweat blood during His agony.[102]

---

101. *The Baltimore Catechism,* 375.

In fact, the inherent veracity of the bloody sweat is affirmed in no small part because this detail *was* at first expunged from some manuscripts. It discomfited some people's ideas of what was seemly for the God-man, and yet the truth survived. Fr. Staudinger continues his description of the agonizing conflict that resulted in this bloody sweat:

> By way of explanation it is sometimes said that fear caused the sweat. But fear drives the blood back to the heart, inducing pallor; whereas in this instance the blood is forced away from the heart to the extremest pores of the body, and that with such violence that the delicate blood vessels could not withstand the pressure but were broken through. Christ's sweat of blood cannot therefore be the result of fear. It was caused rather by the effort to overcome it, and was proof of His determination to make the supreme sacrifice out of love for us. Christ struggled—in the full literal sense of the word—with death for our sakes.[103]

While there are several theories as to the cause of Christ's death, blood loss is one very plausible cause. "Physicians and historians have suggested that Jesus might have died from asphyxiation because breathing was so difficult on the cross. Others say perhaps he had a heart attack after the hours of physical exertion and trauma."[104] But some physicians believe that Jesus likely died from excessive blood loss.

---

102. Josef Staudinger, *Holiness of the Priesthood*, trans. John J. Coyne, (Westminster, MD: 1960, The Newman Press), 409.

103. Josef Staudinger, *Holiness of the Priesthood*, 409-410.

104. Tom Dermody, "Catholic Doctor gives Medical View of Christ's Passion, Crucifixion", *The Catholic Telegraph*, April 10, 2019, accessed May 2024, www.thecatholictelegraph.com/catholic-doctor-gives-medical-view-of-christs-passion-crucifixion/57186.

"Christ emptied himself," Dr. Timothy Millea told about 100 people at his home parish of St. Paul the Apostle in Davenport. "As a surgeon, two words that make our hair stand on end are 'bleeding out,'" he said. "'If you can't stop it, you can't keep that patient alive.'"[105]

If indeed Jesus died of blood loss, as Dr. Millea asserts, then it could be stated that Christ began the process that led to His death in Gethsemane, where the trauma of hematidrosis had set in. Hematidrosis (also spelled hematohidrosis) is a rare condition that "results in the excretion of blood or blood pigment in the sweat. Under conditions of great emotional stress, tiny capillaries in the sweat glands can rupture, thus mixing blood with perspiration. This condition has been reported in extreme instances of stress."[106] Clearly, Jesus went through such extreme stress in the Garden of Gethsemane.

Dr. Millea states, "an adult male has about 1.5 gallons of blood and that the loss of 40 percent of that blood can lead to hypovolemic shock, a life-threatening condition. Jesus likely surpassed that threshold after repeated beatings through the night, an intense scourging at the hands of Roman soldiers that included wearing a crown of thorns and having nails driven through his upper wrists and feet."[107] Millea also referenced modern research on the Shroud of Turin, believed by many to be Jesus' burial cloth.

For example, he said the man whose image is seen on the shroud was 5 feet 10 inches tall and weighed about 175 pounds. While tradition says Jesus was whipped 39 times in his scourging, nearly 400 wound marks are counted on the shroud and "every one of them (was) bleeding" on the day of his death…Millea feels the blood loss theory is not only medically likely but it also corresponds with the theological

---

105. Dermody, "Catholic Doctor gives Medical View of Christ's Passion, Crucifixion".

106. Dave Miller, "Hematidrosis: Did Jesus Sweat Blood?", *Apologetics Press*, July 2017, accessed July 2024, apologeticspress.org/hematidrosis-did-jesus-sweat-blood-5436/.

107. Dermody, "Catholic Doctor gives Medical View of Christ's Passion, Crucifixion".

teachings of atoning sacrifice, with Jesus taking the place of the slaughtered lambs of the Old Testament. Sacrificed animals also died from blood loss. "Jesus was literally the sacrificial lamb," he said."[108] Indeed, this blood loss theory as cause of death reflects a sacrificed lamb. This Lamb of God has begun to bleed in Gethsemane. He is our Eucharistic Host/host, inviting us there in Adoration. Just as in Eucharistic Adoration we strengthen our souls through watching and praying in the presence of the Lamb of God; so too in Gethsemane.

Along with the emotional and psychological pain Jesus was enduring, it is quite possible that physical pain had begun as well during the Agony in the Garden. Regarding episodes of hematidrosis, "while the extent of blood loss generally is minimal, hematidrosis also results in the skin becoming extremely tender and fragile, which would have made Christ's pending physical insults even more painful."[109]

This visceral detail has telling implications for the Second Sorrowful Mystery. Following the Agony in the Garden comes the rough treatment of the soldiers as they imprison Christ, and then the infamous Scourging at the Pillar. To consider that Christ's skin becomes "extremely tender and fragile" due to the Garden Agony prior to the Scourging makes the reality of that torture all the more grievous and hearbreaking.

The Catechism, in responding to the question, "What did Jesus Christ suffer," asserts that "Jesus Christ suffered a bloody sweat, a cruel scourging, was crowned with thorns, and was crucified."[110] It is notable that in the Catechism it is the bloody sweat of Jesus in Gethsemane that is specifically given special focus, right alongside the scourging (which would have been more excruciatingly painful because of the effects of His recent hematidrosis); the crowning with thorns; and crucifixion. This grievous torture demands the presence of

---

108. Dermody, "Catholic Doctor gives Medical View of Christ's Passion, Crucifixion".

109. Miller, "Hematidrosis: Did Jesus Sweat Blood?".

110. *The Baltimore Catechism,* 370.

a Good Samaritan to pour oil and wine into His sores, through the balm He requested of each of us: vigilant prayer.

Jesus was awaiting execution in these three hours of Gethsemane and asked for company; yet it was the time He needed it the most that it was denied Him. Ironically, the consolation through prayerful vigilance that Peter, James, and John were called to give would have been a gift for them, too, strengthening them. "A friend is a friend at all times, and a brother is born for the time of adversity."[111]

Understanding more about the bleeding Host of Gethsemane increases insight into why the host of the faithful are called to offer hospitality to Him as consolation for all He is suffering there for each soul in an agony greater than the sorrowful wretchedness of Job. Yet He is not even given the consolation Job received from his three friends:

> Now when three of Job's friends heard of all the misfortune that had come upon him, they set out each one from his own place: Eliphaz from Teman, Bildad from Shuh, and Zophar from Naamath. They met and journeyed together to give him sympathy and comfort. But when, at a distance, they lifted up their eyes and did not recognize him, they began to weep aloud; they tore their cloaks and threw dust into the air over their heads. Then they sat down upon the ground with him seven days and seven nights, but none of them spoke a word to him; for they saw how great was his suffering.[112]

These friends of Job are by no means perfect. They do not speak wisdom; rather they give inaccurate speeches stating Job must have done something wrong to displease God. They give bad advice and talk when they should listen. They motivate Job to declare, "I have

111. Prov 17:17.
112. Job 2:11-13.

heard this sort of thing many times. Troublesome comforters, all of you!"[113] Like Jesus in Gethsemane, Job had three less-than-ideal friends at his side during his time of trial. Just as Peter, James, and John failed in the Garden; these friends of Job were not, in the end, a comfort. But even *they* did better than Peter, James, and John. The friends of Job cried for him, stayed awake watching with him, did penance for him. They sat quietly and faithfully with him for seven days before they ruined their good efforts with ignorant and inflated speeches. Scripture instructs how to be a good companion: "Rejoice with those who rejoice, weep with those who weep,"[114] and "...Do to others as you would have them do to you."[115] While Job calls his three confounded friends "troublesome comforters," Jesus tells his three friends, "Get up and pray that you may not undergo the test,"[116] warning them of the danger that waits for those who do not watch and pray when called upon to do so. After all, each of these friends would some day face martyrdom.

Augustine asserts, "Our Lord praying with a bloody sweat represented the martyrdoms which should flow from His whole body, which is the church."[117]

As St. Thomas More asserts, "...in this passage about Christ's agony, whichever of these deeds, sufferings, or prayers of His are so lowly that they seem quite incompatible with the lofty height of divinity, let us remember that the same Christ performed them as a man. Indeed, some of them had their origin only in the lower part of His humanity. I mean the part concerned with sensation; and these served to proclaim the genuineness of His human nature and to relieve the natural fears of other men in later times."[118]

---

113. Job 16:2.

114. Rm 12:15.

115. Lk 6:31.

116. Lk 22:46.

117. Aquinas, *Catena Aurea Vol III*, 725.

Since Thomas More was himself imprisoned, awaiting his own martyrdom while writing *De Tristitia Christi*, since he dedicated the majority of his final efforts and time whilst still alive on penning this study of Gethsemane, More ought to know that Christ's suffering in the Garden served to "relieve the natural fears of other men in later times."

"Nothing, then, in these words or in any of all the other things that the sequence of His agony presented as signs of His afflicted humanity, was considered by Christ to be unworthy of His glory; indeed so little did He think so that He Himself took special care to see that they became widely known. For, though everything written by all the apostles was dictated throughout by one and the same Spirit of Christ, still I find it hard to recall any of His other deeds which He took such particular pains to preserve in the memories of men."[119]

Indeed, More asserts that the recounting of the Gethsemane narrative, written by the Evangelists but inspired directly by the Holy Spirit, is extremely detailed and full of poignant description. This is another proof of the Host/host of Gethsemane. It indicates clearly that the invitation is ongoing, since so much detail has gone into setting the scene; that each one of the faithful through the generations, may be motivated to accept the invitation to watch and pray with Christ. St. Thomas More continues:

> To be sure, He told His apostles about His intense sadness, so that they might be able to hand it down from Him to posterity…Certainly they would have been even less able, at that time of night, to make out when He knelt down or when He threw Himself face forward on the ground. As for those drops of blood which flowed like sweat from His whole body, even if they had later clearly seen the stain left

118. More, *Complete Works Volume 14, Part I, De Tristitia Christi*, 185-187.

119. More, *Complete Works Volume 14, Part I, De Tristitia Christi*, 189.

on the ground, I think they would have drawn almost any number of conclusions without guessing the right one, since it was an unprecedented phenomenon for anyone to sweat blood.[120]

St. Thomas More makes an excellent point that it would have been hard for the Apostles to have known the details of what happened. The likelihood of anyone awake or aware to hear Him in the Garden was slim. More asserts that Jesus must have explained His Agony to his disciples and Blessed Mother after the fact, after He rose from the dead when it was now completely clear that He was God, which shows how vitally important it was to our Lord that His Agony be known and that through the narrative of it, others may be invited to watch and pray with Him there. More continues, "Therefore, to those whose hearts are troubled, meditation on this agony provides great consolation, and rightly so, since it was for this very purpose, to console the afflicted, that our Savior in his kindness made known His own affliction, which no one else knew or could have known."[121]

This point by St. Thomas More again proves the Host/host of Gethsemane in that it confirms the Real Presence of Christ's Blood in the Garden. It also confirms the hospitality Jesus is giving, by inviting each one of His followers throughout history to be His guest, watching and praying in the Garden. Through learning of His Agony, they may be better able to empathize with His pain, or learn from Him how to handle their own pain, and in being moved to console Him; in turn, they themselves may be consoled. As Paul instructs the Corinthians:

> Praised be God, the Father of our Lord Jesus Christ, the
> Father of mercies, and the God of all consolation! He
> comforts us in all our afflictions and thus enables us to

---

120. More, *Complete Works Volume 14, Part I, De Tristitia Christi*, 189-191.

121. More, *Complete Works Volume 14, Part I, De Tristitia Christi*, 191-193.

comfort those who are in trouble, with the same consolation we have received from him. As we have shared much in the suffering of Christ, so through Christ do we share abundantly in his consolation.[122]

Gethsemane as a Model of Martyrdom, Whether White or Red

Martyrdom is inevitable for any Catholic who wishes to enter heaven. Although the fearsome honor of execution for the sake of Christ does not come to all, all are called to martyrdom; if not of the body, then of the spirit. If not "red martyrdom," then, nevertheless, we are called to an un-bloody martyrdom.

The degrees of martyrdom in the Catholic Church were assigned by Pope Gregory I, as George Ryan explains, "His work *Homilia in Evangelia* assigns the colors red, blue (or green), and white to represent the varying 'modes' of sacrifice. This classification system by Pope Gregory I helped formalize the understanding of martyrdom within the Church, recognizing the different trials faced by the faithful on their paths to holiness."[123]

Specifically concerning the un-bloody martyrdoms, Ryan writes, "White martyrdom is characterized by a complete separation from worldly attachments for the sake of God. This form of martyrdom does not necessarily involve physical suffering, but

---

122. 2 Cor 1:3-5, from *The Liturgy of the Hours Vol 4*, (New York: Catholic Book Publishing Corp, 1976), Common of Several Martyrs, Morning prayer, 1705.

123. George Ryan, "Did You Know? There Are 3 'Colors' of Catholic Martyrs", *uCatholic*, June 20, 2024, accessed June 2024, ucatholic.com/blog/did-you-know-there-are-3-colors-of-catholic-martyrs/.

demands a life of strict asceticism…Blue martyrdom involves rigorous self-denial through fasting and penance. It requires individuals to control their desires and perform acts of repentance without necessarily withdrawing from society."[124]

We have to die to ourselves, "put off the old man"[125] of sin and become righteous; and "take up (our) cross and follow (Him)."[126] We must be guided as we prepare our souls ever-more deeply for the martyrdom that awaits us, of whichever kind.

Thomas More himself is consoled by Jesus of Gethsemane as he awaits his own martyrdom, so much so that he writes a book about the sadness of Christ there in the Garden. Knowing he himself would be martyred, it must have comforted More that Jesus already went before Him and so made a path for More to follow; and that the pain More would face would be understood completely by Christ.

More asserts that the Gethsemane narrative:

> provides very convincing reasons to believe that no martyr's torments could ever be compared with Christ's suffering, even on this point of the intensity of the pain…I see that Christ, as the thought of His coming passion was borne in upon Him, was overwhelmed by mental anguish more bitter than any other mortal has ever experienced from the thought of coming torments. For who has ever felt such bitter anguish that a bloody sweat broke out all over his body and ran down in drops to the ground? The intensity of the actual pain itself, therefore, I estimate by this standard: I see that even the presentiment of it before it arrived was more bitter to Christ than such anticipation has ever been to anyone else.[127]

---

124. Ryan, "Did You Know? There Are 3 'Colors' of Catholic Martyrs".
125. Eph 4:22-24.
126. Lk 9:23.

It is clear how the Host/host of Gethsemane continues to extend a consoling invitation to keep vigil with Him that is meant to benefit each and every guest, across the generations. St. Thomas More, anticipating his own execution, was comforted that Jesus went before him, and had it worse. Therefore, More could follow His Master host as a dutiful servant guest in the sorrowfully glorious work of martyrdom:

> Nor could this anguish of the mind ever have grown to sufficient intensity to cause the body to sweat blood if He had not, of His own free will, exercised His divine omnipotence, not only to refrain from alleviating this painful pressure, but even to add to its force and strength. This He did in order to prefigure the blood which future martyrs would be forced to pour forth on the ground, and at the same time to offer this unheard of, this marvelous example of profound anguish as a consolation to those who would be so fearful and alarmed at the thought of torture that they might otherwise interpret their fear as a sign of their downfall and yield to despair.[128]

One can hear Saint Thomas More advising himself, taking great consolation in this, knowing he himself stands at the brink of execution:

> At this point, if someone should again bring up those martyrs who freely and eagerly exposed themselves to death because of their faith in Christ, and if he should be of the opinion that they are especially worthy of the laurels of

---

127. More, *Complete Works Volume 14, Part I, De Tristitia Christi*, 231-235.

128. More, *Complete Works Volume 14, Part I, De Tristitia Christi*, 235-237.

triumph because with a joy that left no room for sorrow they betrayed no trace of sadness, no sign of fear, I am perfectly willing to go along with him on that point, so long as he does not deny the triumph of those who do not rush forth of their own accord but who nevertheless do not hang back or withdraw once they have been seized, but rather go on in spite of their fearful anxiety and face the terrible prospect out of love for Christ.[129]

This assertion is composed by a man who became a martyr, revealing something of his own fear and love in this statement, and also shows his ultimate acceptance and reciprocal love of the invitation from the Host, even in the face of his own fears:

Though I grant that God loves a cheerful giver, still I have no doubt that He loved Tobias, and holy Job too. Now it is true that both of them bore their calamities bravely and patiently, but neither of them, so far as I know, was exactly jumping with joy or clapping his hands out of happiness. To expose one's self to death when the case clearly demands it or when God gives a secret prompting to do so, this, I do not deny, is a deed of preeminent virtue. But otherwise I do not think it very safe to do so, and among those who willingly suffered for Christ we find outstanding figures who were very much afraid, who were deeply distressed, who even withdrew from death more than once before they finally faced it bravely.[130]

---

129. More, *Complete Works Volume 14, Part I, De Tristitia Christi*, 237-239.

130. More, *Complete Works Volume 14, Part I, De Tristitia Christi*, 241-243.

St. Thomas More is an exemplar of how the Gethsemane narrative strengthens souls and how the Host/host of Gethsemane's invitation is a lodestar for the Catholic journey. More was an Oxford graduate, lawyer, doting father, author of the famous *Utopia*, and other works; and Lord Chancellor of England. He wrote *The Sadness, the Weariness, the Fear, and the Prayer of Christ Before He Was Taken Prisoner: Matthew 26, Mark 14, Luke 22, John 18*; (that is the entire title as he penned it, though it is now shortened) from his jail cell in the Tower of London as he awaited execution for refusing to acknowledge King Henry VIII as head of Our Lord's Church in England, or to acknowledge Henry's annulment. This makes St. Thomas More a kind of St. John the Baptist of his day, angering royalty over his refusal to accept an adulterous and illicit marriage and putting God before politics. While he was in prison, More discovered a deep consolation and inspiration in Jesus of Gethsemane:

> But whoever is utterly crushed by feelings of anxiety and fear and is tormented by the fear that he may yield to despair, let him consider this agony of Christ, let him meditate on it constantly and turn it over in his mind, let him drink deep and health-giving draughts of consolation from this spring. For here he will see the loving shepherd lifting the weak lamb on his shoulders, playing the same role as he himself does, expressing his very own feelings, and for this reason: so that anyone who later feels himself disturbed by similar feelings might take courage and not think that he must despair.[131]

More knew all too well this anxiety and fear, and yet he writes joyfully:

---

131. More, *Complete Works Volume 14, Part I, De Tristitia Christi*, 253.

Therefore, let us give Him as many thanks as we can (for certainly we can never give him enough); and in our agony remembering His (with which no other can ever be compared) let us beg Him with all our strength that He may deign to comfort us in our anguish by an insight into His; and when we urgently beseech Him, because of our mental distress, to free us from danger, let us nevertheless follow His own most wholesome example by concluding our prayer with His own addition: "Yet not as I will but as you will."[132]

More continues with confidence, stating that if one follows this aforementioned wisdom:

I have no doubt at all that, just as an angel brought Him consolation in answer to His prayer, so too each of our angels will bring us from His Spirit consolation that will give us the strength to persevere in those deeds that will lift us up to heaven. And in order to make us completely confident of this fact, Christ went there before us by the same method, by the same path.[133]

---

132. More, *Complete Works Volume 14, Part I, De Tristitia Christi*, 253-255.

133. More, *Complete Works Volume 14, Part I, De Tristitia Christi*, 255-257.

Living the Our Father

Therefore, it becomes clear how vitally the Host/host of Gethsemane is hosting us. He has invited us, has gone before us, and has taught us what to do in our own Gethsemanes. He is our guide in the Garden, teaching us as a good teacher does, through repetition, reminding us three times to watch and pray so that we can withstand temptation; to be vigilant, to do the Father's Will, to "pray the longer" when we are still fearful, anxious or irresolute. When the apostles said to Jesus, "Lord, teach us to pray,"[134] they little dreamed what they were asking. They scarce imagined that the lesson He would give them would extend much further beyond the Introduction of the Lord's Prayer. They could not have guessed that Jesus *would really* teach them to pray, not only by word...but by example. The Our Father prayer that is prayed at every Mass and countless times a day around the world enjoins, "Thy Kingdom come; Thy Will be done." Jesus lived this in Gethsemane. In order for the Father's Kingdom to come, the Son had to do the Father's will. Jesus lived out each word of that prayer, and because of His Passion, begun in that Garden, we have the model *par excellence* for what exactly to do in the face of any challenge. We must watch and pray...and "pray the longer." The Our Father, as a prayer, comes to its summit and glory in Gethsemane. In Luke 22:42-46, the Host/host shows us how to pray, and it is, I assert, the completion of the lesson He began in Luke 11:

> When you enter upon your agonies, which are piercing enough for you, however slight they may be when compared with the Agony of Jesus, what prayer above all

---

134. Lk 11:1.

will you whisper with anguished heart? Should it not be the prayer the Lord has taught us, the prayer which He may be said to have lived in deed before He put it into words, the prayer He enacted within His Heart in the garden of Mount Olivet, the "Our Father"? Like the hurt child who at once calls to its parent, you will cry "Father" to the God of love.[135]

St. Thomas More worked out the anguish of his impending martyrdom by leaning upon Christ in Gethsemane, by responding to the Host/host's invitation to watch and pray with Him there. Because of this, More died nobly, with an honorable statement declaring himself God's servant and even a bit of endearing humor for his executioner. He had "prayed the longer" and was given the necessary strength. He "ascended the scaffold on July 6, 1535, joking to his executioners to help him up the scaffold, but that he would see himself down. He then made a final statement, proclaiming that he was 'the king's good servant, but God's first.'"[136]

The Eucharistic and Priestly Signs of Melchizedek as related to Gethsemane

Melchizedek is an important and unique Biblical figure in that he is both king and priest. He appears in the Old Testament when Abraham pays a tithe to him and Melchizedek gives Abraham bread and wine, which is seen as a precursor to the Eucharist. For this reason, Melchizedek's very name entered the canon of the Mass.

---

135. Donnelly, *The Our Father in Gethsemane*, 17.

136. Catholic Online, "St. Thomas More", *Catholic Online,* n.d., accessed April 2024, www.catholic.org/saints/saint.php?saint_id=324.

Melchizedek is an old Canaanite name meaning "My King Is [the god] Sedek" or "My King Is Righteousness" (the meaning of the similar Hebrew cognate). Salem, of which he is said to be king, is very probably Jerusalem. Psalm 76:2 refers to Salem in a way that implies that it is synonymous with Jerusalem, and the reference in Genesis 14:17 to "the King's Valley" further confirms this identification. The god whom Melchizedek serves as priest is "El ʿElyon," again a name of Canaanite origin, probably designating the high god of their pantheon.[137]

137. Encyclopaedia Britannica, "Melchizedek", *Encyclopaedia Britannica,* last modified August 2, 2024, accessed August 2024, www.britannica.com/biography/Melchizedek.

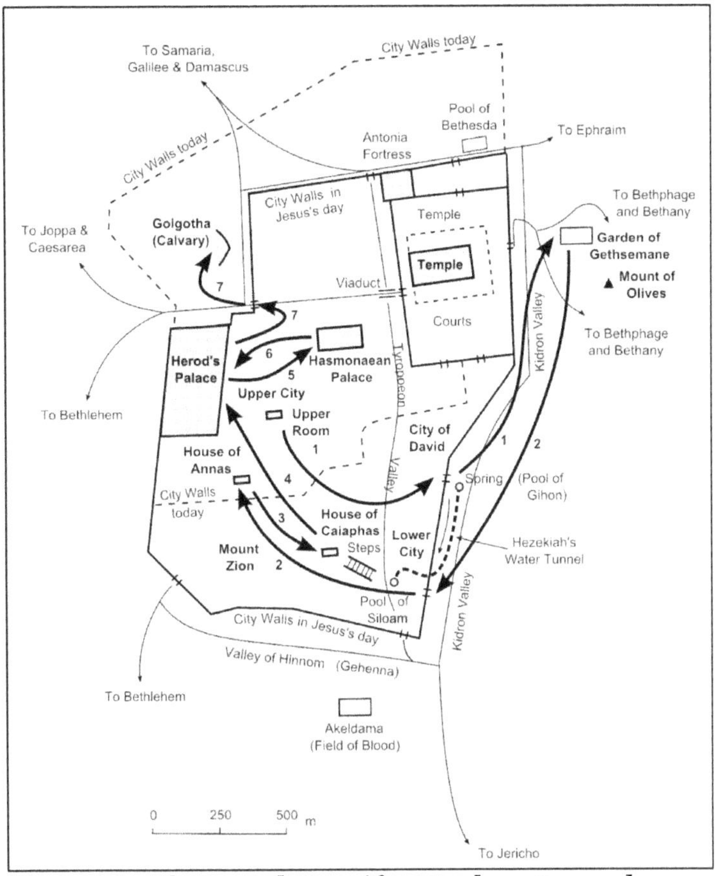

*Figure 3: Chris and Jennifer Taylor, Jerusalem:
The Last 24 Hours*

It is of key interest that the area referred to as "The King's Valley" in Scripture is the same as what is later called The Kidron Valley. "The *Kidron Valley*, otherwise known as '*The King's Valley*,' is beautifully nestled between two historic Holy Land locations within the City of Jerusalem. This picturesque basin is flanked on the West side by the Eastern Gate of the Temple Mount, and on the East side stands the Mount of Olives."[138] The map[139] in Figure 3 shows the proximity:

---

138. My Olive Tree, "Guide to the History of the Kidron Valley", *My Olive Tree,* November 28, 2017, accessed July 2024, www.myolivetree.com/kidron-valley-guide/.

For Abraham to recognize the authority and authenticity of a Canaanite priest-king is startling and has no parallel in biblical literature. This story may have reached its final formulation in the days of King David, serving as an apologia for David's making Jerusalem his headquarters and setting up the priesthood there. Abraham's paying tribute to a Jerusalem priest-king then would anticipate the time when Abraham's descendants would bring tithes to the priests of Jerusalem ministering in the sanctuary at the Davidic capital...Psalm 110, in referring to a future messiah of the Davidic line, alludes to the priest-king Melchizedek as a prototype of this messiah. This allusion led the author of the Letter to the Hebrews in the New Testament to translate the name Melchizedek as "king of righteousness" and Salem as "peace" so that Melchizedek is made to foreshadow Christ, stated to be the true king of righteousness and peace (Hebrews 7:2). According to the analogy, just as Abraham, the ancestor of the Levites, paid a tithe to Melchizedek and was therefore his inferior, so the Melchizedek-like priesthood of Christ is superior to that of the Levites. Furthermore, just as the Old Testament assigns no birth or death date to Melchizedek, so is the priesthood of Christ eternal.[140]

Melchizedek appears in Genesis in this brief exchange between Melchizedek presenting Abraham with bread and wine, and in turn, Abraham giving him a tithe of the spoils of war.[141] He also appears in

139. Chris Taylor and Jennifer Taylor, "Jerusalem: The Last 24 Hours", from "Jesus Crosses the Kidron Valley", *The Bible Journey*, n.d., accessed July 2024, thebiblejourney.org/biblejourney1/6-jesuss-last-journey-to-jerusalem/jesus-crosses-the-kidron-valley/

140. Encyclopaedia Britannica, "Melchizedek".

141. Gn 14:18-20.

Psalm 110 and again in Hebrews in a verse cited at many a priestly ordination: "You are a priest forever according to the order of Melchizedek."[142]

Of great note vis-a-vis Jesus of Gethsemane, Melchizedek, "the king of Salem," gave Abraham bread and wine in the King's Valley. Gethsemane itself is located at the foot of the Mount of Olives, an olive grove on the east side of the Kidron Valley that is at the base of the Mount of Olives. That is why Scripture records Jesus as walking across the Kidron Valley (or King's Valley) on His way to the Garden.

This location where Abraham would not take tribute from the king of Sodom[143]–even as he gave tribute to Melchizedek the priest-king–is the same Kidron Valley where the greatest priest-king, the Second Person of the Trinity, would journey on his way to offer His will to the Father, and sweat blood for humanity as He agonized. The giving of Melchizedek's gifts is Eucharistic in tone and the fact that it was given in the area near Christ's Agony is another reminder of the Eucharistic tone of Christ in the Garden.

Let Every Priest Take Gethsemane as His Own Garden and Let Each Faithful Soul See Gethsemane in Every Mass

In his work, *The Agony of Jesus*, St. Padre Pio writes of the blood shed in Gethsemane, "I want to offer Thee to the Father. It is the Blood of His well-beloved Son, the God-Man, which ascends to His throne to pacify His justice, offended by our sins. He is superabundantly satisfied."[144] St. Padre Pio, a consummate priest,

---

142. Heb 7:17.

143. Gn 14:21-24.

144. Pio, *The Agony of Jesus*, 32.

instinctually desires to offer the blood of Jesus in Gethsemane as a sacrifice to the Father just as he would in a Mass.

As we consider the title of priest/high priest as it relates to Christ in the Garden, both in the subject of his prayer, and the posture of kneeling and laying prostrate before the Father. These are both markers of a Eucharistic theme as it relates to the Host and presiding priest/host of our liturgical celebrations and sacraments. In the Homily of the Most Reverend Placido Rodriguez at the Holy Mass at the Garden of Gethsemane, as part of the Hispanic Bishops' Pilgrimage to the Holy Land on January 22, 2018, he states, "we know that Jesus prayed at this Garden of Gethsemane. We can easily imagine Jesus fully prostrated on this holy monument, where drops of blood make this monument an altar of God, uttering his 'priestly prayers' and truly being heard, piercing the Heavens."[145]

It is *immediately* after the Institution of the Eucharist and the Institution of the Priesthood that Jesus has His Agony in the Garden. This, I assert, must be a lesson to each and every newly-ordained priest. Agony follows ordination; at some point, whether sooner or later: but spending time in Gethsemane is the way to master the agony and bring pain into purpose.

What does our High Priest, Jesus, endure immediately after that Last Supper and first Mass; immediately after the apostles are ordained; immediately after all the luminous grandeur and exultant jubilation of that first Mass…Loneliness, betrayal, sleep in the face of challenge, the betrayal of Judas…agony:

> How often are the sufferings of that night in the Garden of Olives re-enacted in the priest's life! The supports of his human nature threaten to collapse as darkness gathers about his soul; one star alone is visible: the will of the Father. Christ wrestled victoriously with his own sufferings in Gethsemane, but he continues to suffer mystically in the

---

145. Rodriguez, "Garden of Gethsemane".

Gethsemane of each of His priests. The aura of His death-struggle descends on such hours of priestly suffering: the priest should then kneel beside Christ, His High Priest, and share his sentiments.[146]

Let *every* priest take Gethsemane as his own garden, a place set apart, in which to refresh himself when the demands of his vocation bruise and weary and challenge. Let every priest live by the guidance of Christ our Host/host: watch; pray; do the Father's Will; pray the longer. Gethsemane is not a fearful place to avoid, but rather a place to refresh, to return to nightly, to be alone with Christ in the place and way which He Himself requested; to bring Him everything that no one understands but Him…that ought to draw each priestly soul like a magnet.

Let every soul who wants to support the priesthood through prayers for priests enter Gethsemane. Indeed, let every person who suffers or longs or struggles take Gethsemane for his or her refuge. In the Garden, Jesus triumphed, with athletic prowess, so that each soul who follows Him there can triumph, too. Though sorrowful, it is just as beautiful:

> The greatest public prayer of the Church, the Mass, is closely associated with the hour of Jesus in Gethsemane. The Precious Blood was shed mystically at the Last Supper, when the changed substance of the Wine was set apart from the consecrated Bread. Who shall say how often you have seen the priest at the altar bowing over the bread and wine before he hallows them as Minister of Christ. Look now at Jesus bowed in the Garden, while the wine of sacrifice reddens the raiment of His Body.[147]

---

146. Staudinger, *Holiness of the Priesthood*, 412.

147. Donnelly, *The Our Father in Gethsemane*, 64.

The Betrayal of Innocent Blood

While Peter, James, and John were taking their rest, "…Judas the traitor was wide awake and intent on betraying the Lord that the very idea of sleep never entered his mind."[148]

Thomas More asks, "Does not this contrast between the traitor and the apostles present to us a clear and sharp mirror image (as it were), a sad and terrible view of what has happened from those times even to our own? Why do not bishops contemplate in this scene their own somnolence? Since they have succeeded in the place of the apostles, would that they would reproduce their virtues just as eagerly as they embrace their authority…For very many are sleepy…"[149]

Another betrayal of Christ into the hands of sinners is:

…when His most holy body in the sacrament is consecrated and handled by unchaste, profligate, and sacrilegious priests. From the example of bad priests the contamination of vice spreads easily among the people…And the less suitable for obtaining grace those persons are whose duty it is to watch and pray for the people, the more necessary it is for the people to stay awake, get up, and pray all the more earnestly for themselves—and not only themselves but also for priests.[150]

Those who do not believe in the Real Presence but receive the Eucharist anyway, or who receive the Eucharist in a state of mortal sin,

---

148. More, *Complete Works Volume 14, Part I, De Tristitia Christi*, 259.

149. More, *Complete Works Volume 14, Part I, De Tristitia Christi*, 291.

150. More, *Complete Works Volume 14, Part I, De Tristitia Christi*, 353.

without having gone to the Sacrament of Reconciliation are like those who took Jesus prisoner in Gethsemane. "How little difference, I ask you, between them and those who took Christ captive that night?"[151] It is vital, too, then, to understand the Host of Gethsemane as the Eucharistic Host who is betrayed by those who deny and/or abuse the Real Presence of the Eucharist. In understanding the Host/host of Gethsemane, we are called to have a greater zeal for the Eucharist, and increase love of the Real Presence in ourselves and others.

The blood money of the betrayal really *is* blood money. "Then Judas, his betrayer, seeing that Jesus had been condemned, deeply regretted what he had done. He returned the thirty pieces of silver to the chief priests and elders, saying, 'I have sinned in betraying innocent blood.' They said, 'What is that to us? Look to it yourself.' Flinging the money into the temple, he departed and went off and hanged himself."[152]

This assertion by Judas, "I have betrayed innocent blood," reminds that Judas would have seen the face of Jesus in Gethsemane, streaming with the bloody sweat he had just endured. It could even be said that Judas literally betrayed innocent blood, in Gethsemane, when he placed the traitor's kiss upon Christ's face which undoubtedly was still streaked with blood from the Agony. It is indeed tragic that Judas, although guilty enough to admit his sin, is not humble enough to seek atonement, forgiveness, penance. It is a reminder that the Host/host offers mercy and invites us like the Prodigal to return, but we must in return offer penitent hearts. Admitting sin is not enough if we are not humble enough to repent, atone, and trust in God's mercy. Despair is a form of pride.

"The money he received was used to buy the potter's field, which they called the Field of Blood. Yet the question of how did Judas die doesn't quite end there. You must also consider Acts 1:18-19: 'With the payment he received for his wickedness, Judas bought a

---

151. More, *Complete Works Volume 14, Part I, De Tristitia Christi*, 357.
152. Mt 27:1-5.

field; there he fell headlong, his body burst open and all his intestines spilled out. Everyone in Jerusalem heard about this, so they called that field in their language Akeldama, that is, Field of Blood.'"[153]

If there is an opposite of hospitality and friendship, it is betrayal. The Host/host of Gethsemane was betrayed in the Garden on the Mount of Olives, which is all the more reason we are invited to keep company, console and offer reciprocal hospitality to Christ there, through our watchful and prayerful presence. Interestingly, the betrayal of Judas was not the first time God had been betrayed on the Mount of Olives. Some time after Solomon had finished building the beautiful temple for the Lord, he built pagan shrines for false gods on the Mount of Olives, "Solomon then built a high place to Chemosh, the idol of Moab, and to Moloch, the idol of the Ammonites, on the hill opposite Jerusalem."[154] This hill opposite Jerusalem was the Mount of Olives. This angered the Lord, since Solomon's heart had turned away from God, and this terrible act of Solomon led to the divided kingdom, in which all the tribes strayed from God except the faithful tribe of Judah. Contrast this sorrowful scene with the visions of Ezekial in which the prophet saw how "the glory of the Lord rose from the city and took a stand on the mountain which is to the east of the city;"[155] and with the prophecy of Zechariah in which "God's feet will stand on the Mount of Olives, which is opposite Jerusalem to the east,"[156] which describes the coming Day of the Lord.

153. Clarence L. Haynes Jr., 2023, "What Happened to Judas after He Betrayed Jesus?", *Bible Study Tools,* August 30, 2023, accessed May 2024, www.biblestudytools.com/bible-study/topical-studies/what-happened-to-judas-after-he-betrayed-jesus.html.

154. 1 Kings 11:7.

155. Ez 11:23.

156. Zec 14:4.

The Road to Emmaus as a Key to Understanding the Lukan Host/host

Fr. Dennis Billy writes in detail about this connection:

If we return to the Emmaus story, we see that it is very much about Jesus befriending the two disciples on the road and being befriended by them in return. Christianity, in fact, proposes a threefold order of friendship. First, there is the community of friends in the Godhead itself: Father, Son, and Spirit bonded together by their love of what is One, Good, True, and Beautiful; all seek each other's well-being, reciprocate their love for one another, and mutually indwell each other in an intimate embrace of love. Then, there is the individual's friendship with God. The same three characteristics resonate in my relationship with the ground of my being. God seeks my well-being, and I seek God's; we nurture a close, mutual rapport with one another; God dwells in me, and I dwell in God. Finally, there is friendship among Christians themselves. United by their common interest in and friendship with God, Christians forge genuine bonds of friendship that enable them constantly to seek each other's interest in a respectful, reciprocal manner, in the hope of becoming a reflection of the other's love for God. Each of these orders, moreover, somehow interrelates. As the Emmaus story demonstrates, the befriending God fosters befriending Christians, who live in turn for the purpose of an ever-widening circle of

God's friends. Christian friendship is one of the most precious treasures a person can be given…'No one has greater love than this, to lay down one's life for one's friends.' (John 15:13). What does all this say about our befriending God? It tells us that he is a quiet, unpretentious partner in all genuine human friendships.[157]

The significance of Bethany is seen once more at the end of Luke's Gospel. "Besides a number of smaller references to Bethany, one final event took place there. Bethany provided the location for Jesus' final blessing to His disciples and His subsequent parting. The encounter made up the final scene of Ascension in Luke's Gospel."[158] And recalling that Bethany is on the Mount of Olives is deeply significant to a study of the Garden of Gethsemane. The Mount of Olives is the site of the Agony and the Ascension, a sorrowful mystery and a glorious one. The Host/host of Gethsemane has given His guests an important lesson in this. Right before the Ascension, when Jesus appears to His Apostles, they share a meal together. "And they offered him a piece of a broiled fish, and a honeycomb. And when he had eaten before them, taking the remains, he gave to them." In this Gospel of Hospitality, the theme of hospitality is clear with the sharing of this meal. The Host/host still promises them yet more. "I am sending the promise of my Father upon you; but stay in the city until you are clothed with power from on high. Then he led them [out] as far as Bethany, raised his hands, and blessed them. As he blessed them he parted from them and was taken up to heaven. They did him homage and then returned to Jerusalem with great joy, and they were continually in the temple praising God."[159] These last words remind

---

157. Dennis J Billy, *Meeting Jesus on the Road to Emmaus: An Invitation to Friendship, Eucharist and Christian Community*, (Eugene, OR: Wipf and Stock, 2017), 62-63.

158. Butler et al., *Holman Illustrated Bible Dictionary*, 189.

159. Lk 24:49-53.

how the faithful can respond to the Host/host's perpetual invitation: through praising and blessing God via fervent and joyful prayer.

Conclusion

This chapter was focused on the Agony in the Garden in the Gospel of Luke. This chapter was filtered through the lens of this "Evangelist of prayer."[160] This overarching Lukan theme is confirmed in the Lukan Gethsemane narrative in which great emphasis is placed upon the prayer of Christ in the Garden, with details the other evangelists do not include, worded in a way that emphasizes the importance of prayer such as: "And being in agony, he prayed the longer."[161]

St. Luke's Gospel uniquely emphasizes Christ's perseverance in prayer by articulating that His Agony necessitated more time spent, until He was ready, and thus is a lesson for all who pray. St. Luke uniquely mentions the presence of an angel. Of great import, St. Luke is the only Evangelist to include the detail of Jesus sweating blood. Luke's Gospel is "interested in portraying this scene as a cosmic battle"[162] and his Gospel and commentaries upon it will be an important study for this thesis as the shedding of Jesus' blood in the Garden is a vital consideration that points to Him as the Eucharistic Host of Gethsemane. These three unique Lukan details: Jesus praying "the longer;" the ministering angel; and the shedding of blood were all addressed vis-a-vis Jesus as the Host/host of Gethsemane.

The hospitality emphasized in Luke was considered throughout this chapter. Indeed, there are so many examples in this Gospel that I

---

160. Kodell, *The Gospel According to Luke*, 10.

161. Lk 22:43-44 [*Douay-Rheims*].

162. Green and McKnight, *Dictionary of Jesus and the Gospels*, 266.

assert that St. Luke could be called "The Evangelist of Hospitality." His Gospel is the only one to include The Good Samaritan, and also emphasizes the House at Bethany in which Saints Martha and Mary show great hospitality to Jesus. His Gethsemane narrative includes many details that affirm Christ as Host/host of Gethsemane.

As we come to the conclusion of this study of Gethsemane in the Synoptic Gospels that the past two chapters have explored, it is worth pausing to reiterate and expound upon the similarities and differences between the Synoptic Gospels. I assert that Luke's Gospel could be known as the Gospel of Gethsemane, since his is the Gospel which uniquely contains the detail of "withdrawing about a stone's throw from them;"[163] the angel comforting Christ; the mention that being in agony, "He prayed so fervently,"[164] therefore He was persistent in prayer; and "his sweat became like drops of blood falling on the ground."[165] Surely the Eucharistic detail of His blood in Gethsemane, coupled with the hospitality that is emphasized throughout Luke's Gospel, beautifully point to Christ as the Host/host of Gethsemane.

Matthew and Mark both note the site of the Agony as "a place called Gethsemane"[166] while Luke refers to it as "The Mount of Olives."[167] In Matthew's Gospel, Jesus tells the apostles, "Sit here while I go *over there* and pray;"[168] while Mark has Him utter merely, "Sit here while I pray."[169] Matthew records that Jesus took Peter "and the two sons of Zebedee,"[170] while Mark names them: "Peter, James,

---

163. Lk 22:41.
164. Lk 22:44.
165. Lk 22:44.
166. Mt 26:36; Mk 14:32.
167. Lk 22:39.
168. Mt 26:36.
169. Mk 14:32.
170. Mt 26:37.

and John."[171] Luke, however, does not name the three at all. He simply writes, "and the disciples followed him."[172] Luke does not mention "sit here" or "over there," but gets right to this point: "Pray that you may not undergo the test."[173] Then the Lukan Jesus withdraws about "a stone's throw from them."[174] Meanwhile, in Matthew's Gospel, Jesus "began to feel sorrow and distress," and in Mark's, Jesus "began to be troubled and distressed." All three Synoptic Gospels depict Jesus asking the Father to take the cup away from Him, if it is the Father's will. In Matthew, Jesus says it three times. Mark mentions Jesus saying it only twice, but is the only one who includes the detail "Abba," or "Papa," when Jesus calls out to the Father.[175] Both Matthew and Mark note that Jesus tells the apostles to "remain here and keep watch."[176] Both Mark and Matthew specifically mention that Jesus addresses Peter and asks, "you could not keep watch [with me] for one hour?"[177] In Matthew, Jesus "fell prostrate in prayer"[178] while in Mark, Jesus "advanced a little and fell to the ground,"[179] and in Luke Jesus was "kneeling."[180] All three Synoptic Gospels include a word of explanation for the sleeping apostles. Matthew says they were sleeping because "they could not keep their eyes open."[181] Mark says, "they could not keep their eyes open and did not know what to answer him."[182] Luke, however, explains the most poignant reason: "he found

---

171. Mk 14:33.

172. Lk 22:39.

173. Lk 22:40.

174. Lk 22:41.

175. Mk 14:36.

176. Mt 26:38; Mk 14:34.

177. Mt 26:40; Mk 14:37.

178. Mt 26:39.

179. Mk 14:35.

180. Lk 22:41.

181. Mt 26:43.

182. Mk 14:40.

them sleeping from grief."[183] When comparing and contrasting the three side-by-side it is important to remind that Mark's Gospel distinguishes itself in Gethsemane not only by the use of the word "Abba," but by uniquely mentioning, at the close of the Gethsemane narrative, the "young man followed him wearing nothing but a linen cloth about his body. They seized him, but he left the cloth behind and ran off naked."[184]

As Chapter Three comes to its conclusion, it is important to take a moment to reflect upon the fact that all three of the Synoptics place the Garden of Gethsemane narrative in the same chapter as The Last Supper. Thus, even Scripture itself elucidates the fact that Jesus is the Host of Gethsemane, the same Eucharistic Lord who presides over the first Mass in the Upper Room.

As the Gospel of John is examined in the next chapter, it will be revealed that this evangelist also places His Gethsemane narrative in the same chapter as other important reflections, but the emphasis there is not as much the connection to the Eucharistic Host of the Last Supper, as it is the host who has invited guests and initiated hospitality, and has been repeatedly rejected and denied.

---

183. Lk 22:45.
184. Mk 14:51-52.

Chapter 4 The Host of Gethsemane in the Gospel of John

Introduction

"Changing Old Testament water into Messianic wine, consequently, signifies, for John the passing of the old into the new... John wants his audience to think also of *the* Messianic wine that will be the result and Eucharistic sacrament of Jesus' death."[1] Chapter four will be filtered through this lens.

The Gospel of John is dated to "80-110, traditionally [written in] the Ephesys area, but some opt for Syria."[2]

"John is a Gospel where style and theology are intimately wedded. Many scholars recognize a formal poetic style in a few parts of John, for example, the Prologue...and John 17. Some scholars perceive in the Johannine discourses a uniquely solemn semi-poetic pattern marked by rhythm."[3]

The Gospel of John is the "Fourth Gospel account of the New Testament, distinct from the Synoptic Gospels, Matthew, Mark, and Luke...[it is] written by John, the...son of Zebedee...the beloved disciple...The Gospel of John is different from the three Synoptic Gospels...John omits events and references that are extremely important in the others...John has much information that the Synoptics

1. Neal M. Flanagan, *The Gospel According to John and the Johannine Epistles*, (Collegeville, MN: The Liturgical Press, 1983), 13.

2. Brown, *An Introduction to the New Testament*, 117.

3. Brown, *An Introduction to the New Testament*, 116.

leave out. Over 90 percent of John is unique."[4] For example, the Woman at the Well is a story only found in John. This story points to why and how the Host/host of Gethsemane actually offers His guests holy food: it is the food of doing the Father's Will.

Raymond Brown suggested that there were possibly several revisions and additions to John's Gospel over a number of years. Brown "suggested a plausible multiple edition theory to explain how John's Gospel developed over a period of time. In most 'multiple editions' theories there was a single base document which underwent several revisions, possibly at the hand of the original author, over a number of years."[5]

Further, according to Raymond Brown's theory, the audience of John's Gospel is what he refers to as a "Johnannine community" which included Samaritans and Jews who accepted Jesus:

> Discussion of Jesus as Messiah generated a number of "homilies" preserving Jesus' teaching as attempts to convince Jews he was the Messiah. It is possible that some time before A. D. 70 these Jewish Christians were expelled from the synagogue, ostracized and persecuted (as implied in John 1:11, 10:28-29; 15:18, 16:2 and the "not of this world" theme in 15:18, 16:3, 16:33).
>
> The Gospel of John therefore could be aimed at Jewish Christians that are still in the synagogue ("crypto-Christians" in Brown) who are not fully "Christian" in the opinion of the author. They need to come out and be separate from the Synagogue. A second aim would therefore be to continue to try and convince Jews [that]

---

4. Butler et al., *Holman Illustrated Bible Dictionary*, 934.

5. Phillip J. Long, "Origins of the Gospel of John: Raymond Brown", November 29, 2014, accessed June 2024, readingacts.com/2014/11/29/origins-of-the-gospel-of-john/.

Jesus was the Messiah…Raymond Brown and his Johannine community theory is well-respected and is always discussed in recent study of the Gospel of John.[6]

As the Gospel of John is examined, it will be revealed that much can be gleaned by noticing that this evangelist places His Gethsemane narrative within the same chapter as other important reflections; such as the Denials of Peter, the Inquiry before Annas, and the Trial before Pilate. In the Synoptic Gospels, the Gethsemane narratives are found within the same chapter as the Institution of the Eucharist at the Last Supper. In this way, the Synoptics shed light on the Host of Gethsemane, since the same Eucharistic Host of the Last Supper is now sacrificing himself through the Passion of His Soul in Gethsemane, even unto the shedding of His own Blood there, as Luke describes. In John's Gospel, by sharing of the Gethsemane narrative with the Denial of Peter and the Trial before Pilate, he sheds light upon the host of Gethsemane who has invited guests and initiated hospitality, and yet is repeatedly rejected and denied.

Particularly poignant and significant in John's Gospel is "The Prayer of Jesus," which follows John's Last Supper Discourse. This Prayer of Jesus comprises the entire chapter before the Gethsemane narrative. I assert, it is this prayer of fatherly love, immediately preceding Gethsemane, that makes the Garden of Gethsemane the Garden of God's Love. Appropriately, St. John the Evangelist is known as the Beloved Disciple, the one who rested upon the heart of Christ at the Last Supper. The Prayer of Jesus preceding Gethsemane gives a trajectory of love that elucidates Gethsemane, moving the reader into Gethsemane as we encounter the Passion of the Sacred Heart.

In John's Gethsemane narrative, one theme is the betrayal and imprisonment of Jesus. In this chapter, it will be shown in a paramount way how the "Host/host" becomes "Hostage." Importantly, this

---

6. Long, "Origins of the Gospel of John".

chapter through its understanding of "Hostage" will draw out the "Host/host" connection in the context of the Agony in the Garden as it relates to the Passion Narratives…immediately following the Last Supper, and leading up to the moment of Betrayal that will set into motion the Crucifixion.

In a very powerful way, the Gospel of John points to Jesus as the Eucharistic Lord in Gethsemane, bringing to light the seven "I AM" statements of John's Gospel, which this chapter will elucidate. Christ's "I AM" statements culminate, finding their apex in the Garden of Gethsemane narrative of this Gospel, as will be discussed. Also, there are seven signs presented to us by John, beginning with the Wedding at Cana and ending with the Raising of Lazarus. At the Raising of Lazarus, Jesus sheds tears. This is one of the three times in Scripture He does so, and always poignantly, on the Mount of Olives. This leads to a deeper understanding of His Sacrifice as represented by the blood, sweat, and tears of Gethsemane. The Raising of Lazarus is followed, significantly, by the Anointing at Bethany, at which hospitality to the Host/host is exemplified.

Seven is the Biblical number of heavenly completion[7], and so it is of great significance that Jesus says "I AM" seven times in the Gospel of John. However, it is also important to note that these seven "I AM"s are the seven metaphors Jesus gives for Himself, such as "I am the light of the world." However, these seven "I AM"s do not include the other times Jesus uses that phrase in the Gospel of John. He does so three times in the Garden of Gethsemane.

In John's Gospel, he writes of what happens in "the Kidron valley to where there was a garden," and then, the action shifts immediately to the arrest. Once the soldiers say they are looking for Jesus the Nazorean, Jesus responds, "I AM," which refers to the name of God as relayed to Moses in The Old Testament, and when Jesus

---

7. Bible Study Tools, "The Number 7 in the Bible," *Bible Study Tools*, accessed May 2024, www.biblestudytools.com/topical-verses/the-number-7-in-the-bible/.

utters this name, "they turned away and fell to the ground."[8] Here we see the power of our Eucharistic Host, for whom we kneel during the transubstantiation, when we recognize Him through prayer and say, "My Lord and My God." John adds this to the Eucharistic theme in the account of Peter cutting off the slave Malchus' ear: "Put your sword into its scabbard. Shall I not drink the cup that the Father gave me?"[9] This reference to the cup shows our Eucharistic Host. As Jesus puts an end to the violence, his "food is to do his Father's will;"[10] his drink will be that which the Father offers.

Another component which makes John's Gospel special is when he writes of Jesus walking "over the brook Cedron," (which flowed with the blood of temple sacrifice) following the Last Supper Discourse in which Jesus tells of His Love. Still another special component of John's Gospel is the "I AM" of Gethsemane when the soldiers fall down in fear at His name while trying to arrest Him, in so doing making abundantly clear that Jesus is the willing hostage, impelled by love. In the Discourse of Love, Jesus prays,"Those whom thou gavest me, I have kept; and none of them is lost, but the son of perdition…"[11] and then it is clear in the Garden that Jesus is lovingly protecting all to whom He is host: "Let these go their way."[12] What an incredibly perfect and most loving host Jesus is. He takes care of His apostles, He protects them, and this very action completes the prayer for his disciples, to witness a pure act of love.

---

8. Jn 18:6.
9. Jn 18:10-11.
10. Jn 4:34.
11. Jn 17:12.
12. Jn 18:8.

Messianic wine: The result of Jesus' passion (including Gethsemane) and His death

The Wedding at Cana is the first of Jesus' seven signs in the Gospel of John. The Blessed Mother prefigures prominently here as the ideal model of both watcher and pray-er, and she does so with obedience and love. She is vigilant about the situation, notices the problem, and petitions her son, and counsels obedience to Him. "… John's Gospel clearly displays Mary's role as mediator. She presents the need—the lack of wine—to her Son, and teaches the proper attitude toward him: 'Do whatever he tells you.'"[13] There are six stone jars which Jesus has the stewards fill with water. These six jars are linked to the sixth day of creation. "The sixth day, on which God created man, is a prophecy of the sixth day on which he will recreate it, in Christ, at the end of time."[14] As the water is transformed into the best wine imaginable, it recalls other Biblical transformations: "In Egypt the water becomes blood…in Cana the water becomes wine…in the Upper Room the wine becomes blood…In order to liberate his people from slavery, God changes water into blood. For the joy of the wedding feast, Jesus transforms water into wine. And to seal the definitive covenant, the eternal wedding feast, he transforms wine into his blood."[15] The wedding feast of the un-bloody Mass at the Last Supper continues into the Garden; dripping sacrificial blood in Gethsemane and emptying the rest of His blood at the Sacrifice at Calvary. And so, the wedding supper of the Lamb is to be remembered

---

13. Elena Bosetti, *John: The Word of Light*, (Boston: Pauline Books and Media, 2007), 38.

14. Bosetti. *John: The Word of Light,* 38.

15. Bosetti. *John: The Word of Light*, 39-40.

in light of Gethsemane just as much as the Upper Room and Calvary. The blood and water from Egypt to Cana reminds of Christ walking through the Cedron Brook on the way to Gethsemane which was filled with the blood of temple sacrifice, as will be mentioned later; and reminds of Christ's pierced side at the Crucifixion.

The host of Gethsemane's food is to do the will of God

Jesus, the host of Gethsemane, even offers the three disciples in the Garden food and drink. Our good host provides sustenance for them even in His Agony. Recalling that we must imitate the Suffering Servant who is our host, and offer Him food and drink in return, we need only look to John Chapter Four for what this exchange actually is, and what it reveals.

"Give me a drink,"[16] Jesus says to the Samaritan woman at the well, in a story unique to the Gospel of John, reminding of His thirst for souls:

> In the Bible, encounters that take place at wells follow a narrative formula with common features and usually conclude with a marriage, according to this outline: a man travels to a foreign land; he finds a well. A woman arrives…a conversation occurs about the water that is given. A conversation follows about the man's identity. The woman runs home to spread the news. The foreigner is invited to the home; a meal and a wedding follow. The servant of Abraham, sent by the patriarch to the land of his birth in order to choose a wife for his son Isaac, meets the splendid Rebecca at a well (Gen 24:10-51). Jacob meets his

---

16. Jn 4:7.

beautiful shepherd girl, Rachel, at a well (Gen 29:9-14) and Moses meets his future wife at a well (Ex 2:15-22)...But why did the evangelist John set the meeting between Jesus and the Samaritan woman at a well, knowing the reader's expectation for the story's ending? What is he trying to tell us? This question can help us read the text again from a new perspective: the journey of faith leads us to recognize Jesus as Messiah/Bridegroom. The Baptist vouches for this, 'rejoicing with joy at the Bridegroom's voice'(Jn 3:29). The messianic time is the time of the wedding, the time of fidelity to the marital alliance, the time in which the true worshippers "will worship the Father in spirit and truth" (Jn 4:23).[17]

At Jacob's Well, where Christ encounters the Samaritan woman, all faithful souls ought to hear the voice of the Bridegroom seeking them personally, the same Bridegroom who made all the water at Cana turn into the choicest wine.

St. Augustine asserts, "Jesus also thirsted after that woman's faith...He thirsteth for their faith, for whom He sheds His blood."[18] From the account of Luke's Gospel we know Jesus sheds His very blood in Gethsemane, and so we can give Him a drink there through our faith; to slake the deep thirst of He who shed His blood for us. In return, "he would have given you living water...whoever drinks the water I shall give will never thirst; the water I shall give will become in him a spring of water welling up to eternal life."[19]

In case there is any doubt that there is actually a banquet to which the faithful are truly being invited in Gethsemane, of all places, the proof is given later in Chapter Four of John's Gospel, when the

17. Bosetti. *John: The Word of Light*, 55-56.
18. Aquinas, *Catena Aurea Vol. IV*, 139.
19. Jn 4:10,14.

disciples return to Jesus after He has converted the Samaritan woman and they urge Him, "Rabbi, eat. But he said to them, 'I have food to eat of which you do not know.' So the disciples said to one another, 'Could someone have brought him something to eat?' Jesus said to them, 'My food is to do the will of the one who sent me and to finish his work. Do you not say, 'in four months the harvest will be here? I tell you, look up and see the fields ripe for the harvest. The reaper is already receiving his payment and gathering crops for eternal life, so that the sower and the reaper can rejoice together."[20] Gethsemane is the place Jesus most famously does the Father's Will and it is in a garden, thus the very location suited for harvest. In Gethsemane, Jesus lives out the very essence of what He describes at Jacob's well.

Jesus explains that the "food to eat of which you do not know" is "to do the will of the one who sent me and to finish his work." I assert that this one verse, "to do the will of the one who sent me and to finish his work," can be seen as a kind of diptych[21] or two-fold altarpiece of the Agony in the Garden and the Crucifixion. How is this so? "To do the will of the one who sent me," is spoken and embodied in Gethsemane "and to finish his work," is spoken and embodied on the Cross, "when Jesus had taken the wine, he said, 'It is finished.' And bowing his head, he handed over the spirit.'"[22]

And so imagine, if you will, an elaborately carved diptych with Jesus doing the will of the Father in Gethsemane on one side; and finishing the Father's work in Calvary on the other, and recalling the importance of obedience to the will of God as the disposition of Christ's sacrifice and the obliged disposition of the faithful at Mass; the thirst Jesus expresses to the Samaritan woman and the drink He offers her in return. The hidden food of which he speaks, is part of the Eucharistic sacrifice, in Gethsemane as well as Calvary. Calvary is the

---

20. Jn 4:31-36.

21. Merriam-Webster, s.v. "diptych,"
www.merriam-webster.com/dictionary/diptych.

22. Jn 20:30.

place of the Passion of Christ's Body; Gethsemane is the place of the Passion of Christ's Sacred Heart. Fr. Tesniere writes, "That part of the drama of the Passion which was played in Gethsemani[23] may properly be called the Passion of the Sacred Heart. Although the Heart of the Saviour, in all the torments that He underwent for us, ceased not for one instant to suffer, even till the last pulsation with which He breathed forth His soul upon the Cross, yet it was in Gethsemani that every pang sprang from the depths of His Heart, fell back upon His Heart, flowed in torture over His Heart. It was from the Heart alone that His Agony then came, for no external violence…then struck the Divine Victim."[24]

The poignant Scripture passage in which Jesus says "it is finished," begins in this way: "After this, aware that everything was now finished, in order that the scripture may be fulfilled, Jesus said, 'I thirst.'[25] There was a vessel filled with common wine. So they put a sponge soaked in wine on a sprig of hyssop and put it up to his mouth. When Jesus had taken the wine, he said, 'It is finished.' And bowing his head, he handed over the spirit."[26] This passage of Christ's thirst on the cross recalls the story of the woman at the well when Jesus asked her for a drink. It also recalls that at the end of that pericope, Jesus tells His apostles, "My food is to do the will of the one who sent me and to finish his work."[27]Here on the cross, the thirst and what is finished are intrinsically connected. The thirst precedes what is finished. What is between them and what joins them is the will of God, a prime home for this will is Gethsemane, where Jesus thirsts for our vigilance, and does the will of His Father, in obedience, despite the agony.

---

23. An alternate spelling of Gethsemane used by Tesniere.

24. Tesniere, *The Eucharistic Heart of Jesus*, 136.

25. This should recall what Jesus said to the Samaritan woman when He asked for a drink.

26. Jn 20:28-30.

27. Jn 4:34.

Figure 4: Francesco Trevisani, The Agony in the Garden, 1740, oil on copper.

In the notes of the Catholic Study Bible, it is stated: "John does not mention the drugged wine, a narcotic that Jesus refuses as the crucifixion began (Mk 15, 23) but only this final gesture of kindness at the end (Mk 15, 36). Hyssop, a small plant, is scarcely suitable for carrying a sponge (Mark mentions a reed) and may be a symbolic reference to the hyssop used to daub the blood of the paschal lamb on the doorpost of the Hebrews (Ex 12,22)."[28] Also He has now finally drank the last, fourth cup of the Paschal meal begun in the Upper Room, the same chalice looming over his head in Gethsemane that we see in a plethora of religious art[29] (see Figure 4). Now we hear Christ's

---

28. Commentary for John Chapter 19, "The Gospel According to John", *The Catholic Study Bible*, 180.

29. Franceso Trevisani, "The Agony in the Garden", oil on copper, 1740, Glasgow Museums Resource Centre, Glasgow, accessed June 2024, at artuk.org/discover/artworks/the-agony-in-the-garden-86262.

words of Gethsemane echo, "Shall I not drink the cup that the Father gave me?"[30]

Theophylact asserts, "In that He calls it a cup, He shows how pleasing and acceptable death for the salvation of man was to Him."[31] And Augustine teaches, "But the Giver of this cup and the Drinker of this cup are the same; as…the Apostle saith, *Christ loved us, and gave Himself for us.*"[32]

It has been asserted frequently in this work that the Agony in the Garden is Eucharistic because of its link to the Last Supper and the priesthood; it is worth expanding this connection to the Sacrifice of Calvary. As it is taught in the Catechism of the Council of Trent, "The Mass is the same sacrifice as that of the cross: We therefore confess that the Sacrifice of the Mass is and ought to be considered one and the same Sacrifice as that of the cross, for the victim is one and the same, namely, Christ our Lord, who offered Himself, once only, a bloody Sacrifice on the altar of the cross. The bloody and unbloody victim are not two, but one victim only, whose Sacrifice is daily renewed in the Eucharist, in obedience to the command of our Lord: *Do this for a commemoration of me.*"[33]

Fr. William Most writes, "Since the Mass has the same external sign, and the same interior dispositions on the part of Christ, we rightly call it a sacrifice, the continuation of Calvary. It does not need to earn redemption all over—that was done once for all (Hebrews 9:28) by His death. But since the Holiness of God loves everything that is good, and in good order, it pleases Him to have titles or reasons in place for what He will give (cf. Summa I. 19. 5. c). So it pleases Him to have the Mass provide the title for the distribution of what was once for all earned on Calvary."[34]

---

30. Jn 18:11.

31. Aquinas, *Catena Aurea Vol. IV*, 550.

32. Aquinas, *Catena Aurea Vol. IV*, 550.

33. *Catechism of the Council of Trent*, 237-238.

Between what is clearly decided and defined at the Council of Trent that the Mass is the same (un-bloody) sacrifice as that at Calvary, and the way Fr. Most explains it above, one realizes that what happened at the Last Supper, in the Upper Room, was a Mass, the unbloody sacrifice, which was, also, the offering of Calvary which was as yet to happen the next day; and what happened at Calvary was the bloody sacrifice which is daily renewed in the Eucharist in an un-bloody way. What is the greatly significant location in Scripture between the Upper Room and Golgotha? It is Gethsemane. Gethsemane is between the two Eucharistic events: the unbloody sacrifice of the Mass and the bloody sacrifice of Calvary. Gethsemane is the sacrifice of Christ's heart, soul and will. It is the lodestar of Christ's perfect obedience.

"Since the Mass has the same external sign, and the same interior dispositions on the part of Christ, we rightly call it a sacrifice, the continuation of Calvary...Catechists often like to use a memory word ACTS to express the dispositions: adoration, contrition, thanksgiving, and supplication. This is not wrong, but it leaves out the essential disposition, obedience to the Father."[35]

The interior dispositions of Christ and His people are important to consider. "At the Last Supper He ordered, 'Do this in memory of me.' Since we were not there, He wants us to join our dispositions to His. The great Liturgy Encyclical of Pius XII, Mediator Dei, explains well that the people can be said to exercise their royal priesthood, to offer the Mass with the priest: first, 'from the fact that the priest at the altar in offering a sacrifice in the name of all His members, does so in the person of Christ,' whose members they are. (Since only the ordained priest acts 'in the person of Christ,' Vatican II says [LG #10]

---

34. William G. Most, "The Sacrifice of the Mass", n.d., *Eternal Word Television Network*, accessed May 2024, www.ewtn.com/catholicism/teachings/sacrifice-of-the-mass-234.

35. Most, "The Sacrifice of the Mass".

that the ordained priesthood differs from that of the laity in essence, and not only in degree)."[36]

As the Catechism of the Council of Trent explains: "The priest is also one and the same, Christ the Lord; for the ministers who offer Sacrifice, consecrate the holy mysteries, not in their own person, but in that of Christ, as the words of consecration itself show, for the priest does not say: *This is the body of Christ*, but *This is my body*; and thus, acting in the Person of Christ the Lord, he changes the substance of the bread and wine into the true substance of His body and blood."[37]

The people at Mass offer spiritual sacrifices. As Most described:

> These spiritual sacrifices consist of their obedience to the will of the Father, already carried out, and planned for the future. This includes their works, their bearing the troubles of life, their prayers, their apostolic efforts, their living out the duties of their state in life, even their relaxation of body and mind if all these things are done as part of the Father's plan, to enable them to serve Him better...It would be good to take a moment before each Mass to see what one has to join with the obedience of Christ, soon to be offered on the altar. Then Mass cannot be without meaning; rather, it dominates all of life, for we should bring our past obediences, and look ahead to the obedience of the near future...It is good to recall too that His Mother shared in this sacrifice by her obedience (cf. our comments on the Third Article of the Creed) on Calvary, and now, as John Paul II taught, she "is at every altar" because "she was present at the original sacrifice", sharing in it, and now

---

36. Most, "The Sacrifice of the Mass".
37. *Catechism of the Council of Trent*, 237-238.

from heaven, she still joins her will to His, as He offers the flesh and blood He received from her.[38]

This is reminiscent of what was discussed in the previous chapter of why there is a custom of a new priest giving his *maniturgium* to his mother after he is ordained. Further, the presence of Mary at the foot of the cross, still joining "her will to His, as He offers the flesh and blood He received from her," reminds one of this quote from Luke, "My mother and my brothers are those who hear the word of God and act on it."[39] Thus those who do the will of God are Christ's mother and brothers. And so, it becomes clear that the invitation of Gethsemane is one to a banquet of the food that is to do the will of God; shared with the family of those who do the will of God, and that the obedience to the will of God is an indispensable part of the disposition for those who attend Mass.

The Fiat of Gethsemane

Cardinal Joseph Siri states:

In the Mystery of Gethsemane the two greatest, most poignant, and sweetest mysteries are unveiled: the Incarnation of God in perfect man in Mary, and the engendering of holy Church in the relativity of temporal man…The Fiat of the Virgin Mary had as immediate consequence, an event in the nature of the human being, an event ontologically new. The words by which Christ abandons himself totally to the will of the Father constitute

---

38. Most, "The Sacrifice of the Mass".
39. Lk 8:21.

the second Fiat of the economy of man's salvation. The Fiat of Gethsemane was the consequence in a new period, of the first Fiat of the human being Mary. The second Fiat pronounced and accomplished by the Being begotten by God in human nature, had as outcome the union of God with the existences of all men, that is, with the existence of all beings constituting the History of men.[40]

Siri continues:

...We have difficulty in conceiving the mysterious act of love and harmony which was accomplished with the first Fiat of the Virgin Mary. Nevertheless, it is that act which permitted the Being who was praying, his face covered with a sweat of blood, to unite himself ontologically to the existence of each man, an anarchic and sorrowful disorder of History...and it is this union which gives man the possibility of becoming a new being and to know that a second will is rising up in him, which is in struggle with the first will of his nature in disorder; the disorder of sin. It is this particular union which was accomplished by the Fiat of Gethsemane: not as I will, but as Thou wilt. For it is this union which was the subject of the prayer of the agony and of the Fiat; and it was the cause of the Cross which must follow. The agony of Gethsemane in its ontologic mystery, would not have been possible if the Being of the agony had not been the Being of the Incarnation.[41]

---

40. Joseph Siri, *Gethsemane: Reflections on the Contemporary Theological Movement*, (Chicago, IL: Franciscan Herald Press, 1981), 364-365.

41. Siri, Gethsemane, 368-371.

The student of Gethsemane, "will understand why, in the race of men, there is a privileged being. It is the being who spoke the first Fiat in the history of salvation, Mary; and he will understand why it is not a question of the literature compassed by a pious sentimentality, when the Church calls the Virgin Mary, Mother of God. He will understand that no urgency, no personal or general danger, no hostility towards the Incarnate Word and the Mother of the Incarnate Word, must alter, in the mind and heart, the real basis of holy Theology and unique finality; that is, the Incarnation of the Word, of Christ Jesus in the Blessed Virgin Mary."[42]

The connection between the Fiat of the Annunciation and the Fiat of Gethsemane is punctuated by the fact that, "the chosen place for Mary's burial lies, perhaps not coincidentally, just a few meters from the Garden of Gethsemane, at the foot of the Mount of Olives."[43]

The Raising of Lazarus

Preceding the anointing at Bethany was the raising of Lazarus from the dead. Lazarus had been dead already four days when Jesus arrived. According to Fr. David Stanley:

> When he was confronted with his enemy death in the presence of the bereaved sisters, Martha and Mary, and their grieving friends, Jesus (the evangelist observed) "shuddered to the depths of his soul and was deeply troubled" (Jn 11:33). For his reserved description now of Jesus; struggle in the face of his hour, John borrows an

---

42. Siri, Gethsemane, 376.

43. Joseángel Domínguez, "The Mother in Heaven", *St. Josemaria Institute*, August 11, 2023, accessed May 2024, stjosemaria.org/the-mother-in-heaven/.

expression of the psalmist, "My soul is deeply troubled within me" (Ps 41:7), the source of the Matthean and Markan phrase "sorrowful unto death." As the crowd at Bethany observed Jesus' distressing reactions and later were privileged to witness his prayer before the tomb (Jn 11:35, 44), so also in this moving episode the crowd, apparently forgotten for the moment, are seemingly witnesses of Jesus' struggle and prayer, like the disciples in the Synoptic Gethsemane.[44]

For John, Gethsemane is present at the Raising of Lazarus. Although John's description of Jesus in Gethsemane is brief compared to the Synoptics, John has references to what Jesus was feeling in Gethsemane in other places within his Gospel, such as Christ's reaction at the tomb of Lazarus.

"When Martha heard that Jesus was coming, she went to meet Him; but Mary sat at home. Martha said to Jesus, 'Lord, if you had been here, my brother would not have died. But even now I know that whatever you ask of God, God will give you.' Jesus said to her, 'Your brother will rise.' Martha said to Him, 'I know he will rise, in the resurrection on the last day.' Jesus told her, 'I am the resurrection and the life; whoever believes in me, even if he dies, will live, and everyone who lives and believes in me will never die. Do you believe this?' She said to Him, 'Yes. Lord. I have come to believe that You are the Messiah, the Son of God, the one who is coming into the world.'"[45]

In the previous chapter discussing the Gospel of Luke vis-a-vis the Gethsemane narratives, the house at Bethany's role in providing hospitality for Christ was discussed at length. But whereas the Martha of the Lukan House of Bethany narrative was still somewhat short-sighted in her service, leaving Christ's side and resenting her sister for remaining with Him rather than helping her, the Martha of this

---

44. Stanley, *Jesus in Gethsemane*, 240.

45. Jn 11:20-27.

Johannine sign of the Raising of Lazarus has matured in faith. She speaks confidently that Lazarus would not have died had Christ been there, and that Jesus is the Messiah:

> When she had said this, she went and called her sister Mary secretly, saying, "The teacher is here and is asking for you." As soon as she heard this, Mary rose quickly and went to Him. For Jesus had not yet come into the village, but was still where Martha had met Him. So when the Jews who were with her in the house comforting her saw Mary get up and go out, they followed her, presuming she was going to the tomb to weep there. When Mary came to where Jesus was and saw Him, she fell at his feet and said to Him, "Lord, if You had been here, my brother would not have died."[46]

Blood, Sweat, and Tears on the Mount of Olives

The Raising of Lazarus pericope continues, "When Jesus saw her weeping and the Jews who had come with her weeping, He became perturbed and deeply troubled, and said, 'Where have you laid him?' They said to Him, 'Sir, come and see.' And Jesus wept."[47]

---

46. Jn 11:28-32.
47. Jn 11:20-35.

Figure 5. Enrique Simonet Lombardo, Flevit Super Illam, 1892, oil on canvas.

At this recollection of the tears of Christ, it is important to notice that all three times in Scripture that Jesus weeps are on the Mount of Olives. The first time is at the death of Lazarus, in Bethany, which is on Mount Olivet. He weeps even though He will resurrect Lazarus mere moments later. It is as though in this moment, Jesus covers each death of each of His faithful, each grief that would ever be endured, with His tears. God who created us for such perfect happiness weeps over the bodily death that we must suffer after the Fall. The second time Jesus cries in Scripture is His lamentation over Jerusalem.[48] There, too, He is upon the Mount of Olives. In this we are reminded that Jesus weeps over the chastisements that befall humanity. There is a work of art that depicts this moment of Jesus mourning Jerusalem. "Flevit super illam," by Enrique Simonet[49] (see Figure 5),

48. Lk. 19:41-44.

49. Enrique Simonet Lombardo, "Flevit Super Illam", 1892, oil on canvas, Museo del Prado, Madrid, accessed May 2024, at www.museodelprado.es/en/the-collection/art-work/flevit-super-illam/498b0344-ee49-435c-bfd7-ff707d728975

which translates "He wept over it," depicts the hands of Christ reaching out as though He wants to gather Jerusalem like a bird gathers her young under her wings.[50]

The third time that Jesus weeps is in the Garden of Gethsemane. Surely, it can be reasoned that someone distraught enough to shed a bloody sweat also would have shed tears. But there is even a clearer proof, one drawn from the words of Scripture.

John Piper writes convincingly of the tears Jesus must have shed in Gethsemane, connecting verses found in the Letter to the Hebrews with the Agony in the Garden. He writes:

> Hebrews 5:7 says, "In the days of his flesh, Jesus offered up prayers and supplications, with loud cries and tears, to him who was able to save him from death, and he was heard because of his reverence." He was heard. He got his request. What does this refer to in Jesus's life? Nothing in Jesus's experience comes closer to this description than the prayers of Gethsemane. "Jesus offered up prayers and supplications, with loud cries and tears" corresponds emotionally to Luke 22:44: "Being in agony he prayed more earnestly; and his sweat became like great drops of blood falling down to the ground." "Loud cries and tears" is a description of the "agony" of Jesus. Hebrews 5:7 says, "Jesus offered up prayers and supplications, with loud cries and tears, to him who was able to save him from death, and he was heard because of his reverence." If "save him from death" does not mean "Remove this cup from me," what does it mean? For he was certainly heard and received this request…This was the greatest act of obedience that Christ was to perform. He prays for strength and help, that his poor feeble human nature might be supported, that he might

---

50. Mt. 23:37.

213

not fail in this great trial, that he might not sink and be swallowed up, and his strength so overcome that he should not hold out, and finish the appointed obedience."[51]

Piper continues his assertion:

…therefore he offered up strong crying and tears unto him that was able to strengthen him, and support, and save him from death, that the death he was to suffer might not overcome his love and obedience, but that he might overcome death, and so be saved from it. ("Christ's Agony"). Jesus did not go on praying for the cup to pass. He went on praying for success in drinking it. When Paul says of Jesus's resurrection, "Therefore God has highly exalted him" (Philippians 2:9), the "therefore" refers to Jesus's unwavering obedience unto death: "Being found in human form, he humbled himself by becoming obedient to the point of death, even death on a cross. Therefore…" (Philippians 2:8). God saved Jesus from death because he was obedient. His prayers were answered.[52]

This is, too, a reminder for each follower of Christ that Gethsemane is a proper location to prayerfully cultivate the necessary disposition of obedience which must be present as we participate at Mass. It is also a further example of Jesus as the Host of Gethsemane, for the tears shed by Our Lord, just as His bloody sweat, is an effluence which makes a pleasing sacrifice to the Father. Jesus gives forth His blood, His sweat, doubtless His tears upon Calvary. So, too, it can reasonably be understood, does this happen in Gethsemane.

51. John Piper, 2014, "The Greatest Prayer in the World: Maundy Thursday," *Desiring God*, April 17, 2014, accessed June 2024, www.desiringgod.org/articles/the-greatest-prayer-in-the-world/.

52. Piper, "The Greatest Prayer in the World: Maundy Thursday".

A common idiomatic expression when achieving something difficult and seemingly impossible is to say, "I gave my blood, sweat, and tears."[53] Gethsemane, we recall, means "place of the olive press," and one can picture the image of being crushed beneath the heavy olive press as a fitting metaphor for the Agony. When one discovers how olives are harvested and made into olive oil, it is clear that "it is hard work. Before you get to indulge in that delicious olive oil, you have to go through the long hard process of sawing off- and lifting up huge branches, dragging them through a machine that constantly tries to pull you in as well, and dragging huge nets and bags full of olives across a slightly muddy field. Unsurprisingly, there is a common saying in Greece 'μου έβγαλε το λαδί,' which roughly translates to something along the lines of 'it squeezes the olive oil out of me,' meaning something that takes extreme effort to do–the Greek equivalent of 'blood, sweat, and tears.'"[54] There is no experience that is more worthy of the expression, "I gave my blood, sweat and tears" or "it squeezed the olive oil out of me," than Christ's Agony in the Garden of Gethsemane.

The most extreme effort, going beyond what is described above, happens in Gethsemane in the very blood Jesus sheds. The Baltimore Catechism teaches that, "Our Lord suffered the 'bloody sweat' while drops of blood came forth from every pore of His body, during His agony in the Garden of Olives, near Jerusalem, where He went to pray on the night His Passion began."[55] The image of Christ shedding blood in Gethsemane *from every pore of His body*, as the Church teaches, shows that when St. Luke writes of the bloody sweat,

53. Cross Idiomas, "Understanding the Idiom: 'blood, sweat and tears'," *CrossIdiomas.com*, accessed May 2024, crossidiomas.com/blood-sweat-and-tears/.

54. The Glutton Life, "The Olive Harvest and Making Greek Olive Oil,' *The Glutton Life*, December 12, 2018, accessed May 2024, www.thegluttonlife.com/2018/12/04/the-olive-harvest-and-making-greek-olive-oil/.

55. *The Baltimore Catechism*, 371.

we must understand this is not a metaphor nor is it a few drops falling here and there. It is, as the Catechism asserts, an effluence from every pore, a giving to the very limit.

Here is yet another reason that Gethsemane is a Eucharistic account. Jesus sweated blood. To understand the significance of this, one must consider: what is sweat? It is mostly composed of water.[56] Earlier in this chapter, as the Messianic wine was discussed, an understanding of the significance of the water, blood, and wine was explored.

I assert there is indeed water and blood shed for us in the Garden of Gethsemane. Consider this in light of the rubrics at Mass. At Mass, it is required to add water to the wine in the chalice:

> The mixing of the water and wine in the chalice before its consecrated is required. While failure to add the water is illicit, it does not affect the validity of the sacrament. What makes this act significant is what it represents: the water is Christ's humanity and the wine his divinity. The mingling of the water and wine in the chalice symbolizes the Incarnation of Christ. It also recalls Christ's Passion when the soldiers pierced his side with a spear and out flowed blood and water (John 19:34), thus signifying baptism and Eucharist.[57]

Just as Christ shed water and blood at Calvary, the Host of Gethsemane also sheds water and blood in the Garden vis-a-vis His bloody sweat. As I describe earlier in my introduction to this work, in

---

56. Lindsay Baker, "Physiology of sweat gland function: The roles of sweating and sweat composition in human health", *Temperature,* July 17, 2019, accessed July 2024,
www.ncbi.nlm.nih.gov/pmc/articles/PMC6773238/.

57. Peggy Frye, "Water Added to the Wine During Mass", *Catholic Answers,* September 20, 2017, accessed July 2024,
www.catholic.com/qa/water-added-to-the-wine-during-mass.

my discussion of the doctrine of the two wills, Jesus has a human will and a divine will, and Jesus draws both into union in the Garden. It is in Gethsemane that we see the most clear struggle and triumph of that reality as Jesus chooses to do the Will of the Father. I assert that the co-mingling of blood and water in His bloody sweat symbolizes the human and divine Christ and the Eucharistic Lord.

As described earlier in this chapter, the Catechism of the Council of Trent describes the cross of Jesus at Calvary as "the altar of the cross." In a similar way, we might refer to "the altar of Gethsemane," for the very stone and soil of the place which absorbed His blood, sweat, and tears would surely be the most consecrated of altars. Indeed, as I asserted earlier in this work, the chrism which consecrates each altar of every church and each hand of every priest is surely first born in Gethsemane, where the place of the olive press, in the Agony of Christ, made the first and perpetual oil of chrism.

Piper continues, "Evidently, by the time Jesus was done praying in Gethsemane, the Father had not only made clear that there is no other way than the cross, but also that this way would succeed. The Lamb would have the reward of his suffering. He will 'see his offspring; he shall prolong his days; the will of the Lord shall prosper in his hand. Out of the anguish of his soul he shall see and be satisfied' (Isaiah 53:10–11). Surely this is why Hebrews 12:2 could say, 'For the joy that was set before him [he] endured the cross.' Beneath the terrors of present agony was the taste of future joy. The angel had come, 'strengthening him' — clarifying, confirming, connecting the coming joy."[58]

---

58. Piper, "The Greatest Prayer in the World: Maundy Thursday".

Hospitality and The Anointing at Bethany

"…A woman (recognized as Mary in John 12:3) gave Jesus His 'burial anointing.' Coming to Jesus in the sight of all, she brought a costly alabaster vial of perfume and emptied its contents upon Jesus' feet in John 12:3."[59] This was six days before his passion.[60] This number again recalls the six days of creation, which "symbolize the six ages of the world, or the six millennia in which God brings the work of his hands to perfection."[61]

The Anointing at Bethany takes place at the celebratory dinner in honor of Jesus for having raised Lazarus from the dead. This was the seventh and greatest of the seven signs of Jesus described in the Gospel of John. St. John Chrysostom writes of this: "No other miracle of Christ excited such rage as this. It was so public, and so wonderful, to see a man walking and talking after he had been dead four days. And the fact was so undeniable. In the case of some other miracles they had charged Him with breaking the sabbath, and so diverted people's minds: but here there was nothing to find fault with, and therefore they vent their anger upon Lazarus."[62]

"Six days before Passover, Jesus came to Bethany, where Lazarus was, whom Jesus had raised from the dead. They gave a dinner for him there, and Martha served, while Lazarus reclined at table with him. Mary took a liter of costly perfumed oil made from genuine aromatic nard and anointed the feet of Jesus and dried them

---

59. Butler et al., *Holman Illustrated Bible Dictionary*, 189.
60. Jn 12:1-8.
61. Bosetti. *John: The Word of Light*, 38.
62. Aquinas, *Catena Aurea Vol. IV*, 399.

with her hair."[63] It may be easy to overlook, but just as Mary anointed Jesus with oil, "Martha served." And so, it is clear that once again the woman who welcomed Jesus into her home as described in the Gospel of Luke is serving a meal in his honor. But this time, Jesus is not chiding her or telling her Mary has chosen the better part; because Martha has learned and grown, and is serving this meal for Christ, with love and not any resentment in her heart, offering every action for Him and thereby, spiritually, remaining at His side and choosing the better part, too. In this same scene, Mary anoints the Anointed One, the Christ. The very use of oil in this pericope reminds of the oil of Gethsemane. Also, I assert that together the Bethany sisters are the perfect hostesses of the Host/host of Gethsemane. Mary of Bethany, anointing with oil the Christ who will soon endure the agony of the olive press in Gethsemane, the Passion, Cross and Death; is honoring and serving the Eucharistic Host of Gethsemane with a sacramental kind of loving attentiveness. Martha of Bethany, serving the meal, is honoring and serving the host of Gethsemane, who invites others to gain strength through watching and praying with Him there; who invites others to eat the food of doing His Father's Will there at His side, but is rejected. Just as Martha gives the Son of Man a place to rest His head through her hospitality in Bethany, (and He is so accustomed to rejection and homelessness) she now again shows the kind of servitude that would be appropriate to give the Son of Man in Gethsemane, where He was abandoned and betrayed. When a faithful soul enters Gethsemane in prayer, he or she must, like Mary, anoint Christ with the oil of obedient prayer. He or she must, like Martha, serve Christ the food of doing God's will.

This sign or miracle or raising Lazarus from the dead inspires the dinner at which Martha serves and Mary anoints Jesus and "the house was filled with the fragrance of the oil. Then Judas, the Iscariot, one of his disciples, and the one who would betray him, said, 'Why was this oil not sold for three hundred days' wages and given to the

---

63. Jn 12:1-3.

poor?' He said this not because he cared about the poor but because he was a thief and held the money bag and used to steal the contributions. So Jesus said, 'Leave her alone. Let her keep this for the day of my burial. You always have the poor with you, but you do not always have me.'"[64]

Mary of Bethany is in sharp contrast to Judas at this dinner in celebration of the raising of Lazarus, as Elena Bosetti explains:

> Judas loudly protests against the wastefulness of this gesture. From his point of view, he is right. That perfume could indeed have been sold for "three hundred denarii": ten times the price he accepted to "hand over" the Master! The contrast could not be any more strident. If Mary is an eminent example of agape, Judas is the opposite. But Jesus defends Mary (Jn 12:7-8). After silently receiving the eloquent gesture of love, he now speaks in her defense. Hadn't Jesus dedicated his entire life to the poor? But who is poorer than he, about to be sold by Judas, abandoned by his own disciples, and handed over to death? Mary has understood what is happening. This woman resembles Jesus in that her love knows no limits and she spares no expense…Here the "wastefulness" shows the measure of love. The logic of love is to give everything, without measure.[65]

---

64. Jn 12:3-7.

65. Bosetti. *John: The Word of Light*, 91.

This is the way we ought to love Jesus in Gethsemane. This is the Garden in which He is betrayed with a kiss and arrested. Mary of Bethany has provided us with an image of how to console Christ in Gethsemane: to love Him so lavishly that we anoint Him with precious oil; He who provides the very oil of love with the agonizing pressing, He, the most perfect olive branch, the Prince of Peace, endures upon the Mount of Olives.

For, after all, when Noah and his family had endured forty days of the Flood, as the waters diminished, He sent a dove to see if the waters had completely receded. The dove returned. Seven days later, He sent it again and "in the evening the dove came back to him, and there in its bill was a plucked-off olive leaf! So Noah knew the waters had lessened on the earth."[66] This was foreshadowing Our Lord in Gethsemane, among the olive trees, the Prince of Peace beginning His Passion that would put an end to the flood of unredeemed sin. The Hour that Jesus speaks of so often in the Scriptures comes to a head in Gethsemane. In John's Gospel, Jesus declares, "Amen, amen, I say to you, unless a grain of wheat falls to the ground and dies, it remains just a grain of wheat; but if it dies, it produces much fruit. Whoever loves his life loses it, and whoever hates his life in this world will preserve it for eternal life. Whoever serves me must follow me, and where I am, there also will my servant be. The Father will honor whoever serves me."[67] These verses provide a kind of bridge between the account of the Anointing at Bethany, of Mary serving Jesus through her lavish anointing; and the next chapter, Chapter 13, which begins with Jesus washing the disciples' feet. It is a bridge between the servant serving Our Lord and Our Lord serving His servants. The Olive Branch of Gethsemane continues after describing that the Father will honor who ever serves Jesus, and what He says is an encapsulation of John's depiction of Jesus' feelings in Gethsemane, and in John it can be described as simultaneously sorrowful and heroic: "I am troubled now.

66. Gn 9:11-12.
67. Jn 12:23-36.

Yet what should I say? 'Father, save me from this hour'? But it was for this purpose that I came to this hour. Father, glorify your name."[68] In just four lines, John encapsulates the struggle and resolution of Gethsemane.

The Lord Becomes a Servant

John's "Book of Glory" begins with Holy Thursday, with the Washing of the Disciples' Feet in the Upper Room, the same evening as the Agony in the Garden. It is profound that the sorrows of this chapter are titled, "Book of Glory," and so they are indeed glorious.

In the Washing of the Feet, Jesus, the Master shows that He is the Willing Servant, and He is setting the example for all His servants, including all who heed His call from the Garden to watch and pray.

At the Washing of the Feet, Jesus bends down to wash Peter in fullness of love and humility. "Peter wants to draw back; he does not accept that Jesus would lower himself like a slave. He calls him 'Lord,' a title that clearly contrasts with the washing of feet, the task of a slave. Humility is one thing, but this gesture is excessive. The Master's response explains that this is not simply a matter of 'humility.' What is at stake is having a part in him, sharing his plan for the Kingdom, which is decisively different from the world's parameters. For Jesus, the greatest one is the one who serves."[69]

Holy Thursday, the night on which this occurs is also known as Maundy Thursday, which comes from the word "Mandatum," which refers to the Mandate Jesus gives to His disciples upon washing their feet: "I give you a new commandment: love one another. As I have

---

68. Jn 12:27-28.

69. Bosetti. *John: The Word of Light*, 97.

loved you, so you also should love one another. This is how all will know that you are my disciples, if you have love for one another."[70]

> Guests at an important Jewish meal washed. They washed for ritual purification and they washed to feel better after trudging the dusty roads of Israel. This was a sign of hospitality, though one usually left to servants if the host had any...Jesus recognizes the meaning in terms of status of his washing of his Apostles' feet and enjoins this group —which has spent no small amount of time these past three years arguing among themselves over their rankings—to do likewise. He likewise recognizes the meaning of his act in terms of its significance of cleansing. He wants his Apostles to be "clean" as they sit down to Passover and the first Eucharist. He is preoccupied not with physical dirt but with moral purity; as he once reminded the Pharisees who took him and his Apostles to task for their lapses in ablutions, "Nothing that enters one from outside can defile that person; but the things that come out from within are what defile" (Mark 7:15).

"'But not all are clean.' For he knew who would betray him."

Moral goodness is essential to entering into communion with God and, therefore, to receiving Communion. That does not mean we are perfect. But it does mean, according to consistent Catholic teaching, that one must be free from mortal sin, because it is impossible to be attached to God and anti-God at the same time. If one has committed mortal

---

70. Jn 13:34-35.

sin, recourse to sacramental Confession must precede reception of Communion.

The Eucharist is medicine: that is the teaching of the Fathers of the Church. But it is not magic. It is not the purpose of the Eucharist to re-establish ruptured communion with God. There's another sacrament for that: Penance.

That's why moral uprightness bookends the Paschal Triduum. Tonight, at the Last Supper, John reminds us that we need to be "clean" before partaking of the Eucharist. Three nights from now, when Jesus first encounters his Apostles altogether on Easter Sunday night, he will give them the means to cleanse others by instituting the sacrament of Penance (John 20:22-23). We should also note that immediately following the selection of First Corinthians which is our Second Reading—the institution of the Eucharist (vv. 23-26)—Paul himself solemnly warns against unworthy and sacrilegious reception of the Eucharist and its fatal spiritual consequences (vv. 27-32). There's a basic imbalance between the phenomena of frequent Communion and infrequent Confession.[71]

---

71. John Grondelski, "Holy Thursday: The Washing of the Disciples' Feet", *National Catholic Register*, April 6, 2023, accessed May 2024, www.ncregister.com/blog/scriptures-and-art-holy-thursday-washing-of-the-feet.

The Seven Signs

The seven signs of the Gospel of John are: the water turned to wine at the Wedding at Cana; the healing of the Nobleman's son near death; the healing of the Lame Man at the Pool; the Feeding of the Five Thousand; the Walking on Water; the Healing of the Man Born Blind; The Raising of Lazarus from the Dead. "Now Jesus did many other signs in the presence of his disciples that are not written in this book. But these are written that you may come to believe that Jesus is the Messiah, the Son of God, and that through this belief you may have life in his name."[72] So the purpose of these seven signs in the Gospel of John is that the reader or listener of the Gospel may have life. The first sign, as discussed earlier in this chapter, is the Wedding at Cana which highlights the Messianic wine. The final sign is the Raising of Lazarus. "The primary event in the New Testament taking place in Bethany involved the raising of Lazarus from the dead (John 11-12). This magnificent miracle by Jesus demonstrated His authority, prepared for His resurrection, and was even magnified through the name of His friend, Lazarus (an abbreviation of Eleazor, 'God has helped')."[73] Both the first and last signs are Eucharistic signs of the Host of Gethsemane because one deals mostly with wine and the other with rising from the dead, a foreshadowing of what Jesus Himself would do for us in the Paschal Mystery of His suffering, death, and resurrection. The signs in between are signs of the host of Gethsemane as they include healings and an act of saving (Peter, in the Walking on the Water pericope) and an act of feeding (in the sign of the Feeding of

---

72. Jn 20:30-31.

73. Butler et al., *Holman Illustrated Bible Dictionary*, 189.

the Five Thousand). The good host of Gethsemane heals and saves and feeds His guests.

The Seven "I Am"s of John

The Gospel of John points to Jesus as the Eucharistic Lord in Gethsemane in a very powerful way through the use of seven "I AM" statements, which I will elucidate in this chapter. Seven is the biblical number of heavenly completion, and so it is of great significance that Jesus says "I AM" seven times. However, it is important to note that these seven "I AM"s are the seven metaphors Jesus gives for Himself, such as "I am the light of the world," but these seven "I AM"s do not include the other times Jesus uses that phrase in the Gospel of John, such as the three times He does so in the Garden of Gethsemane.

The seven "I AM"s of John's Gospel are "I am the Bread of Life;" "I am the Light of the World;" "I am the Door;" "I am the Good Shepherd;" "I am the Resurrection and the Life;" "I am the Way and the Truth and the Life;" "I am the True Vine."[74] Then, there are the other "I am" statements:

> The other "I am" statements of Jesus in the Gospel of John are not metaphors; rather, they are declarations of God's name, as applied by Jesus to Himself. The first instance comes as Jesus responds to a complaint by the Pharisees. "I tell you the truth," Jesus says, "before Abraham was born, I am!" (John 8:58). The verbs Jesus uses are in stark contrast with each other: Abraham was, but I am. There is no doubt that the Jews understood Jesus' claim to be the eternal God

---

74. Got Questions Ministries, "What are the seven I AM statements in the Gospel of John?", *Got Questions Ministries*, 2022, accessed April 2024, www.gotquestions.org/seven-I-AM-statements.html.

incarnate, because they took up stones to kill Him (verse 59)" and an other instance "of Jesus applying to Himself the name I AM comes in the Garden of Gethsemane. When the mob came to arrest Jesus, He asked them whom they sought. They said, "Jesus of Nazareth," and Jesus replied, "I am he" (John 18:4–5). Then something strange happened: "When Jesus said, 'I am he,' they drew back and fell to the ground" (verse 6). Perhaps explaining the mob's reaction is the fact that the word he has been provided by our English translators. Jesus simply said, "I am." Applying God's covenant name to Himself, Jesus demonstrated His power over His foes and showed that His surrender to them was entirely voluntary (see John 10:17–18; 19:11).[75]

There is another "I AM" moment in the Gospel of John. It comes right before the announcement of Judas's Betrayal. Jesus says, "But so that the Scripture might be fulfilled, "the one who ate my food has raised his heel against me."[76] This reference is to King David and his son, the betrayer, Absalom. David writes of this betrayal in Psalm 41. When King David's son, Absalom, initiated a rebellion against the King, "fearing for his life, David led his fighting men and members of his family out of Jerusalem and up the Mount of Olives."[77]

After Jesus says at the Last Supper, "But so that the Scripture might be fulfilled, "the one who ate my food has raised his heel against me..." (this affirms how Jesus considers Judas a betraying son) "... From now on I am telling you before it happens, so that when it happens you may believe that I AM."[78]

---

75. Got Questions Ministries, "What are the seven I AM statements in the Gospel of John?".

76. Ps 41:9.

77. 2 Sam 15:13-37.

78. Jn 13:18-19.

Jesus continues, "Amen, Amen, I say to you, whoever receives the one I send receives me, and whoever receives me receives the one who sent me."[79] This reference to receiving Him is a reference to proper hospitality given to the host.

In Gethsemane, Jesus's final utterance of "I AM", with its powerful effect upon the soldiers, makes it abundantly clear that Jesus is the willing hostage, impelled by love.

The Garden of Gethsemane is the Garden of God's Love

The Garden of Gethsemane narrative in John is part of "The Book of Glory," which begins with the Washing of the Disciples' Feet. This action shows Jesus the host of Gethsemane as the Servant, and reminds that the best host is the one who best serves his guests.

The name of this book. "The Book of Glory," is in notably sharp contrast to the pain that is endured in this book, such as the Passion of Christ, from the Agony to Crucifixion; yet still it is called The Book of Glory, a name of great hope and one that explains that the sorrowful mysteries make the glorious ones possible. Stanley writes:

> It will be recalled that The Book of Glory begins with the observation that Jesus, "having loved his own who were in the world, loved them to *the end* (13:1), to his dying breath *and* to perfection. If then one asks how God has brought Jesus' earthly life to its "perfect fulfillment," John provides the answer with the second part of the verse which describes Jesus' death: "And bowing his head *he handed over the Spirit*" (19:30). The dying breath of Jesus has

79. Jn 13:20.

228

become a symbol of the Spirit promised by Jesus to his disciples at the Last Supper. Thus John provides his solution to the puzzle he created at the outset of his Gospel (1:14). It is for John at this very moment, when Jesus reveals his own identity as "God's only Son" (3:16) whose "flesh" is given "for the life of the world" (6:51) through the supreme act of love, that he "handed over the Spirit," that "other Paraclete" and "life-giver," the cause of the apostolic "remembering."[80]

The Gospel of John states, "and whatever you ask in my name I will do it, in order that the Father may be glorified in the Son, if you ask me anything in my name I will do it."[81] Stanley also explains:

The evangelist later represents Jesus as returning to the theme of love to clarify once more the meaning of Christian love in which his disciples must continue to abide (Jn 15:9). As with all he does and is, Jesus' love for them springs from the Father's love for himself. To discern whether one's love of Jesus is genuine and not mere sentimentality, the keeping of his commands is imperative (v. 10). This means in effect obedience to the single command of Jesus: love for the community, made possible by his laying down his life for his dearly loved friends (vv.12-13). This love evinced by Jesus depends upon no quality of lovableness in his disciples; it is totally free because it is creative. Jesus shows his love by communicating to his beloved followers "all I have heard

---

80. Stanley, *Jesus in Gethsemane*, 83.
81. Jn 14:13-14.

from my Father (v. 15). Hence it is undeniably clear that their following of Jesus is totally his doing.[82]

Again, the Host of Gethsemane shows every good thing every one of the faithful receives is because He, the Host, has invited them or blessed them. The words "dearly beloved friends" are used, and these words are highly relevant to the Gethsemane invitation. Stanley writes:

> You have not chosen me; it is I myself who have chosen you, and I have determined that you should go and bear a rich harvest, and that your harvest should abide, so that whatever you ask the Father in my name, he will give you" (Jn 15:16). The evangelist now points the direction in which prayer in Jesus' name is intended to develop by his insistence, as has been seen, upon acquiring the love of friendship for Jesus…through prayer the believer is led to love Jesus for himself, to enter into a profoundly personal relationship with Jesus…[83]

This assertion of Christ from John's Gospel: "I have chosen you, and I have determined that you should go and bear a rich harvest," is exceedingly important vis-a-vis the Host/host of Gethsemane. The invitation is apparent; the initiative of the host is clear. The garden location of Gethsemane is all the more relevant that the apostles were called there, when Jesus determines that there will be a rich harvest. If "the blood of the martyrs is the seed of the church," what is the seed of the martyrs? I assert it is the blood of Christ in Gethsemane, where his red drops fell in a literal garden; and there, the King of Martyrs and Master Gardener, through His agony, planted the seeds of his blood, prayed for the church, and planned his rich harvest.

---

82. Stanley, *Jesus in Gethsemane*, 231.
83. Stanley, *Jesus in Gethsemane*, 231-232.

The host has initiated hospitality and been denied

John places His Gethsemane narrative in the very same chapter as the Denials of Peter, the Inquiry before Annas, and the Trial before Pilate; whereas in the Synoptic Gospels, the Gethsemane narratives share a chapter with the Institution of the Eucharist. The Gethsemane chapter-placement in the Synoptics sheds light on the Host of Gethsemane as Eucharist; and in John's Gospel, the sharing of the Gethsemane narrative, with the Denial of Peter and Trial before Pilate, also sheds light upon the host of Gethsemane who has initiated hospitality and has been repeatedly rejected and denied.

In John's Gospel it is uniquely mentioned that on His way to Gethsemane, Jesus walked "across the Kidron Valley"[84] over the Cedron Brook. When walking over that stream, Jesus walked over the very waters through which the blood of the sacrificial, unblemished lambs of the temple, the blood guilt, spilled into the stream and ran out of Jerusalem. Now the passionate agony of this Lamb moves Him to give forth a stream of His own blood, as described in the Gospel of Luke "over the brook Cedron," (which flowed with the blood of temple sacrifice) following the prayer of Love (the Last Supper Discourse in which Jesus tells of His Love). Walking through the Kidron Valley meant walking "where there would be a tremendous amount of blood drained from 250,000 lambs along with the water used in the ritual cleansings."[85] Further, "The Old Testament tells us that during the period of the divided kingdom, there were at least three cleansings of the Temple and the Jerusalem rooftops to remove the

---

84. Jn 18:1.

85. Arthur J. Licursi, "Gethsemane and the Kidron Valley," artlicursi.com, accessed May 2024, artlicursi.com/articles/gethsemane-and-kidron-valley.

altars of idols that have been erected during times of Israel's great sins and spiritual backsliding. First was King Asa (third king of Judah) who destroyed the idols and burned them in the Kidron Valley."[86]

In His love, therefore, Jesus accepts and approached His sacrifice, walking through a valley of sin and a brook of the blood of sin offering. This is a reference to Christ as the Lamb of God. It is also the original Eucharistic Procession in which Jesus walks from the Mass of the Upper Room, to the Tabernacle of Gethsemane.

There is a true living structure to Gethsemane, an abode of sorts which would, by its very nature, call out for hospitality. I have spoken throughout this work of the stones which build Gethsemane's "walls," including the stone that the builder rejected, and the rock leaned upon by Christ, the stone's throw away, the very ground of this hallowed place as the holiest of altars. I have spoken of the roof of each believer into which Christ is invited in each holy receipt of Communion and how each believer is as though a walking tent able to offer hospitality even when he or she is far from their brick-and-mortar abode. I have spoken of Gethsemane as a place set apart to which Jesus invites His disciples and hosts them. Now I add that the Letter to the Hebrews refers to the "perfect tent, or tabernacle, not made by human hands"[87] that Jesus, the high priest, passed through to bring salvation. And in the tenth chapter of the Letter to the Hebrews it is written:

For this reason, when he came into the world, he said:

"Sacrifice and offering you did not desire, but a body you prepared for me; holocausts and sin offerings you took no delight in. Then I said, 'As is written of me in the scroll, Behold, I come to do your will, O God.'"

---

86. Licursi, "Gethsemane and the Kidron Valley".
87. Heb 9:11.

232

First he says, "Sacrifices and offerings, holocausts and sin offerings, you neither desired nor delighted in." These are offered according to the law. Then he says, "Behold, I come to do your will." He takes away the first to establish the second. By this "will," we have been consecrated through the offering of the body of Jesus Christ once for all.[88]

Gethsemane is a tabernacle, consecrated with the chrism of Christ pressed in the olive press of His Agony. There, Jesus the High Priest does the will of the Father and consecrates us through the offering of His very body, as the Letter to the Hebrews describes. It is a tabernacle and thus must be a location of hospitality. Yet He is in that very place rejected and denied.

"The daring figure of a 'tent which was not made with hands and does not belong to this creation,' which seems so strange to us, is intended to be a theological description of Christ's entire historical existence.'"[89] Christ Himself is a tent or tabernacle; then He deserves hospitality wherever He is present; and even more where He is suffering. Indeed, Gethsemane is a place of consecration: holy chrism made from the olive oil sweetened by the balsam of Christ's love. But in John's Gospel the action moves swiftly into rejection of the Host/host, as Judas "got a band of soldiers and guards from the chief priests and the Pharisees and went there with lanterns, and torches, and weapons."[90] When accepting the invitation of a host, one brings food to supplement a feast, or at least a humble gratitude for the invitation. In contrast, the host of Gethsemane is brought weapons by those who meet him there, the betrayal of Judas, and soon thereafter, the threefold denial of Peter.

---

88. Heb 10:5-10.
89. Stanley, *Jesus in Gethsemane*, 96.
90. Jn 18:3.

Host becomes Willing Hostage

In John's Gethsemane narrative, one theme is the betrayal and imprisonment of Jesus. In this chapter, it will be shown in a paramount way how the "Host/host" becomes a *willing* "Hostage." Importantly, this chapter through its understanding of "Hostage" will draw out the "Host/host" connection in the context of the Agony in the Garden as it relates to the Passion Narratives…it is just after the Last Supper, and leading up to the moment of Betrayal that will set into motion the Crucifixion.

The definition of "hostage" is "someone who is taken as a prisoner by an enemy in order to force the other people involved to do what the enemy wants."[91] Indeed, the enemy, Satan, who had entered Judas,[92] has Jesus arrested in order to, in capturing Him, not only to hurt Him but create evil havoc in others as a result, and thus please the enemy. But the enemy has no power over Jesus which Jesus does not permit for some greater good. Within the English word, "hostage" are hiding the English words "host" and "Host." And indeed, there is a common thread between the arrested Jesus and the Real Presence of Our Lord in every tabernacle. In both cases, He is a willing prisoner. In Gethsemane, His would-be captors fall to the ground as His very name is spoken upon His very lips, which proves He could have escaped from them, but instead chose to be imprisoned by them; for love of man, desire to save humanity, and obedience to the will of the Father.[93] The Catechism explains, "Christ could, if He pleased, have escaped

---

91. Cambridge Dictionary, s.v. "hostage," dictionary.cambridge.org/dictionary/english/hostage/.

92. Jn 13:26.

93. Jn 18:6.

the tortures of His Passion, because He foresaw them and had it in His power to overcome His enemies."[94]

In the Eucharist, He is a willing Divine Prisoner, allowing His Body, Blood, Soul, and Divinity to be humbly imprisoned, if you will, under the meek appearances of bread and wine; and He waits for us patiently, in every tabernacle. As Saint Teresa of the Andes puts it, "I don't know what happens to me when I contemplate Our God exiled in the tabernacles for love of His creatures who forget and offend Him. I'd like to live till the end of the world by suffering with the Divine

Figure 6. The Little Flower of the Divine Prisoner.

Prisoner."[95]

When St. Thérèse was a little girl she was shown an image of "The Little Flower of the Divine Prisoner."[96] (see Figure 6) St. Thérèse of Lisieux contemplated deeply about the Divine Prisoner in the

---

94. *The Baltimore Catechism,* 378.

95. Hearthcake and a Jug of Water, "Sunday, March 13th", *Hearthcake and a Jug of Water*, n.d., accessed April 2024, hearthcake.com/sunday-march-13th/.

tabernacle who waits for visits from his creatures, who knocks at the door of each of our hearts, hoping to find a tabernacle in that heart in which He can rest:

> In this image, Jesus is depicted as a prisoner, looking out of His cell through a barred window at a single white flower placed on the ledge of the window. The prison was meant to depict the Tabernacle containing the divine presence of our Lord. The little white flower was to depict the consolation given to Jesus every time He was visited in the Tabernacle. Thérèse spent much time meditating upon this image, "gazing at it in a kind of ecstasy." Through her meditation, Thérèse grew in a desire to be that "Little Flower" outside the cell of Jesus, consoling Him in His imprisoned state.[97]

Drawing this theology of the Little Flower further, as I am apt to do as a Third Order Carmelite who, upon my Profession, took the name "Annabelle-Thérèse of Gethsemane," I cannot help but be struck by the realization that Jesus is a willing prisoner of Gethsemane. This is the place He allows Himself to agonize and even be arrested for our sakes. Gethsemane, being a garden, is the perfect location for a Thérèsian "Little Flower of the Divine Prisoner," a soul of consolation, watching and praying in obedience to the Lord. In that same spirit, on Holy Thursday, the Church in her wisdom has both the Chrism(Oil) Mass that takes place in the morning, and the Mass of the Lord's

96. "The Little Flower of the Divine Prisoner," print, ca. 1800s, accessed June 2024, at mycatholic.life/books/lessons-saint-therese-wisdom-gods-little-flower/chapter-four-first-communion-confirmation/.

97. John Paul Thomas, *Lessons from St. Therese: The Wisdom of God's Little Flower*, (2017, My Catholic Life!), Lesson 32, accessed May 2024, mycatholic.life/books/lessons-saint-therese-wisdom-gods-little-flower/chapter-four-first-communion-confirmation/.

Supper in the evening. "The day commemorates the institution of the sacraments of Holy Orders and the Holy Eucharist."[98]

After the evening Mass on Holy Thursday, the Eucharist is carried to the Altar of Repose, re-creating another Gethsemane. There the faithful worship the humble Lord who not only abased Himself in love in the Garden, but further humbles Himself now by taking the form of bread. Pastophoria is a word which can denote "the watcher's chamber," of the temple; in the outward court.[99] "Noting St. Jerome's use of the word Pastophoria in his commentary to denote a "bridal chamber for the Eucharist to be preserved outside of the liturgy... [there is a] rich history of adoration of the Most Holy and the long-standing tradition of devotion to the Eucharist."[100]

There is truly a correlation between the Garden of Gethsemane and the Altar of Eucharistic Adoration. The Divine Prisoner of the tabernacle of Gethsemane (or in the church tabernacle or monstrance) waits for the visits of the faithful to watch and pray with Him. "Whoever loves me will keep my word, and my Father will love him, and we will come to him and make our dwelling with him."[101] And "Behold, I stand at the door and knock. If anyone hears my voice and opens the door, [then] I will enter his house and dine with him, and he with me."[102] We are invited to a messianic banquet through the invitation of Christ which makes a dwelling for God in each of our hearts. He knocks at the door of each heart looking for a tabernacle in which to rest. "I offered myself to Our Lord to be His Little Flower; I

---

98. Maria Cintorino, "What Happens on Holy Thursday?", *National Catholic Register*, April 6, 2023, accessed April 2024, www.ncregister.com/blog/what-happens-on-holy-thursday.

99. StudyLight Bible Encyclopedia, s.v. "Pastophoria," www.studylight.org/encyclopedias/eng/mse/p/pastophoria.html.

100. Bénédicte Cedergren, "Keeping Eucharistic Vigil at Rome's Altars of Repose", *National Catholic Register*, March 29, 2024, accessed May 2024, www.ncregister.com/features/keeping-eucharistic-vigil-at-rome-s-altars-of-repose.

101. Jn 14: 23.

102. Rev 3:20.

longed to console Him, to draw as near as possible to the Tabernacle, to be looked on, cared for, and gathered by Him."[103]

Meanwhile, Jesus in Gethsemane protects those He was hosting. The soldiers trying to arrest Him fall down, unable to stand in the presence of God's Holy Name, and at the same time making abundantly clear that Jesus is the willing hostage, impelled by love. In the Discourse of Love, Jesus prays, "Those whom thou gavest me, I have kept; and none of them is lost, but the son of perdition…"[104] and then it is clear in the Garden that Jesus is lovingly protecting all of whom He is host: "Let these go their way."[105] What an incredibly perfect and most loving host Jesus is. He takes care of His apostles, protecting them, and this action completes the prayer for his disciples, an act of love.

This shows the power of our Eucharistic Host, for whom we kneel during the transubstantiation, when we recognize Him through prayer and say, "My Lord and My God." John adds this to the account of Peter cutting off the slave, Malchus', ear: "Put your sword into its scabbard. Shall I not drink the cup that the Father gave me?"[106] This reference to the cup shows our Eucharistic Host. As Jesus puts an end to the violence, his "food is to do his Father's will;"[107] his drink will be whatever the Father offers.

---

103. Thomas, *Lessons from St. Therese*, Lesson 32.
104. Jn 17:12.
105. Jn 18:8.
106. Jn 18:10-11.
107. Jn 4:34.

238

Christ, The Glorious Gardener

It was a grave within a garden, a garden-grave in which the body of Christ was buried, as though a seed planted in the ground. The new sepulcher where Jesus was buried, was within view of the site of the Crucifixion, where the Tree of Life broke open the barrier between heaven and earth that had existed since Adam's Fall.

As the Resurrected Christ emerges and then appears to Mary Magdalene's eyes like the gardener, one can imagine the gardens of Scripture coming to life around Him: the cedars of Lebanon; the staff of Aaron budding and producing almonds; the rose of Sharon in the Song of Solomon; the lilies of the field in the Sermon on the Mount; the branches of palm waved on Palm Sunday; the bitter herbs eaten at Passover; the fig tree bearing figs; and the tiny mustard seed; the olive trees of Gethsemane. When Mary Magdalene encounters first the Risen Lord, she does not know Him.

"Thinking it was the gardener, she said to him, 'Sir, if you have taken him hence, tell me where you have laid him and I will take him away.' Jesus said to her: 'Mary.' She turning, said to him, 'Rabboni' (which is to say Master)."[108]

Jesus said to Mary Magdalene, "Do not touch me, for I am not yet ascended to my Father. But go to my brethren and say to them: I ascend to my Father and to your Father, to my God and your God."[109]

Scripture reveals a truth in that seemingly extraneous detail that Mary thought Jesus was the Gardener. That is because Jesus has become the Gardener. He agonized in a garden, was forsaken and betrayed in a garden, died on the crossed limbs of a tree overlooking a

---

108. Jn 20:16-16.
109. Jn 20:17.

239

garden, was buried in a garden, was willingly trampled like an innocent olive branch of peace, crushed beneath the feet of sinners, then He rose from the dead in a garden.

Jesus accomplished what any good gardener strives for: to bring order and beauty and growth to what is wild or choked by weeds; to bring beauty and good fruit where was once only overgrowth or the smallest of seeds. The Master Gardener indeed flowered forth from the grave in Easter triumph. The sorrowful mysteries yielded to the glorious ones.

Many great churches display the fourteen Stations of the Cross and often conclude with what is known as the Fifteenth Station: The Resurrection. Rembrandt's painting, "Christ and St Mary Magdalen at the Tomb"[110] (see Figure 7) depicts the image of Jesus as the Gardener. How refreshing to the soul to see the beauty, and even whimsy, of Christ, now past all of the suffering, depicted in a jaunty gardener's hat, with triumph in his eyes. No more is He shedding blood in the agony of the Garden of Gethsemane.

"He will blossom like a lily. Like a cedar of Lebanon, he will send down his roots; his young shoots will grow. His splendor will be like an olive tree, his fragrance like a cedar of Lebanon."[111] He is no longer bleeding in the Garden of His Agony; He is the pruner of the Garden. Each faithful soul before His Majesty in the Garden of Resurrection may well reply: "I am like a green olive tree in the house of God: I trust in the mercy of God forever and ever."[112]

---

110. Rembrandt van Rijn, "Christ and St Mary Magdalen at the Tomb", 1638, oil on panel, the Picture Gallery at Buckingham Palace, London, accessed July 2024, at www.rct.uk/collection/404816/christ-and-st-mary-magdalen-at-the-tomb.

111. Hosea 14:6-7.

112. Psalm 52:8.

Figure 7. Rembrandt van Rijn, Christ and St. Mary Magdalene at the Tomb, 1638, oil on board.

The Epilogue of John: Three Calls to Love that Echo the Calls of the Host/host of Gethsemane

In the Epilogue of the Gospel of John, Jesus appears to seven disciples at the Sea of Tiberius. It is no coincidence, in this Gospel that emphasizes the importance of the Seven Signs of Jesus and the Seven "I AM" statements of Christ; that Jesus appears for the last time to seven disciples. In this account, Jesus provides a charcoal fire with fish on it, and bread; He invites them to have breakfast:

> When they had finished breakfast, Jesus said to Simon Peter, "Simon, son of John, do you love me more than these?" He said to him, "Yes, Lord, you know that I love you." He said to him, "Feed my lambs." He then said to him a second time, "Simon, son of John, do you love me?" He said to him, "Yes, Lord, you know that I love you." He said to him, "Tend my sheep." He said to him the third time, "Simon, son of John, do you love me?" Peter was distressed that he had said to him a third time, "Do you love me?" and he said to him, "Lord, you know everything; you know that I love you." Jesus said to him, "Feed my sheep. Amen, amen, I say to you, when you were younger, you used to dress yourself and go where you wanted; but when you grow old, you will stretch out your hands, and someone else will dress you and lead you where you do not want to go." He said this signifying by what kind of death he would glorify God. And when he had said this, he said to him, "Follow me."[113]

This death refers to Peter's crucifixion. In the words of St. John Chrysostom: "Our Lord having made Peter declare his love, informs him of his future martyrdom; an intimation to show us how we should love."[114]

St. John Chrysostom asserts, "a third time our Lord asks Peter whether he loves Him. Three confessions are made to answer to the three denials; that the tongue might shew as much love as it had fear, and life gained draw out the voice as much as death threatened. A third

---

113. Jn 21:15-19.
114. Aquinas, *Catena Aurea Vol. IV*, 625.

time He asks the same question, and gives the same command; to show of what importance He esteems the superintendence of His own sheep, and how He regards it as the greatest proof of love to Him."[115]

As St. John Chrysostom makes clear, the three "I love you"s of Peter on the beach are penance for the three denials of Peter upon Christ's Arrest. But significant here too are the three calls from Gethsemane to watch and pray that are ignored by Peter as he sleeps in the Garden. And so, the invitation here on the beach is verbalizing more of the invitation from Gethsemane: the threefold call to watch and pray so that one is strengthened, in love, to feed the sheep. This feeding is the two types of hosting: feeding as the Host with the Eucharist and feeding as the host bringing the guest to understand and do and be fed by the will of the Father. Surely the three calls of Gethsemane and three denials of Peter (because he didn't keep vigil and thus failed the test) and the three acts of love upon the beach are linked.

After all, the Garden of Gethsemane in the Gospel of John is the Garden of God's Love. The words which immediately precede "When he had said this, Jesus went out with his disciples across the Kidron valley to where there was a garden…"[116] are "Righteous Father, the world also does not know you, but I know you, and they know that you sent me. I made known to them your name and I will make it known, that the love with which you loved me may be in them and I in them."[117] It is not singing a hymn in John's Gospel but "when he had said this" that Jesus goes to Gethsemane. This love is the catalyst. And so the three questions of Peter, "do you love me?" echo the three times in the Book of Matthew that Jesus came to rouse the apostles from sleep…to rouse their love. To watch and pray with Jesus is to love Him. A priest, still more a Pope, like Peter, must not just feed the sheep and lambs. He must do so because He loves Christ. And He

---

115. Aquinas, *Catena Aurea Vol. IV*, 623-624.

116. Jn 18:1.

117. Jn 17: 25-26.

must stoke this love with vigilant prayer. To cease having an active prayer life, for a prelate or any person, is to have the coals of love for God gradually burn out. Prayer is the coal that feeds the fire of love. Gethsemane is part of the same call to the disciple that Jesus teaches upon the beach of the Sea of Tiberius. "Do you love me?" Christ may as well be asking each time he wakes the sleeping apostles. "If so, then watch and pray." For if Peter had fed the fire of his love with the coals of vigilant prayer, he would not have denied Jesus at the charcoal fire in the courtyard of the high priest. As it transpires, Jesus re-creates a charcoal fire upon the beach to give Peter a new chance to verbalize his love with the same tongue with which he had denied.

"Then the maid who was the gatekeeper said to Peter, 'You are not one of this man's disciples, are you?' He said, 'I am not.' Now the slaves and the guards were standing around a charcoal fire that they had made, because it was cold, and were warming themselves. Peter was also standing there keeping warm."[118] This passage shows the coldness of Peter's denial, the coldness of the lack of love that would have been formed through vigilant prayer. It is also another detail which sheds light upon Christ's suffering in Gethsemane. As He shed blood, sweat and tears, as He agonized and lay prostrate on the ground praying in the darkness, He would have also been cold.

The Host/host of Gethsemane has, in the end, as John's Gospel reveals, primarily invited us to love Him as He loves us. It is cold and lonely in Gethsemane, and what can console and warm Him? Three watches of love over three hours is one way. Another is to harvest three fruits of Gethsemane that Jesus recommends and exemplifies: prayer, watchfulness (or vigilance) and obedience. And do we not need these qualities at Mass? Do we not need them at Adoration of the Most Blessed Sacrament? How we respond to the Host/host of Gethsemane is the key to how we respond to our Eucharistic Lord, how we honor and adore Him. Tesniere writes:

---

118. Jn 18:17-18.

Instituted to be the perfect and perpetual memorial of the Passion of the Saviour, the Eucharist carries down through the centuries the remembrance of the prayer and the agony of Gethsemani. It recalls the fact itself together with the sorrow and the love. It applies its virtues, and confers its fruits. It continues it in reality, but under conditions compatible with the glorified and impassible state which the immortal Christ retains even under the sacramental veil of death. Of the mental and physical sufferings, of the bloody sweat, of the abandonment of His Father which marked His agony, the Eucharistic Christ retains only the remembrance, a remembrance blessed and recompensed. But desirous to perpetuate as much of His Passion as is possible, He continues His prayer in the lowliness of a state of inertia, which abases Him before His Father even below that of Gethsemani.[119]

It is abundantly clear how humble is the Second Person of the Trinity. Tesniere continues:

---

119. Tesniere, *The Eucharistic Heart of Jesus*, 145.

There, the pallor of His divine countenance, the agony and the blood, without doubt, disfigured Him; but here, He is no longer human, He is but a little dust. He dwells alone, abandoned by indifferent, ungrateful, or hostile men, an abandonment far more displeasing to Him than was the sleep of the Apostles; and there He will remain night and day until the consummation of ages. Every morning, at the Consecration, He descends, perseveringly overcoming all repugnance, into the Gethsemani of the Sacrament, there to resume His prayer, in the humility of His attitude and the ardor of His desires for the redemption of the world and the coming of His Kingdom.[120]

In the words of St. Francis of Assisi: "What wonderful majesty! What stupendous condescension! O sublime humility! That the Lord of the whole universe, God and the Son of God, should humble Himself like this under the form of a little bread, for our salvation."[121]

Three times we call before the Altar of God: "Holy, Holy, Holy, Lord God of Hosts, Heaven and earth are full of your glory!" This is "the hymn of the seraphim in Isaiah 6:3 and Revelation 4:8." "*Sanctus, Sanctus, Sanctus, Dóminus Deus exercituum...*"[122] This phrase is part of the Eucharistic prayer which in the Mass precedes the epiclesis, the calling down of the Holy Spirit, and the Institution Narrative.[123] Why should we not see that thrice-acclaimed call "Holy,"

120. Tesniere, *The Eucharistic Heart of Jesus*, 145-146.

121. Louis J. Tofari, "St. Francis of Assisi and the Roman Liturgy", *Catholic Family News*, November 8, 2018, accessed April 2024, catholicfamilynews.com/blog/2018/11/08/2018-11-8-st-francis-of-assisi-and-the-roman-liturgy/.

122. Isaiah 6:3 [*Douay-Rheims, Latin Vulgate*].

123. Our Catholic Faith, "Mass – Eucharistic Prayers", *Our Catholic Faith*, n.d., accessed May 2024, ourcatholicfaith.org/mass/eucharisticprayers.html.

as a fitting response to Christ in the Garden of Gethsemane? Are we not kneeling with Him in the Garden with each word, "Holy," each *Sanctus* uttered? Are we not making reparation for His lonely agony there if we offer each word of the Sanctus as part of a threefold "Lord, you know I love you," with as much zeal as Peter's responses by the shore of the Sea of Tiberius? Each time we kneel at the Sanctus, could it not be offered as a way to kneel with and for our Lord who is on His knees in Gethsemane? There, the Lord God of Hosts is not recognized; He is abandoned and betrayed. How often the Eucharist is not recognized as the Body, Blood, Soul, and Divinity of Christ; as the Real Presence.[124] That is the challenge that the final chapter of this work will address: how study of the Host/host of Gethsemane must lead us to a more fitting Eucharistic devotion.

Conclusion

This chapter studied the Fourth Gospel account of the New Testament as distinct from the Synoptic Gospels, Matthew, Mark, and Luke, focusing on unique information John shares but that the Synoptics leave out, such as the Samaritan woman at the well, and how the host of Gethsemane teaches through that Bible story, how He offers food to those He invites to Gethsemane: the food of doing the will of the Father.

Much was gleaned by noticing that this evangelist places His Gethsemane narrative in the same chapter as other important reflections such as the Denials of Peter, the Inquiry before Annas, and

---

124. Gregory A. Smith, "Just one-third of U.S. Catholics agree with their church that Eucharist is body, blood of Christ", *Pew Research Center*, August 5, 2019, accessed May 2024, www.pewresearch.org/short-reads/2019/08/05/transubstantiation-eucharist-u-s-catholics/.

the Trial before Pilate, shedding light upon the host of Gethsemane who has invited guests to join Him and initiated hospitality; but has been repeatedly rejected and denied. In John's Gethsemane narrative, a theme is the betrayal and imprisonment of Jesus. In this chapter, it was shown how the "Host/host" becomes "Hostage."

"The Prayer of Jesus," follows John's Last Supper Discourse and comprises the entire chapter prior to the Gethsemane narrative of John, and makes the Garden of Gethsemane of John's Gospel into the Garden of God's Love, giving a trajectory of love that elucidates Gethsemane as truly the Passion of the Sacred Heart.

The Gospel of John points to Jesus as the Eucharistic Lord in Gethsemane. This has to do with the seven "I AM" statements of John's Gospel, which this chapter will elucidate. Christ's "I AM" statements culminate, finding their apex in the Garden of Gethsemane narrative of John, as was discussed. Also, there are seven signs in the Gospel of John beginning with the Wedding at Cana and ending with the Raising of Lazarus. In this chapter, the great importance of the sign of the raising of Lazarus was explored. It is one of the three times Jesus sheds tears, and all three of those times are upon the Mount of Olives. The blood, sweat, and tears of the olive press of Gethsemane were explored. The anointing at Bethany that follows the raising of Lazarus was discussed, especially vis-a-vis hospitality to the Host/host.

Seven is the Biblical number of heavenly completion,[125] and so it is of great significance that Jesus says "I AM" seven times in the Gospel of John. However, it is important to note that these seven "I AM"s are the seven metaphors Jesus gives for Himself, such as "I am the light of the world," but these seven "I AM"s do not include the other times Jesus uses that phrase in the Gospel of John, such as the three times He does so in the Garden of Gethsemane.

John's Gospel ends on hopeful and poetic notes for the lover of Gethsemane and for those who hope to serve the Host/host. The

---

125. Bible Study Tools, "The Number 7 in the Bible".

Resurrected Christ in John's Gospel is the Gardener, displaying a glorious mystery coming forth from the sorrowful mystery of the Garden Agony. The Epilogue of John contains three calls to love that echo the calls of the Host of Gethsemane. They are also beautifully echoed in the "*Sanctus*" at Mass, once again joining Jesus of Gethsemane to our Eucharistic Lord.

The final chapter of this work will be conclusions and a summary of The Host of Gethsemane. It will also address the challenge: how does study of the Host/host of Gethsemane draw us to a renewed and more fitting Eucharistic devotion, and what form that should take.

Chapter 5 Summary and Conclusions

Introduction

This chapter of *The Host of Gethsemane* will give a summary of this work and draw conclusions. It will show that what was set out to be accomplished in this work was, in fact, accomplished. It will also address the challenge of how this study of the Host/host of Gethsemane impels one to go forward with a more fitting Eucharistic devotion and what form that should take.

What Chapter One Accomplished

Chapter One of this work demonstrated the authenticity of the title of Jesus as the "Host/host" of Gethsemane. I introduced the title of Jesus as "Host/host" of Gethsemane, and why and how it is appropriate to refer to Jesus in this manner. He is truly the Sacrificial Lamb as He offers His Body, "the Host" to His apostles and this continues in Gethsemane. I showed how the New Covenant which began at the Last Supper continues in Gethsemane as Jesus prays and bleeds and agonizes alone, and as His hostly appeal for company from His guests is denied Him. Jesus' role of high priest, so evident at the Last Supper, continues into Gethsemane through the events that take place there.

I asserted the significance of olives and considered the relevance of the name "Christ," which means "anointed," as our

Eucharistic Lord is indeed the anointed one; and I considered such words as "hostly," which means behaving in a hospitable way toward guests. Jesus is the Host/host of Gethsemane and He welcomes guests to join Him there; to watch and pray. It has been made apparent that the proper response to the Host/host of Gethsemane is hospitality in return. In that way, the role of host is then transferred to the faithful, the large group of those called to keep watch and to pray with Jesus as we, the church, worship and offer hospitality. Indeed, we, too, are the host of Gethsemane, the army of souls called as guests to enter Gethsemane, just as Peter, James, and John were. Jesus offers an invitation to each of us there. Throughout the chapters of this work, we saw how this invitation unfolds in each of the Gospel accounts of Gethsemane.

What Chapter Two Accomplished

Chapter Two of *The Host of Gethsemane* focused on the Agony in the Garden as told in the Gospel of Matthew and in the Gospel of Mark. There are similarities and differences. Matthew's is a very similar narrative to that of Mark, but there are some key differences that help emphasize Jesus of Gethsemane as the Host/host. Each Gospel has a distinct lens and focus, and brings forth salient points to consider vis-a-vis the Gethsemane narratives.

In Matthew's Gethsemane narrative, Jesus was shown to be the fulfillment of the Scriptures. Gethsemane's connection to Eden was addressed. In Matthew's Gospel, we saw how the drowsiness factor of those who should have been awake watching and praying impacted the situation, allowing evil to run its course. Thus, the examination of Matthew's Gethsemane narrative asserted that watchmen are needed. The Transfiguration's connection to the Agonizing Host of

Gethsemane was explored, as were the images of the Rock of Gethsemane, the Olive Tree, and the oil, each with deeply symbolic implications for Christ and His Church. This chapter illustrated how the Suffering Servant in Matthew's Gospel is also the Lord of Hosts.

Also discussed was how Mark's Gospel shows, with its own style and motion distinct from Matthew's, the bridge between the Upper Room of the Last Supper and the Gethsemane narrative. In the Markan pericope, the treatment of Peter was explored. The fascinating and unique character of the young man in Mark's Gethsemane was also discussed in depth.

To summarize the similarities and differences of how Gethsemane is discussed in these Gospels, both the Gospels of Matthew and Mark, the site of the Agony was noted as "a place called Gethsemane."[1] While in Matthew, Jesus tells the apostles, "Sit here while I go *over there* and pray,"[2] in Mark, Jesus says, "Sit here while I pray."[3] Matthew says Jesus took Peter "and the two sons of Zebedee,"[4] while Mark states their names: "Peter, James, and John."[5] Meanwhile, in Matthew, Jesus "began to feel sorrow and distress," and in Mark, Jesus "began to be troubled and distressed."

Both the Gospels of Matthew and Mark depict Jesus asking the Father to take the cup away from Him, if it is the Father's will. In Matthew, Jesus says it three times. Mark mentions Jesus saying it only twice, and is the only one who includes the detail "Abba," or "Papa," when Jesus calls out to the Father.[6] In both Matthew and Mark, Jesus tells the apostles to "remain here and keep watch."[7] Both Mark and Matthew specifically mention that Jesus addresses Peter and asks,

---

1. Mt 26:36; Mk 14:32.
2. Mt 26:36.
3. Mk 14:32.
4. Mt 26:37.
5. Mk 14:33.
6. Mk 14:36.
7. Mt 26:38; Mk 14:34.

"you could not keep watch [with me] for one hour?"[8] Matthew tells us, Jesus "fell prostrate in prayer,"[9] while in Mark's version, Jesus "advanced a little and fell to the ground."[10] Both Gospels include a word of explanation for the sleeping apostles. Matthew writes they were sleeping because "they could not keep their eyes open."[11] Mark explains, "they could not keep their eyes open and did not know what to answer him."[12] When examining the two Gospels side-by-side it is important to remind that Mark's Gospel distinguishes itself in Gethsemane not only by the use of the word "Abba," but by uniquely mentioning, at the close of the Gethsemane narrative, the "young man followed him wearing nothing but a linen cloth about his body. They seized him, but he left the cloth behind and ran off naked."[13]

The student of Gethsemane may be encouraged to consider this image of the young man, running off naked from Mark's Garden of Gethsemane, in sharp contrast to the way Adam and Eve, formerly innocent; now clothed in their shame, were banished from the Garden of Eden, with an angel holding a flaming sword barring their re-entry. Since Our Lord, the Host/host of Gethsemane, has agonized in this new garden, there is now a sheathed sword and a man running out naked, an image of innocence instead of sin; a reminder that through Christ's Paschal Mystery, heaven will no longer be barred from the one who follows Christ purely. Mark is an author who shows immediate action, and we followed this scene of his Gospel's young man, running with him, as we entered Luke's Gethsemane narrative, where we learned even more details of how Gethsemane begins the re-gaining of what we lost in Eden; through such details as Christ's perseverance in

---

8. Mt 26:40; Mk 14:37.
9. Mt 26:39.
10. Mk 14:35.
11. Mt 26:43.
12. Lk 22:45.
13. Mk 14:51-52.

prayer; the anointing of the priesthood in Gethsemane; and the very shedding of His Blood.

What Chapter Three Accomplished

Chapter Three of this work focused on the Agony in the Garden, as told by Luke, the "Evangelist of prayer."[14] This overarching Lukan theme was confirmed in the Lukan Gethsemane narrative in which great emphasis is placed upon the prayer of Christ, throughout His ministry, and rising to a crescendo in the Garden, which is a *vade mecum* of prayer, with details the other evangelists do not include, worded in a way that emphasizes the importance of prayer such as: "And being in agony, he prayed the longer."[15]

It was discussed that St. Luke's Gospel uniquely emphasizes Christ's perseverance in prayer by articulating that His Agony necessitated more time spent, until He was ready, and thus is a lesson for all who pray. St. Luke uniquely mentions the presence of an angel. Of great import, St. Luke, the doctor, is the only Evangelist to include the detail of Jesus sweating blood. Luke's Gospel is "interested in portraying this scene as a cosmic battle,"[16] and his Gospel and commentaries upon it will be an important study for this thesis as the shedding of Jesus' blood in the Garden is a vital consideration that points to Him as the Eucharistic Host of Gethsemane. These three unique Lukan details: Jesus praying "the longer;" the ministering angel; and the shedding of blood were all addressed vis-a-vis Jesus as the Host/host of Gethsemane.

---

14. Kodell, *The Gospel According to Luke*, 10.

15. Lk 22:43 [*Douay-Rheims*].

16. Green and McKnight, *Dictionary of Jesus and the Gospels*, 266.

The hospitality emphasized in Luke was considered throughout this chapter. Indeed, there are so many examples in this Gospel that I assert that St. Luke could also be called "The Evangelist of Hospitality." His Gospel is the only one to include The Good Samaritan, and also emphasizes the House at Bethany in which Saints Martha and Mary show great hospitality to Jesus. His Gethsemane narrative includes many details that affirm Christ as Host/host of Gethsemane.

As we come to the conclusion of this study of Gethsemane in the Synoptic Gospels which the past two chapters have explored, it is worth pausing to reiterate and expound upon the similarities and differences, not just between Matthew and Mark, but now also between the three Synoptic Gospels. I assert that Luke's Gospel, in light of this work, could be known as the Gospel of Gethsemane, since his is the Gospel which uniquely contains the detail of "withdrawing about a stone's throw from them;"[17] the angel comforting Christ; the mention that, being in agony, "He prayed so fervently,"[18] therefore He was persistent in prayer; and "his sweat became like drops of blood falling on the ground."[19] Surely the hospitality that is emphasized throughout Luke's Gospel coupled with the Eucharistic detail of His blood in Gethsemane beautifully point to Christ as the Host/host of Gethsemane.

Matthew and Mark both note the site of the Agony as "a place called Gethsemane"[20] while Luke refers to it as "The Mount of Olives."[21] In Matthew's Gospel, Jesus tells the apostles "Sit here while I go *over there* and pray;"[22] while in Mark, He utters, "Sit here while I

---

17. Lk 22:41.

18. Lk 22:44.

19. Lk 22:44.

20. Mt 26:36; Mk 14:32.

21. Lk 22:39.

22. Mt 26:36.

pray."[23] Matthew says Jesus took Peter "and the two sons of Zebedee,"[24] while Mark names them: "Peter, James, and John."[25] Luke, however, does not name the three at all. He simply writes, "and the disciples followed him."[26] Luke does not mention "sit here" or "over there," but gets right to this point: "Pray that you may not undergo the test."[27] Then the Lukan Jesus withdraws about "a stone's throw from them."[28] Meanwhile, in Matthew, Jesus "began to feel sorrow and distress," and in Mark, Jesus "began to be troubled and distressed." All three Synoptic Gospels depict Jesus asking the Father to take the cup away from Him, if it is the Father's will. In Matthew, Jesus says it three times. Mark mentions Jesus saying it only twice, but is the only one who includes the detail "Abba," or "Papa," when Jesus calls out to the Father.[29] In both Matthew and Mark, Jesus tells the apostles to "remain here and keep watch."[30] Both Mark and Matthew specifically mention that Jesus addresses Peter and asks, "you could not keep watch [with me] for one hour?"[31] In Matthew, Jesus "fell prostrate in prayer,"[32] while in Mark, Jesus "advanced a little and fell to the ground,"[33] and in Luke, Jesus was "kneeling."[34] All three Synoptic Gospels include a word of explanation for the sleeping apostles. Matthew says they were sleeping because "they could not keep their

---

23. Mk 14:32.
24. Mt 26:37.
25. Mk 14:33.
26. Lk 22:39.
27. Lk 22:40.
28. Lk 22:41.
29. Mk 14:36.
30. Mt 26:38; Mk 14:34.
31. Mt 26:40; Mk 14:37.
32. Mt 26:39.
33. Mk 14:35.
34. Lk 22:41.

eyes open."[35] Mark says, "they could not keep their eyes open and did not know what to answer him."[36] Luke, however, explains the most poignant reason: "he found them sleeping from grief."[37] When comparing and contrasting the three side-by-side it is important to remind that Mark's Gospel distinguishes itself in Gethsemane not only by the use of the word "Abba," but by uniquely mentioning, at the close of the Gethsemane narrative, the "young man followed him wearing nothing but a linen cloth about his body. They seized him, but he left the cloth behind and ran off naked."[38]

As Chapter Three (which addressed Luke, the last of the Synoptic Gospels) came to its conclusion, reflections were provided regarding the fact that all three of the Synoptics place the Garden of Gethsemane narrative in the same chapter as The Last Supper. Thus, even Scripture itself elucidates the fact that Jesus is the Host of Gethsemane, the same Eucharistic Lord who presides over the first Mass in the Upper Room.

What Chapter Four Accomplished

Chapter Four of this work discussed the Fourth Gospel account of the New Testament as distinct from the Synoptic Gospels (Matthew, Mark, and Luke), focusing on unique information John shares, but that the Synoptics do not address, such as the Samaritan Woman at the Well, and how the host of Gethsemane teaches through that Scripture passage, how He offers food to those He invites to Gethsemane: that is, the food of doing the will of the Father.

---

35. Mt 26:43.
36. Mk 14:40.
37. Lk 22:45.
38. Mk 14:51-52.

Much was gleaned by noticing that John places His Gethsemane narrative in the same chapter as other important reflections such as the Denials of Peter, the Inquiry before Annas, and the Trial before Pilate; shedding light upon the host of Gethsemane who has invited guests to join Him and initiated hospitality; but sadly has been repeatedly rejected and denied. Within John's Gethsemane narrative, there is a theme of the betrayal and imprisonment of Jesus. In this chapter, it became clear that the "Host/host" becomes "Hostage."

"The Prayer of Jesus," follows the Last Supper Discourse and comprises the entire chapter prior to the Gethsemane narrative of John, and makes the Garden of Gethsemane of his Gospel into the Garden of God's Love, giving a trajectory of love that elucidates Gethsemane as truly the Passion of the Sacred Heart.

The Gospel of John points to Jesus as the Eucharistic Lord in Gethsemane. This is elucidated through the seven "I AM" statements of John's Gospel. Christ's "I AM" statements culminate, finding their apex in the Garden of Gethsemane narrative of John, as was discussed. Also, there are seven signs in the Gospel of John, beginning with the Wedding at Cana and ending with the Raising of Lazarus. In this chapter, the raising of Lazarus was explored as a sign of great importance. It is one of the three times Jesus sheds tears, and each of those times is upon the Mount of Olives. The significance of the blood, sweat, and tears of the olive press of Gethsemane were explored. The anointing at Bethany that follows the raising of Lazarus was discussed, especially vis-a-vis hospitality to the Host/host.

Seven is the Biblical number of heavenly completion,[39] and so it is of great significance that Jesus says "I AM" seven times in the Gospel of John. However, it is important to note that these seven "I AM"'s are the seven metaphors Jesus gives for Himself, such as "I am the light of the world," but these do not include the other times Jesus

---

39. Bible Study Tools, "The Number 7 in the Bible".

uses that phrase in the Gospel of John, such as the three times He does so in the Garden of Gethsemane.

The discussion of Gethsemane in John's Gospel ended on hopeful and poetic notes for the lover of Gethsemane and for whoever hopes to serve the Host/host. The Resurrected Christ in John's Gospel is the Gardener, ironically displaying a glorious mystery in a garden, rising from the sorrowful mystery of the Garden Agony. The Epilogue of John contains three calls to love that echo the calls of the Host of Gethsemane. They are also echoed in the "*Sanctus*" at Mass, once again joining Jesus of Gethsemane to our Eucharistic Lord.

Similarities in all Four Gospels showing Christ as the Host/host of Gethsemane

What all four Gospels have in common is that each and all point to Jesus as the Host/host of Gethsemane. They illuminate that Jesus is the Host of Gethsemane because in their narratives, all show, as my previous pages have elucidated, that Jesus did the will of the Father. Obedience is the necessary disposition of the faithful at Mass. Obedience is extolled in the Book of Hebrews, as the necessity of following the will of God is described: "First he says, 'Sacrifices and offerings, holocausts and sin offerings, you neither desired nor delighted in.' These are offered according to the law. Then he says, 'Behold, I come to do your will.' He takes away the first to establish the second. By this 'will,' we have been consecrated through the offering of the body of Jesus Christ once for all."[40] Therefore the offering of the body of Jesus Christ, which is the Eucharist, the Host, is connected to doing the will of God.

---

40. Heb 10:8-10.

As a strengthening background to this study of the Host of Gethsemane, it is important to understand the Christology of the Doctrine of the Two Wills, as developed by St. Maximus the Confessor, and also to understand the theology of what the Church teaches on the human will of Christ and His divine will. As the Catechism of the Second Vatican Council states:

> In Christ, and through his human will, the will of the Father has been perfectly fulfilled once for all. Jesus said on entering into this world: "Lo, I have come to do your will, O God." Only Jesus can say: "I always do what is pleasing to him." In the prayer of his agony, he consents totally to this will: "not my will, but yours be done." For this reason, Jesus "gave himself for our sins to deliver us from the present evil age, according to the will of our God and Father." And by that will we have been sanctified through the offering of the body of Jesus Christ once for all.[41]

Jesus was the model of obedience par excellence in the way He suffered:

> How much more reason have we sinful creatures to learn obedience—we who in him have become children of adoption. We ask our Father to unite our will to his Son's, in order to fulfill his will, his plan of salvation for the life of the world. We are radically incapable of this, but united with Jesus and with the power of his Holy Spirit, we can surrender our will to him and decide to choose what his Son has always chosen: to do what is pleasing to the Father.[42]

---

41. *CCC,* 2824.
42. *CCC,* 2825.

The Third Council of Constantinople (680-681) "condemned the monothelites…and asserted two wills and two operations of Christ. Monothelites were largely Eastern Christians who, forbidden to talk of the monophysite concept of a single nature of Christ, thought to enforce the unity of the person of Christ by proposing that Christ had one will (thelēma) and one operation (energeia) from his two natures."[43]

This is what the Third Council of Constantinople taught:

We announce the whole in these brief words: Believing our lord Jesus Christ, even after his incarnation, to be one of the holy Trinity and our true God, we say that he has two natures [naturas] shining forth in his one subsistence [subsistentia] in which he demonstrated the miracles and the sufferings throughout his entire providential dwelling here, not in appearance but in truth, the difference of the natures being made known in the same one subsistence in that each nature wills and performs the things that are proper to it in a communion with the other; then in accord with this reasoning we hold that two natural wills and principles of action meet in correspondence for the salvation of the human race.[44]

When St. Maximus argued against the "one operation" to assert that Jesus has two natural wills, he cited Gethsemane as a proof. "… He pointed to the Garden of Gethsemane in which Jesus prayed, 'not

---

43. Encyclopaedia Britannica, "Third Council of Constantinople", *Encyclopaedia Britannica,* last modified April 13, 2023, accessed June 2024, www.britannica.com/event/Third-Council-of-Constantinople-680-681.

44. Papal Encyclicals, "Third Council of Constantinople: 680-681 A. D.", *Papal Encyclicals,* last modified February 20, 2020, accessed June 2024, www.papalencyclicals.net/Councils/ecum06.htm.

my will but thine be done.' Here the human will of Jesus shows its full integrity by freely conforming its will to the divine will."[45]

Aquinas asks this question:

"Was there any contrariety of wills in Christ?" in the Summa. After citing the definition of Constantinople III, which shows that the "two natural wills" are "not in opposition," St. Thomas Aquinas probes into the mystery and concludes that "The agony in Christ was not in the rational soul, in as far as it implies a struggle in the will arising from a diversity of motives…Nevertheless, there was an agony in Christ as regards the sensitive part [of the soul], inasmuch as it implied a dread of coming trial, as Damascene says.[46]

As Michael Dauphinais asserts:

An important example of the conformity of human and divine in Christ is shown in his agony in the garden of Gethsemane, on the night before he was crucified. Sometimes Christ's agony is depicted as the breakdown of this conformity, but in fact the contrary is the case. Since the contemplative union of his human intellect with his divine intellect was unbroken, his ability to suffer intense sorrow–even agony–at Gethsemane was greatly intensified. In the garden of Gethsemane, Christ knew, far more than we ever could, what it means for humankind to reject his love. Likewise, his human will, while fully submitting to

---

45. André Marie, "Saint Maximus the Confessor, Saint Thomas Aquinas, and Christ's Two Wills", *Catholicism.org,* November 14, 2007, accessed May 2024, catholicism.org/saint-maximus-the-confessor-saint-thomas-aquinas-and-christs-two-wills.html.

46. André Marie, "Saint Maximus the Confessor".

his divine will, fully experienced the natural human aversion to death.[47]

All four Gospels also show Jesus as the host of Gethsemane because in all four the disciples have been invited to pray with Him. The Synoptics all include a direct invitation from Jesus, through His loving ever-present hospitality, to come in to the Garden and sit over here while I go over there…and in the Gospel of John, His invitation comes through prayer itself, as Jesus prays to the Father for them. As a strengthening background to this study of the Host of Gethsemane, it is important to understand the theology of Prayer and how Gethsemane is a *vade mecum* of prayer, as Christ's model of prayer there is one to which we must personally keep returning in our own prayer lives.

Prayer is defined in the Catechism of the Second Vatican Council as "the raising of one's mind and heart to God or the requesting of good things from God…humility is the foundation of prayer,"[48] and prayer is also "a covenant relationship between God and man in Christ. It is the action of God and of man, springing forth from both the Holy Spirit and ourselves, wholly directed to the Father, in union with the human will of the Son of God made man."[49] In Chapter Three, "The Life of Prayer", the Catechism continues, "To his disciples, drawn by their Master's silent prayer, Jesus teaches a vocal prayer, the Our Father. He not only prayed aloud the liturgical prayers of the synagogue but, as the Gospels show, he raised his voice to express his personal prayer, from exultant blessing of the Father to the agony of Gethsemani."[50]

Ultimately, the Gethsemane themes of prayer, and of the will of God (including the understanding of the two wills of Jesus) are joined in this Garden. Jesus prays, after all, to do the Will of the Father. The

---

47. André Marie, "Saint Maximus the Confessor".
48. *CCC*, 2559.
49. *CCC*, 2564.
50. *CCC*, 2701.

prayer *par excellence*, the one which Jesus himself teaches us to pray, the Our Father, prays, "Thy Kingdom come, Thy will be done, on earth as it is in heaven." Gethsemane is an apex of prayer and of doing the will of God, and the two are inherently joined. After all, when we don't know what the will of God is for our lives, we must pray more. When the will of God is difficult to bear, we must pray more. When we persevere in prayer, God's will, even the cross, becomes an easier yoke, a lighter burden.

William Barclay considers Gethsemane the ultimate place of prayer, and as he writes of the courage of Jesus in Gethsemane, shows how strong prayer provides for strong action. We see the courage of Jesus. Barclay writes:

> "Rise," said Jesus, "let us be going. He who betrays me is near"…"Rise," he said. "The time for prayer, and the time for the garden is past, Now is the time for action. Let us face life at its grimmest and men at their worst." Jesus rose from his knees to go out to the battle of life. That is what prayer is for. In prayer a man kneels before God that he may stand erect before men. In prayer man enters heaven that he may face the battles of earth.[51]

Pope Benedict XVI puts it this way:

> In Jesus' prayer to the Father on that terrible and marvelous night in Gethsemane, the "earth" became "heaven"; the "earth" of his human will, shaken by fear and anguish, was taken up by his divine will in such a way that God's will was done on earth. And this is also important in our own prayers; we must learn to entrust ourselves more to divine Providence, to ask God for the strength to come out of ourselves to renew our "yes" to him, to say to him, "thy

---

51. Barclay, *The Gospel of Matthew,* 350.

will be done," so as to conform our will to his. It is a prayer we must pray every day because it is not always easy to entrust ourselves to God's will, repeating the "yes," of Jesus, the "yes" of Mary…Dear friends, let us ask the Lord to enable us to keep watch with him in prayer, to follow the will of God every day even if he speaks of the Cross, to live in ever greater intimacy with the Lord, in order to bring a little bit of God's "heaven" to this "earth."[52]

The Gethsemane of the Host

It is important, upon concluding this study of *The Host of Gethsemane*, to address this challenge: what does this study of the Host/host of Gethsemane impel us to do? I assert it calls for a renewed and more fitting Eucharistic devotion, and I will provide examples. [For the importance of Gethsemane as affirmed by theologians and saints, see Appendix A. For the presence of Gethsemane in the Mass, see Appendix B. For the Holy Hour as a way to watch and pray with Jesus in Gethsemane, see Appendix C.]

But, following the logic of the Host of Gethsemane; allow me now to examine the inverse, and I will show where that logic leads. Is there, I ask, a Gethsemane of the Host? I answer in the affirmative. Indeed, the Eucharist, in tabernacles all across the earth, from the rising of the sun to its setting, often endures a Gethsemane. For in Gethsemane, Jesus was abandoned, without consolers. The friends he had invited fell asleep.

St. Manuel Gonzalez Garcia writes of the Abandoned Tabernacle:

---

52. Benedict, *The Prayer of Jesus*, 67-68.

The Evangelists are the ones who taught me the word "abandonment." I decided to use this word, not to speak of the hatred, envy, or persecution of the enemies of Jesus, but rather in reference to the disloyalty, coldness, ingratitude, inconstancy, insensitivity, indelicacy, and cowardice that Jesus experiences from his friends. This leaving him at the moment when they should all have been with him, this failure to assist him with their presence and their unconditional loyalty when he needed it most is what the Evangelists call abandonment and flight. "And they all forsook him, and fled" (Mark 14:50).[53]

Saint Manuel Gonzalez Garcia is referring to Gethsemane in this preceding quote. This saint was known as the Bishop of the Abandoned Tabernacle, and for a strong devotion to the Eucharist. "In his writings, he always conveyed his extraordinary love for the Blessed Sacrament, providing a Eucharist formation for the faithful… yet it was especially upon….the Real Presence in the Tabernacle that the bishop founded the message of adoration and reparation which constitutes the central point of his teaching."[54] St. Manuel was born in Seville, Spain, in 1877 and was ordained a priest in 1901.[55] In 1902, he was sent for his first parish mission, to an impoverished rural church. Upon his arrival, he found the church in disarray, and the tabernacle covered in dust and cobwebs. As he knelt in prayer, he had a mystical experience of Jesus gazing at him through that tabernacle with sorrow and abandonment. From that point on, the mission of his priestly ministry was made clear to him.

He remained committed to this mission, even upon becoming a bishop, and his dying wish was: "I ask to be buried next to a

---

53. Manuel González García, *The Bishop of the Abandoned Tabernacle*, trans.Victoria Schneider, (New York: Scepter Publishers, 2018), 32-33.

54. García, *The Bishop of the Abandoned Tabernacle*, 28-29.

55. García, *The Bishop of the Abandoned Tabernacle*, 19-20.

tabernacle, so that my bones, after death, as my tongue and my pen in life, are saying to those who pass: there is Jesus! There it is! Do not leave him abandoned!"[56]

Saint Manuel asserts:

> There are two ways in which the tabernacle is abandoned. One, exterior: habitual and voluntary absence of Catholics who know Jesus but do not visit him. I am not speaking of unbelievers, or of the irreligious, or of uncatechized Catholics, from whom Jesus in the Blessed Sacrament will feel persecuted, hated, slandered, or unrecognized, rather than abandoned. I am speaking of Catholics who believe, and know that Our Lord Jesus Christ, true God and true Man is really present and alive in the Blessed Sacrament. But they do not receive him in Holy Communion, nor visit him, nor have a friendly relationship with him—even though they live close to a church, and otherwise have time and energy for recreational activities.[57]

Saint Manuel continues, "The second way is by interior abandonment. It is to go to him but not to really be with him. It is to receive him with the body, but not with the heart...It is when we do not meditate on what we are receiving. It is when we do not prepare ourselves to receive him with a clean heart and with great spiritual hunger...It is when we do not talk to or listen to the Guest who is visiting us."[58]

Saint Manuel clearly affirms my assertion connecting the Host with hospitality in the preceding quote. In the Eucharist, the Host is also our guest. In Gethsemane, we are the guest of the Host, and our response to that should be to treat Him as our Divine Guest in the

---

56. García, *The Bishop of the Abandoned Tabernacle*, 27.

57. García, *The Bishop of the Abandoned Tabernacle*, 33-34.

58. García, *The Bishop of the Abandoned Tabernacle*, 34.

Eucharist. Jesus washed the apostles' feet, and we also recall, as discussed in chapter 3 of this work, how St. Mary washed the feet of Jesus with her tears, and anointed them with the precious ointment. Truly, we must give the Eucharist loving and reciprocal hospitality.

Saint Peter Julian Eymard insists, "...our Lord in the Most Blessed Sacrament is not loved!"[59] He continues:

> We do not love our Lord in the Most Blessed Sacrament because we ignore or do not sufficiently look into the sacrifices made by His love for our sake...It cost our Savior the whole Passion to institute the Eucharist. How is that? Because the Eucharist is the sacrifice of the New Law. Now, there is no sacrifice without a victim, there is no immolation without the death of the victim, and to share in the merits of the sacrifice we must share in the victim by eating of it. All this takes place in the Eucharist...The Eucharist cost our Lord the Agony in the Garden of Olives, the humiliations He had to undergo before the tribunals of Caiphas and of Pilate, and His death on Calvary. The Victim had to pass through all these immolations in order to reach the sacramental state and come to us. By instituting His Sacrament, Jesus perpetuated the sacrifices of His Passion. He condemned Himself to undergo desertions as heart-breaking as the one He suffered in the Garden of Olives; the treachery of His friends and disciples...[60]

Saint Peter Julian Eymard continues, emphatically:

> In His Passion, to which His great love for us led Him, Jesus Christ was outlawed. His people disowned Him and

---

59. Peter Julian Eymard, *The Real Presence (Vol 1)*, (Cleveland, OH: Emmanuel Publications, 1938), 148.

60. Eymard, *The Real Presence*, 151-152.

calumniated Him; He did not say a word in self-defense. He was delivered into the hands of His enemies without any protection whatsoever. He did not demand for Himself what is the right of the most common defendant. Out of love for His people and for their salvation He sacrificed His rights as a citizen and an honest man. In the Eucharist, Jesus Christ accepts again this immolation of His civil life. He is there without any rights whatsoever. The law does not give Him recognition. He, God made man, the Savior of the human race, has scarcely a word in the code of the nations He has redeemed...the Eucharist is without defense, without protection. Provided you do not publicly disturb divine worship, you may abuse the Eucharist and commit sacrileges with impunity; that is no one's business but your own. Jesus Christ is then without any protection from man.[61]

Regarding whether or not heaven will take up his defense, Saint Peter Julian Eymard responds, "No! Jesus is delivered up by His Father to the caprice of sinners just as He was to Caiphas and Pilate. *Tradidit Jesum vero voluntati eorum!* 'But Jesus he delivered up to their will!' What! Jesus knew all this when He instituted the Eucharist, and He freely chose this state? Yes, in order to be our Model, our consolation in our sorrows and in the persecutions of the world. And He will remain in this state even to the end of the world as an example and grace for everyone of His children. He loves us."[62]

It was during His Passion, according to St. Peter Julian Eymard:

Jesus Christ added to the sacrifice of His civil rights the immolation of everything that was human in Him: the

61. Eymard, *The Real Presence*, 59-61
62. Eymard, *The Real Presence*, 59-61.

immolation of His will and of the beatitude of His soul, which He allowed to be overwhelmed with sadness unto death; the immolation of His life on the Cross. It was not enough for His love to have done this once; in the Eucharist He perpetuates this natural death. In order to immolate His will He, God, obeys His creature; He, a King, obeys His subject; He a Liberator, obeys His slave! He obeys priest and people, saint and sinner. He obeys without making any resistance, without our having to force His obedience. He obeys even His enemies. He obeys everybody with the same promptness. He obeys not only at Mass when the priest pronounces the words of the consecration, but at every moment of the day and night, whenever the faithful need Him. His permanent state is one of genuine and simple obedience. Is all this really possible? Oh! If man but understood the love of the Eucharist![63]

It is clear that there is a Gethsemane of the Host, an abandonment suffered by Our Eucharistic Lord due to chains of love. St. Peter Julian Eymard explains:

During His Passion Jesus was bound; He lost His liberty. In the Eucharist He is the One that binds Himself. He has chained Himself with the unconditional and perpetual chains of His promises. He has chained Himself to the Sacred Species to which the sacramental words bind Him inseparably. In the Eucharist as on the Cross or in the Tomb He has no movement, no action of His own, although He possesses within Himself the fullness of the risen life. He is fully dependent on man like a Prisoner of love. He cannot break His bonds, or leave His Eucharistic prison; He is our

---

63. Eymard, *The Real Presence*, 61-62.

Prisoner to the end of time. He pledged Himself to this; His contract of love goes as far as that....As to His soul's beatitude, Jesus is no longer able, as at Gethsemane, to suspend its raptures and its joys, for He is risen and in glory. But He loses it in man, in the Christian, who is an unworthy member. How often Jesus has to suffer ingratitude and insult![64]

We are called to respond to the ingratitude and insult He receives with the time we spend watching and praying in Gethsemane. In the Gospel of Luke, there is a particularly resounding exhortation to watch and pray, which echoes even as it foreshadows the exhortation of Christ in Gethsemane: "Be on guard so that your hearts are not weighed down with dissipation and drunkenness and the worries of this life, and that day catch you unexpectedly like a trap. For it will come upon all who live on the face of the whole earth. Be alert at all times, praying that you may have the strength to escape all these things that will take place, and to stand before the son of Man."[65]

The stakes are high in Gethsemane. Each one of us is invited and each of us finds there the great privilege of answering Christ's invitation to share His Eucharistic, Hostly Presence with our presence; thereby reciprocally hosting Him, offering Him our very souls to slake His thirst while we eat of the food of doing His will.

The food of doing the will of God tastes sweet. Jesus's instruction to watch and pray with Him in Gethsemane, immortalized in the Word of Scripture, ought to lead our souls to repeat the words of the prophet Jeremiah: "When I found your words, I devoured them; your words were my joy, the happiness of my heart."[66] The directives of Christ in Gethsemane are given in a time of His own lamentation

---

64. Eymard, *The Real Presence*, 62.

65. Lk 21:34-36.

66. Jer 15:16.

and agony, yet following these words of His is sweet. This calls to mind the words of the prophet Ezekial:

> He unrolled it before me; it was covered with writing front and back. Written on it was: Lamentation, wailing, woe! He said to me: Son of man, eat what you find here: eat this scroll, then go, speak to the house of Israel. So I opened my mouth, and he gave me the scroll to eat. Son of man, he said to me, feed your stomach and fill your belly with this scroll I am giving you. I ate it, and it was as sweet as honey in my mouth.[67]

Therefore, following the will of God and eating the very food of doing His will, despite Gethsemane being a word of lamentation; it will taste sweet. Furthermore, each of us also finds a training ground in this Garden as a place in which time spent watching and praying ensures that we are not "put to the test"; that we may "stand before the son of Man."

No wonder Christ checks on the sleeping apostles three times, hoping they will wake up. The tenderest parent could not rouse their children with more love. Even as He hopes for their consolation, He aches that much more for their conversion of heart, for an increase in watchfulness, for the sake of the strengthening of their souls.

Immediately after this verse: "Be alert at all times, praying that you may have the strength to escape all these things that will take place, and to stand before the son of Man," Luke gives the following information, which assures the student of the school of Gethsemane of how very important it is to spend time there giving, receiving and sharing hospitality with the Host: "Every day he was teaching in the temple, and at night he would go out and spend the night on the Mount of Olives, as it was called."[68] *Every night* he would spend his hours on

---

67. Ez 2:10; 3:1-3.
68. Lk 21:37.

273

the Mount of Olives. And so ought each of us, through our watchful prayers.

We give our thanks by watching and praying, with obedient love. The philosopher Pascal has something to motivate this endeavor as he meditates on the agony of Jesus asserting, "Christ will be in agony until the end of the world. During this time, we must not sleep."[69]

Pascal continues this meditation written from the perspective of Our Lord:

> I was thinking of you in my agony: Those drops of blood I shed for you. Do you always want to cost me the blood of my humanity, without you shedding a tear? I am more of a friend to you than this or that one, because I have done more for you than they, and they would never suffer what I have suffered for you, they would never die for you in the moment of your infidelity and cruelties, as I have done and am willing to do in my chosen ones and in the Holy Sacrament.[70]

Let us not sleep. The Host of Gethsemane is waiting for us to receive Him.

---

69. Pascal, Pensées n. 553.
70. Pascal, Pensées n. 553.

Appendix A: The Importance of Gethsemane as Sanctuary; and as Home Offered and Home Received

According to Cardinal Joseph Siri, Gethsemane is "the door of the sanctuary by which History finds again its true visage and its true order in the understanding and consciousness of the liberated man. It is the sanctuary where, in solitude, the supreme offering has been spiritually accomplished, so that man each time unique, and the whole race of men can find again the eternal order of their creation, and thus have the possibility of entering by grace, into the joy of direct contemplation of the Creator."[1]

Cardinal Siri very well articulates my assertion that Jesus is the Host of Gethsemane, by calling Gethsemane "the door of the sanctuary." The sanctuary, of course, is the most sacred part of a Catholic church, in which the altar is placed. So already, this quote evokes Gethsemane as a place of holiness and the dwelling place of the Eucharist, the Host. But why does Siri specifically refer to Gethsemane as "the door of the sanctuary"? In the First Book of Kings, as Solomon builds the dwelling place of God, it is written: "At the entrance of the sanctuary, doors of olive wood were made; the doorframes had beveled posts. The two doors were of olive wood, with carved figures of cherubim, palm trees, and open flowers. The doors were overlaid with gold, which was also molded to the cherubim and the palm trees. The same was done at the entrance to the nave, where the doorposts of olive wood were rectangular."[2] And so, the olive wood of Solomon's sanctuary doors foreshadow Gethsemane.

Siri referring to Gethsemane as "the door of the sanctuary" brings to mind the "I AM" statements of John's Gospel, one of which is "I am the door." And so, Gethsemane represents not only the door of the sanctuary at Mass, but the very Door Himself. In some translations

---

1. Siri, *Gethsemane*, 365.
2. 1 Kings 6:31-33.

it is written "gate" and in others it is the "door," Jesus says in this translation,"I am the door; if anyone enters through Me, he will be saved, and will go in and out and find pasture."[3] This door reference is very significant in light of Gethsemane, when it considered that Gethsemane is the door of the sanctuary, and an entryway for access to the Host. It is also a symbol of welcoming into one's domicile, which references the good host of Gethsemane. In John's Gospel, just after this reference to being the door, Jesus continues by insisting also:

> I am the good shepherd, and I know mine and mine know me, just as the Father knows me and I know the Father; and I will lay down my life for the sheep. I have other sheep that do not belong to this fold. These also I must lead, and they will hear my voice, and there will be one flock, one shepherd. This is why the Father loves me, because I lay down my life in order to take it up again. No one takes it from me, but I lay it down on my own. I have power to lay it down, and power to take it up again. This command I have received from my Father.[4]

This too is evocative of Gethsemane. In Gethsemane the Good Shepherd indeed lays His life down for the sheep and where Jesus makes abundantly clear that He has the power to lay down His life and take it up again; when at His arrest in the Garden He says "I AM" to the prison guards and they fall down, showing He could escape if He wanted to.

In this moment of looking more closely at each of the "I AM" statements in John's Gospel, it is amazing that each of the statements is closely linked to Gethsemane, so much so that I assert that when Jesus speaks the great "I AM" of Gethsemane, it is encapsulating all of the I AM statements of John that preceded it. For example, Jesus says,

---

3. Jn 10:9 [*New American Standard Bible, 1995*].
4. Jn 10:14-18.

"I am the Bread of Life; whoever comes to me will never hunger, and who believes in me will never thirst…and I will not reject anyone who comes to me, because I came down from heaven not to do my own will but the will of the one who sent me. And this is the will of the one who sent me, that I should not lose anything of what he gave me, but that I should raise it on the last day. For this is the will of my Father, that everyone who sees the Son and believes in him may have eternal life, and I shall raise him on the last day."[5]

Note that in the Gethsemane narrative of John, which states "I AM" three times, Jesus answers the soldiers, "I told you that I AM. So if you are looking for me, let these men go,"[6] and John's Gospel teaches that "this was to fulfill what he had said, 'I have not lost any of those you gave me.'"[7] This references not only the Bread of Life discourse of John 6 (where Jesus mentions the will of the Father is that none shall be lost), but also the Prayer of Jesus in John 17, where again Jesus mentions that, except the son of destruction, none were lost.

Where do we see the apex of Jesus doing the will of the Father? Gethsemane. Where do we see the apex of Jesus not losing anyone the Father gave Him? Gethsemane, as St. John's Gospel specifically indicates in The Prayer of Jesus. Therefore, it is also in Gethsemane that Jesus is the Bread of Life. Truly, Jesus of Gethsemane is the Eucharistic Lord, our Host.

Although many scholars note that in John's Gethsemane pericope, Jesus appears to speak less than in the Synoptics, nevertheless I assert that Jesus is speaking even more. Because by saying "I AM" in Gethsemane, which sends the guards falling to the ground, Jesus is in those two words reiterating all of the I AM statements of John's Gospel.

What are the other "I AM" statements of John's Gospel and do they point to the Host/host? Indeed they do. "I am the light of the

---

5. Jn 6:35-40.

6. Jn 18:8.

7. Jn 18:9.

world. Whoever follows me will not walk in darkness, but will have the light of life."[8] Gethsemane is an undoubtedly dark location, happening at night, after the Last Supper, after sunset, spanning three hours, which tradition holds was approximately from nine o'clock to midnight. Jesus Himself is born during the darkest part of the year, "at *midnight* in Bethlehem in piercing cold," at the same hour He will later be arrested. Jesus could have been born at any time of year, but comes to us in the darkest time to bring us the light. In a similar way, He chooses the darkness and cold and abandonment of Gethsemane (we know it was a cold night because Peter has to warm himself by the charcoal fire as he denies Christ) to emphasize in drastic contrast that He is the light, in even in one's loneliest agony.

In John's Gospel Jesus also says, "I am the resurrection and the life,"[9] which teaches that even in the Sorrowful Mystery of Gethsemane the great I AM points to the Good News of the Resurrection and Life that He is in His very nature and that He will accomplish. He says "I am the way and the truth and the life,"[10] which also underscores the importance of the I AM taking place in that important location of Gethsemane. Jesus also states, "I am the true vine."[11] These words teach us: Like a branch cannot bear fruit unless it is joined with the vine, only Christians joined to Christ produce fruit. There is another I AM statement in the Gospel of John: "These are not metaphors; rather, they are declarations of God's name, as applied by Jesus to Himself. The first instance comes as Jesus responds to a complaint by the Pharisees. "I tell you the truth," Jesus says, "before Abraham was born, I am!" The verbs Jesus uses are in stark contrast with each other: Abraham was, but I am. There is no doubt that the

---

8. Jn 8:12.

9. Jn 11:25.

10. Jn 14:6.

11. Jn 15:1,5.

Jews understood Jesus' claim to be the eternal God incarnate, because they took up stones to kill Him (verse 59)."[12]

Finally, "in the Garden of Gethsemane, when the mob came to arrest Jesus, He asked them whom they sought. They said, 'Jesus of Nazareth,' and Jesus replied, 'I am he' (John 18:4–5). Then something strange happened: 'When Jesus said, "I am he," they drew back and fell to the ground' (verse 6). Perhaps explaining the mob's reaction is the fact that the word 'he' has been provided by our English translators. Jesus simply said, 'I am.' Applying God's covenant name to Himself, Jesus demonstrated His power over His foes and showed that His surrender to them was entirely voluntary (see John 10:17–18; 19:11)."[13]

Cardinal Siri referring to Gethsemane as "the door of the sanctuary" reminds of the "I AM" statements of John's Gospel, one of which is "I am the door." And so, Gethsemane represents not only the door of the sanctuary at Mass, but the very Door Himself. In some translations it is written "gate" and in others it is the "door," Jesus says in this translation,"I am the door; if anyone enters through Me, he will be saved, and will go in and out and find pasture."[14] This door reference is very significant in light of Gethsemane, when it considered that Gethsemane is the door of the sanctuary, and access to the Host.

Cardinal Siri reminds that Gethsemane is not only the "door of the sanctuary, but also is "the sanctuary," and so, as I asserted earlier, Gethsemane is an altar, a place of sacrifice. Siri continues:

> It is only in Gethsemane's enclosure that theology can be divested of all vain, intellectual dilection, of all dead letter and of all scheme of congealed thought, of all dryness of

---

12. Got Questions Ministries, "What are the seven I AM statements in the Gospel of John?".

13. Got Questions Ministries, "What are the seven I AM statements in the Gospel of John?".

14. Jn 10:9 [*New American Standard Bible, 1995*].

heart, of all illusion of autonomy and all torpor of feverish naturalist activity. It is only there that the understanding and the will are liberated by the truth according to the word of Christ (John 8:32), because it is there that the Redeemer lived in his human intimacy, with all his divine love, the Cross of the history of men. And it is in the secret of the agony of Jesus of Nazareth that one can glimpse the meaning of man in the mystery of the history of men...The nocturnal agony on the Mount of Olives...not only concerns every man, but is ontologically linked to every man. Man is not linked to the agony of Christ only by imagination and compassion towards someone who suffers unjustly. Man is linked to it because he has been the subject of the solitary offering in the garden of Gethsemane, which was not a moral act, but an action of being.[15]

Indeed, the very nature of being human is tied to Gethsemane. It is true that prayerful time spent in Gethsemane increases our compassion. It is also true that meditating upon Gethsemane is vital because each one of us was, personally, the subject of what Jesus suffered and offered there.

In Gethsemane, Jesus accepted in advance all the suffering of the Cross. Cardinal Siri addresses whether Jesus struggled with being the Savior, which of course, He did not. The quote from Siri begins with the famous prayer of Jesus in Gethsemane, and continues in Siri's own words:

"My Father, if it be possible, let this cup pass from me; nevertheless, not as I will, but as thou wilt." When Jesus spoke this "if it be possible" was he asking to be liberated from the burden of saving souls? When his spirit had

---

15. Siri, *Gethsemane*, 364.

uttered that appeal, had he suddenly preferred, be it only for a moment, to disengage himself from his mission and then to live, grow old and one day pass away, according to the lot of every man? Those are some of the thoughts which fade away like empty fabrications of men's pride, they fade away when our understanding and our heart penetrate humbly and with abandon into the enclosure of Gethsemane. There the categories according to which we perceive and judge grow dim, or are transformed, taking on another tenor and another fullness. And it is thus that the understanding as well as the heart, in a harmony of peace, receive the mystery of the Being who prayed, prostrate on the ground, for the salvation of men. For the cry of "if it be possible" did not mean lassitude and that Christ preferred that another take on the salvation of men. Christ did not pray only for himself; he prayed in the name of all men, to whom he had linked himself by his offering: "as thou wilt." Christ, unique Person of divine essence, lived interiorly as Redeemer of men in his human fullness, the suffering by inconceivable love, before the wickedness and sin which engendered his passion and his death.[16]

Cardinal Siri even advocates for peace regarding the upheavals and problems within the Church; that one should not abandon the Lord in His Church because:

> ...it is a vain or perverse fiction to oppose the identity and mission of the Church to the real, natural and social good of men; it is an empty fiction to alter her mission and to adapt it to the temporal perspectives which are always temporary...all the known or unknown betrayals of few or

16. Siri, *Gethsemane*, 365-366.

many members of the Church, the pettiness of soul, the narrowness of spirit, the cruelty and all infidelity that the Church may have had and lived within herself, are only the correspondence to the sweat of blood at Gethsemane and to the wounds and blood of the Cross. That is why one must think of the holy Being of the God-man. One can neither change nor abandon the Lord because of his wounds.[17]

That last sentence is one worth memorizing and given as an answer to whomever is distressed about the latest drama in the Church and considering jumping ship. For indeed, one cannot abandon the Lord because of His wounds.

According to Cardinal Siri, the one who reflects upon Gethsemane:

...will be able to find, in the mystery of the "Fiat" of Gethsemane, the way of knowledge, of the mystery of man in History, a hidden way, but full of light. And he will see illumined before him the enigma of the Church, and he will know a deep joy, the joy which Christ said no one can take away. And he will have great certainties about natural and supernatural realities. And he will have great peace, the peace of truth, which only Christ gives. He will understand with his whole being that the mystery of the Incarnation of the inconceivable God, in our poor, weak flesh, contains the whole secret of the origin of man, of the sorrow of the earth and of the true final ends.[18]

It is clear that the Mystery of the Agony in the Garden is well worth reflecting upon, daily.

---

17. Siri, *Gethsemane*, 374-376.
18. Siri, *Gethsemane*, 372-373.

In considering the Host/host of Gethsemane, we are called to reflect upon the Eucharistic Lord of the Agony, and the hospitality He offers us there; an invitation to which we must respond. The Son of Man has no place to rest His Head, we are told; and even now He is abandoned and alone in Gethsemane through the Eucharist when it is abandoned in many tabernacles and monstrances. This should be a call to "watch and pray" that becomes a catalyst to build Him a home.

Interestingly, the altar of Gethsemane, which I have in the preceding pages proven to be an altar, a sanctuary…it is outdoors. It is cold and dark and roofless except for the branches of trees. How can we build our Eucharistic Lord a refuge in Gethsemane? Surely it is to offer him the very home of our own bodies as we receive Him in the Eucharist; the very home of our hearts as we adore Him. I assert there is a concrete model for this in the Book of Chronicles, in the loving gesture of King David. It is written that David:

> …left Asaph and his brethren there before the ark of the covenant of the Lord to minister before the ark regularly according to the daily ritual; he also left there Obededom and sixty-eight of his brethren, including Obededom, son of Jeduthun, and Hosah, to be gatekeepers. But the priest Zadok and his priestly brethren he left before the Dwelling of the Lord on the high place of Gibeon, to offer holocausts to the Lord on the altar of holocausts regularly, morning and evening, and to do all that is written in the law of the Lord which he has decreed for Israel. With them were Heman and Jeduthun and the others who were chosen and designated by name to give thanks to the Lord, "because his kindness endures forever," with trumpets and cymbals for accompaniment, and instruments for the sacred chant. The sons of Jeduthun kept the gate.[19]

---

19. 1 Chron 16:37-42.

It is worth observing how appropriately lavishly the ark of the covenant is attended, how well cared for is the Dwelling of the Lord in the Book of Chronicles. There are gatekeepers, daily offers of holocausts both morning and evening, trumpets and chants. Compare this to the sacristy of Gethsemane or the tabernacle in the deserted church in which the Real Presence in the Eucharist remains, night and day.

David, after preparing all these acts of love for the Presence of the Lord, went home. "After David had taken up residence in his house, he said to Nathan the prophet, 'See I am living in a house of cedar, but the ark of the covenant of the Lord dwells under tentcloth.'"[20] David wanted to build the Lord a home, and he told Nathan this.

This loving observation of David resounds like a call to each of the faithful. It is a reminder of what God humbly endures for his people and what the thoughtful servant is motivated to offer in return. About the Heart of Jesus in the Tabernacle, St. Peter Julian Eymard writes, "Do you want to know what is His life? It is divided between His Father and us. Our Savior watches over us; and though He seems wrapped in impotent sleep, while enclosed in the frail Host, His Heart is awake…He keeps watch both when we think of Him and when we do not. He does not rest. He pleads with His Father for forgiveness in our behalf. Jesus shields us with His Heart…"[21]

God responds to the desire of His servant David to build Him a house. He does so through the prophet Nathan. It is written: "But that same night the word of God came to Nathan." The use of the phrase "word of God" denotes the Second Person of the Trinity and thus foreshadows the Son of Man, Jesus Christ. The word of God tells Nathan, "…I have never dwelt in a house, from the time when I led Israel onward, even to this day, but I have been lodging in tent or

---

20. 1 Chron 17:1-6.

21. Peter Julian Eymard, *In the Light of the Monstrance (Vol 9)*, (Cleveland, OH: Emmanuel Publications, 1947), 226.

pavilion as long as I have wandered about with all of Israel. Did I ever say a word to any of the judges of Israel whom I have commanded to guide my people such as, 'Why have you not built me a house of cedar?'"[22] What the word of God says here foreshadows Jesus and his would-be followers. "As they were proceeding on their journey someone said to him, 'I will follow you wherever you go.' Jesus answered him, 'Foxes have dens and birds of the sky have nests, but the Son of Man has nowhere to rest his head.'"[23] As discussed in Chapter Three, not long after this is said; in fact, in the very next chapter, Martha welcomes Him into her home. And we must read therein the call to do likewise.

The word of God continues to tell Nathan: "Therefore, tell my servant David, Thus says the Lord of hosts...I declare to you that I, the Lord, will build *you* a house."[24] He explains to Nathan that this house will be through David's son, Solomon, who will build the great Temple. God will establish His kingdom forever through this line of Solomon.

I assert that the logic of Scripture applied to the life of each of the faithful dictates that for each of us who sets forth with the desire to build God a house in Gethsemane, a tabernacle for the Eucharistic Lord...it is God who will build us a house. And, "Behold, I stand at the door and knock. If anyone hears my voice and opens the door, then I will enter his house and dine with him, and he with me."[25] Or St. Josemaria Escriva puts it this way:

This is the source of the joy we feel on Holy Thursday— the realization that the creator has loved his creatures to such an extent. Our Lord Jesus Christ, as though all the other proofs of his mercy were insufficient, institutes the

---

22. 1 Chronicles 17:6.
23. Lk 9:57-58.
24. 1 Chronicles 17:7,10.
25. Rev 3:20.

Eucharist so that he can always be close to us. We can only understand up to a point that he does so because Love moves him, who needs nothing, not to want to be separated from us. The Blessed Trinity has fallen in love with man, raised to the level of grace and made "to God's image and likeness." God has redeemed him from sin—from the sin of Adam, inherited by all his descendants, as well as from his personal sins—and desires ardently to dwell in his soul: "If anyone love me, he will keep my word; and my Father will love him, and we will come to him and make our abode with him."[26]

With God, there is reciprocity always, yet we always are given back more than we gave. It is like unto the lessons I have observed in accounts of heaven-sent food in Sacred Scripture.

In the Book of Kings, "twenty barley loaves made from the first fruits, and fresh grain in the ear" was given, at Elisha's insistence, to a crowd of a hundred. "For thus says the Lord, 'They shall eat and there shall be some left over.' And when they had eaten, there was some left over, as the Lord had said."[27]

In the famous "Loaves and Fishes" passage, Jesus provides food (with leftovers) for a massive crowd from five barley loaves and two fish.[28]

In the Book of Exodus, God's response to the hunger of the Israelites reads like poetry: "In the evening quail came up and covered the camp. In the morning a dew lay all about the camp, and when the dew evaporated, there on the surface of the desert were fine flakes like hoarfrost on the ground. On seeing it, the Israelites asked one another,

---

26. Josemaria Escriva, "The Eucharist, Mystery of Faith and Love", *St. Josemaria Institute*, April 5, 2023, accessed June 2024, stjosemaria.org/the-eucharist-holy-thursday/.

27. 2 Kings 4:42-44.

28. Jn 6:1-15.

'What is this?' for they did not know what it was. But Moses told them, 'This is the bread that the Lord has given you to eat.'"[29]

Here are the rules of heaven-sent sustenance as gleaned from the aforementioned readings and others on this topic: In times of scarcity or want, God provides. We ought not worry about food that perishes, but rather work for permanent food. There will be leftovers. The food will be better than our wildest dreams. God always gives more back than He is given. And we are left, mouths agape in joy, to give thanks.

David, ever thankful and loving, responds to God this way. "Then David came in and sat in the Lord's presence"[30] and said, "Because you, O my God, have revealed to your servant that you will build him a house, your servant has made bold to pray before you. Since you, O Lord, are truly God and have promised this good thing to your servant, and since you have deigned to bless the house of your servant, so that it will remain forever—since it is you, O Lord, who blessed it, it is blessed forever."[31]

Through an exchange of hospitality, we must build the host of Gethsemane a house by offering Him the home of our very hearts, whether we invite Him there as we receive Holy Communion, or as we kneel at Eucharistic Adoration. We do so knowing that our extended hospitality to Our Lord is not something we should boast of, for if we call to Him, we know He first called us. Another way of saying this is that our invitation to God to dwell within us is actually a response to His invitation, His complete offering of Himself on our behalf, from the Last Supper, to the Agony, to the Cross, and now to the Eucharist. When we offer Him the house of our hearts, He will never be outdone in generosity, but will instead build us a house as He did for David.

---

29. Ex 16:2-4, 12-15.
30. 1 Chron 17:16, 25-27.
31. 1 Chron 17:25-27.

Appendix B: Gethsemane in the Mass

The Eucharistic Handbook for the Members of the People's Eucharistic League states that there is a method for hearing and participating well at Mass through the way we meditate upon the Passion. It states:

> The priest comes to the altar dressed in his priestly vestments…carrying the chalice and the matter for the Sacrifice. Jesus goes to the Garden of Olives to offer Himself to His Father for the Sacrifice of Calvary. Accompany this good Savior; pray and watch with Him; reject all distractions and all other thoughts. The priest prays and humbles himself at the foot of the altar. Jesus, on His knees and with His face bowed to the ground in the grotto of Gethsemane, prays to His Father in His agony of blood and takes all the sins with their bitterness upon Himself; to expiate them, He will drink the chalice to its dregs. Drink this chalice of the Savior; His love has sweetened it. The priest goes up to the altar. Jesus in chains returns to Jerusalem to be brought before His enemies. And He goes there as meek as a lamb.[1]

Peter Julian Eymard narrates key elements of the Mass and states the correlation between that particular part of the Mass and various elements of the Passion, notably including Gethsemane:

> *The priest enters and goes to the altar, bearing the chalice.* –Behold Jesus going to the Garden of Gethsemane to begin His loving Passion; follow Him with the Apostles, but watch and pray with Him. Reject every distraction, put

---

1. Peter Julian Eymard, *A Eucharistic Handbook (Vol 6)*, (Cleveland, OH: Emmanuel Publications, 1948), 86-87.

aside every thought that does not pertain to the august Mystery. *The priest prays at the foot of the altar and, bowing low in deep humility at the thought of his own sins, says the Confiteor.*–In the Garden Jesus, casting Himself face downward upon the earth, abases Himself for sinners, taking upon Himself all our sins and the bitterness of them. A bloody sweat, pressed forth by His immeasurable suffering, stains His garments and falls to the earth. With the priest, make confession of all your sins, humbly ask for pardon from them, and receive the absolution, that you may participate with purity in the Holy Sacrifice. Without doubt, this one consideration would be enough to occupy you for the entire duration of the Mass. If you enter into the intentions of Jesus in His agony, if you find yourself held fast by grace at His side, remain there…The priest goes up to the altar and kisses it.–Judas repairs to the Garden of Olives and gives Jesus the kiss of betrayal. Ah, how many times has Jesus been betrayed by a kiss by the unfaithful among His children and His servants! Alas, have I not myself betrayed Him? Have I never given Him up to His enemies, to my passions?…Yet how much He has loved me![2]

The Catechism teaches:

The cup of the New Covenant, which Jesus anticipated when he offered himself at the Last Supper, is afterwards accepted by him from his Father's hands in his agony in the garden at Gethsemani, making himself "obedient unto death." Jesus prays, "My father, if it be possible, let this cup pass from me…" Thus he expresses the horror that

2. Eymard, *Holy Communion*, 4-36.

death represented for his human nature. Like ours, his human nature is destined for eternal life; but unlike ours, it is perfectly exempt from sin, the cause of death. Above all, his human nature has been assumed by the divine person of the "Author of life," the "Living One." By accepting in his human will that the Father's will be done, he accepts his death as redemptive, for "he himself bore our sins in his body on the tree."[3]

"The cup of the New Covenant" is specifically mentioned in all four of the Institution Narratives of Eucharistic prayers. What he offered at the Last Supper is accepted in Gethsemane and included as part of the Eucharistic prayer at Mass and thus we see how Gethsemane is present in the Mass and the Mass, the very Eucharist, is present in Gethsemane: "TAKE THIS, ALL OF YOU, AND DRINK FROM IT: FOR THIS IS THE CHALICE OF MY BLOOD, THE BLOOD OF THE NEW AND ETERNAL COVENANT, WHICH WILL BE POURED OUT FOR YOU AND FOR MANY FOR THE FORGIVENESS OF SINS. DO THIS IN MEMORY OF ME."[4]

---

3. *CCC*, 612.

4. Catholic Resources, "Eucharistic Prayers I – IV", n.d., accessed June 2024, catholic-resources.org/ChurchDocs/RM3-EP1-4.htm.

Appendix C: The Holy Hour: a Way to Watch and Pray with Jesus in Gethsemane

The answer on the part of the faithful to such Eucharistic abandonment is to make reparation through frequently making a Holy Hour. As St. Peter Julian Eymard writes: "In His agony He sought a consoler; on the Cross He asked for someone to sympathize with His afflictions. Today, more than ever, we must make amends, a reparation of honor, to the adorable Heart of Jesus. Let us lavish our adorations and our love on the Eucharist. To the Heart of Jesus living in the Most Blessed Sacrament be honor, praise, adoration, and kingly power for ever and ever!"[1]

An invaluable way to make amends, a reparation of honor, and to give lavish love to the Eucharistic Heart of Jesus is through the Holy Hour. The Holy Hour may be done at church as part of Adoration of the Blessed Sacrament, or through an at-home Holy Hour. In any case, praying a Holy Hour fulfills the marks of a good servant as described by St. Peter Julian Eymard. "But what are the marks of a good servant? They are three. First he is always near his master and at his disposition. Second, he obeys all his commands promptly and affectionately. Third, he works only for his master's glory."[2] And indeed each praying soul who makes a Holy Hour draws near the Lord, obeys the request to watch and pray, and in so doing gives prayerful fruit to the glory of God.

There are different types of Holy Hours recognized by the Church, and they are related, too. The first kind of Holy Hour is more well-known. It's the most important of all the Holy Hours in a way because, this is, after all, adoring the Real Presence. It is the most well known of all Holy Hours. Venerable Fulton Sheen was an enthusiastic

---

1. Eymard, *The Real Presence*, 285.

2. Peter Julian Eymard, *Holy Communion (Vol 2)*, (Cleveland, OH: Emmanuel Publications, 1940), 199.

proponent of Eucharistic Adoration, and he made a daily Holy Hour before the Blessed Sacrament every day of his priesthood.

Archbishop Sheen wrote that there are three main reasons he revolved his day around the Eucharist and taught others to do the same. First, he saw it as a "sharing in the work of redemption," giving us an opportunity to remain with Christ despite the evil in the world around us. He also saw that the only time recorded in Scripture that Jesus asked something of his Apostles was when He brought them to pray with Him in the Garden of Gethsemane. Our Lord asked, "Could you not watch one hour with Me?" and we have an opportunity to answer that question during our own time of Adoration. A third reason Archbishop Sheen gave is that by spending time with Jesus in the Eucharist we become more and more formed in His likeness, much like Moses was transformed when he returned after his time on Mount Sinai seeing God face to face. Our hearts are changed by remaining with the Heart of God present in every tabernacle and within every monstrance. Both priests and laity alike, as well as non-Catholics, were encouraged by Archbishop Sheen to adopt the practice of the Holy Hour.[3]

The next type of Holy Hour, which is far less well-known, may be made at church and even at home. There is a special day and time for this Holy Hour. It is on Thursdays at eleven o'clock at night. Due to the hour of night, it is far more often prayed at home, at least for the laity who often do not have nighttime access to a church. This Holy Hour was instituted thanks to the private revelation, fully accepted by

3. Katie Bogner, "The Hour that made Fulton Sheen's Day", *The Catholic Post*, July 3, 2019, accessed May 2024, thecatholicpost.com/2019/07/03/the-hour-that-made-fulton-sheens-day/.

the Church, of the great saint, Margaret Mary Alacoque, who famously brought the Sacred Heart devotion to prominence in the Catholic Church. Jesus asked her to pray the Holy Hour as a meditation on His Agony in the Garden from 11 pm-12 am on Thursday nights.

Jesus told her, "Here I suffered inwardly more than in the rest of my passion because I was totally alone, abandoned by heaven and earth, burdened with the sins of mankind...In order for you to be united with me, in the humble prayer that I presented to my Father in the midst of all that anguish, you will arise between eleven o'clock and midnight, and prostrate yourself in adoration for one hour with me."[4]

The Third Type of Holy Hour is made at home and can be done any time that is convenient. A Holy Hour can be made at any time of the day or week because God cherishes all devout prayer, though there are special graces attached to the eleven o'clock hour on Thursday given by Christ to St. Margaret Mary. "...This homage of reparation, which is the hour of night adoration, is the very same which the Sacred Heart asked of St. Margaret Mary. In union, then, with His confidante and apostle of Paray-le-Monial, gather up in the chalice of a contrite and loving heart all the tears and countless griefs of our Savior, that in this hour of intimacy, you may be 'completing what is lacking in Christ's afflictions for the sake of his body, that is, the church' (Colossians 1:24)."[5]

Father Mateo Crawley-Boevey (1875-1960), the great founder of the Nocturnal Adoration Holy Hour in the home, called the Sacred Heart Night Adoration Holy Hour in the home "the most beautiful flower of his work." It was an outgrowth of his love for the Sacred Heart and also that wondrous devotion we also owe to Fr. Mateo's apostolate: the Home Enthronement of the Sacred Heart. For this Holy

---

4. Annabelle Moseley, "This classic devotion will bring Holy Thursday to your home", *Aleteia*, April 6, 2023, accessed May 2024, aleteia.org/2023/04/06/this-classic-devotion-will-bring-holy-thursday-to-your-home.

5. Mateo Crawley-Boevey, *Holy Hour for Night Adoration in the Home*, (Fairhaven, MA: National Center of the Enthronement, 2000), 9.

Hour devotion, an image of the Sacred Heart should be displayed and enthroned in the home and be the focus of the Nocturnal Adoration.

The Passion of our Lord, specifically Gethsemane; the Sacred Heart; and the Eucharist are inexorably linked, as was addressed in this work. As the great advocate of the Holy Hour in the 1930's, Father Francis P. Donnelly, once wrote, "In practice, the faithful should be recommended to entertain thoughts of sympathy with Christ suffering, of hatred for sin, of reparation to Christ for the ingratitude and indifference of mankind."[6]

This Nocturnal Adoration in the Home is a way for faithful Catholics to respond to the sorrow of Jesus in the Garden of Gethsemane by answering Our Lord's call to "watch and pray" for one hour with Him: by staying awake. Best of all, the devotion can be prayed *anywhere*, does not require access to a church (only the *domestic* kind) and can provide a deep sense of purpose to whatever challenge one is traversing. It is deeply relevant to this work because it focuses its attention on Jesus in Gethsemane, and through consoling Him there, one is also consoling the Eucharistic Lord, an act of adoration. Upon reflecting on the Gospel of Matthew's Gethsemane narrative, William Barclay asserts, "Surely this is a passage which we must approach upon our knees. Here, study should pass into wondering adoration."[7]

In the Sixth Station of the Cross, St. Veronica offers her veil to wipe the face of Jesus on the Via Dolorosa, and Jesus rewarded her act with the image of His Holy Face, left behind upon her veil. In the Garden of Gethsemane, Jesus fell prostrate, His face to the ground, and so it must have become smeared with dirt. He sweated blood, and its clear that tears fell as He prayed in His Agony. Then there was Judas, who placed a kiss on His face…a kiss of betrayal. The Veronica of Gethsemane who steps forward to wipe that Holy Face, now may be

---

6. Francis P. Donnelly, *The Holy Hour in Gethsemane*, (North Haven, CT: CreateSpace/public domain, 2023), 16.

7. Barclay, *The Gospel of Matthew,* 348.

you or I. Jesus calls to each of us from Gethsemane, speaking directly: *My soul is sorrowful even unto death. Sit here and keep watch with me.*[8] What more direct invitation can we receive from our host?

In watching and praying during a Holy Hour, one's personal loneliness and abandonment can be surrendered to Jesus in compassion and solidarity with all He suffered in Gethsemane. To pray as He did there, telling God, "Not my will but Yours be done," will lead one to "the peace of God which surpasses all understanding."[9] For it is indeed true that a bond is made between someone who can't sleep and the one who stays awake to assist; or between the one who is sick or worried or grieving and the caretaker or good friend who stays awake to help or comfort. One must not let the word "Agony" scare one off the trail! Though The Agony in the Garden is a Sorrowful Mystery, it brings the kind of joy that transfigures and heals, the kind of joy impossible to find without Christ. "This may not be the fruit every time, but the openness remains the goal of the exercise: to await the self-disclosure of God," said Father Mateo Crawley-Boevey (1875-1960), the great founder of the Nocturnal Adoration Holy Hour in the home.

Father David Reid, National Director of the Center of the Enthronement writes, "Jesus is appealing to us…for the consolation of the Spirit which leads to sympathy and empathy for others…The word consolation has a long history in spirituality which goes to the making of community at a very deep level (see 2 Corinthians 1:3-7). To be with others in the midst of their solitude respecting the integrity of their stillness before God (called hesychia in eastern spirituality) is indeed a profound sharing; to be given entry into such interiority of the heart of Jesus is a pearl of great price."[10] It may be observed even in this author's prayer life that truism that Jesus is "never outdone in generosity." Spending regular time with Jesus in the Garden, whatever

---

8. Mt 26:38.

9. Phil 4:7.

10. Crawley-Boevey, *Holy Hour for Night Adoration in the Home*, iv.

one is experiencing (whether one is heartbroken, burdened, even feeling numb); leads to a life-changing and lasting peace.

Bibliography

Primary Sources

Angelico, Fra. "Christ in Garden of Gethsemane", fresco, 1450, Museum of San Marco, at useum.org/artwork/Christ-in-Garden-of-Gethsemane-Fra-Angelico-1450.

Aquinas, Thomas. *Catena Aurea: Commentary on the Four Gospels Vol. I, St. Matthew, trans. John Henry Newman. London: Baronius Press, 2022.*
——. *Catena Aurea: Commentary on the Four Gospels Vol. III, St. Luke, trans. John Henry Newman. London: Baronius Press, 2022.*
——. *Catena Aurea: commentary on the Four Gospels vol. IV, St. John, trans. John Henry Newman. London: Baronius Press, 2013.*

Benedict. "The Reception of Guests," from *The Rule of St. Benedict*, ed. Timothy Fry. Collegeville, Minnesota: The Liturgical Press, 1982.

Benedict XVI. *Jesus of Nazareth.* New York: Rizzoli, 2009.
——. *The Prayer of Jesus.* Washington, DC: United States Catholic Conference Inc–Libreria Editrice Vaticana, 2013.

Catholic Church. *The Liturgy of the Hours Vol 2, Large Type Edition.* New York: Catholic Book Publishing Corp, 1976.
——.*The Liturgy of the Hours Vol 3, Large Type Edition.* New York: Catholic Book Publishing Corp, 1976.
——.*The Liturgy of the Hours Vol 4, Large Type Edition.* New York: Catholic Book Publishing Corp, 1975.
——.*Catechism of the Catholic Church.* Washington, DC: United States Catholic Conference Inc–Libreria Editrice Vaticana, 1994.

Catechism of the Council of Trent. London: Baronius Press, 2018.

Hofmann, Heinrich. "Christ in Gethsemane", oil on canvas, 1890, Riverside Church, New York. www.heinrichhofmann.net/christ-in-gethsemane.html.

John, Paul II. *On the Eucharist: Ecclesia de Eucharistia.* Washington, D.C: USCCB, 2003.

Lombardo, Enrique Simonet. "Flevit Super Illam", oil on canvas, 1892, Museo Del Prado, Madrid. www.museodelprado.es/en/the-collection/art-work/flevit-super-illam/498b0344-ee49-435c-bfd7-ff707d728975

Pontifical Biblical Commission, *The Interpretation of the Bible in the Church.* Vatican City: Libreria Editrice Vaticana, 1993.

Papal Encyclicals, "Third Council of Constantinople: 680-681 A. D.",last modified February 20, 2020. www.papalencyclicals.net/Councils/ecum06.htm.

Third Council of Baltimore, *The Baltimore Catechism*

Trevisani, Franceso. "The Agony in the Garden", oil on copper, 1740, Glasgow Museums Resource Centre, Glasgow. artuk.org/discover/artworks/the-agony-in-the-garden-86262.

Unknown. "The Little Flower of the Divine Prisoner," print, ca. 1800s. mycatholic.life/books/lessons-saint-therese-wisdom-gods-little-flower/chapter-four-first-communion-confirmation/.

USCCB, "The Blessing of the Oils and the Consecration of the Chrism", *United States Conference of Catholic Bishops*, n.d. https://www.usccb.org/prayer-and-worship/sacraments-and-sacramentals/sacramentals-blessings/blessing-of-oils-and-consecration-of-chrism.

van Rijn, Rembrandt. "Christ and St Mary Magdalen at the Tomb", oil on panel, 1638, Buckingham Palace, London. www.rct.uk/collection/404816/christ-and-st-mary-magdalen-at-the-tomb.

Secondary Sources

Armstrong, Patti Maguire. "Holy Cloth for Mom", *National Catholic Register*, May 21, 2017. https://www.ncregister.com/features/holy-cloth-for-mom/.

Ayre, Harrison. "Christology 101: Christ's Two Wills." *Simply Catholic,* June 6, 2023. https://simplycatholic.com/christology-101-christs-two-wills/.

Barclay, William. *The Gospel of Matthew, volume 2.* Philadelphia, PA: Westminster Press, 1976.

Barres, John O. "The Great Week: A Pilgrimage with the Lord in Holy Week: A Pastoral Letter from Bishop John O. Barres to the People of God of the Diocese of Rockville Centre." *The Long Island Catholic,* March 3, 2020.

Baker, Lindsay. "Physiology of sweat gland function: The roles of sweating and sweat composition in human health." *Temperature,* July 17, 2019. https://www.ncbi.nlm.nih.gov/pmc/articles/PMC6773238/.

Bible Study Tools, "The Number 7 in the Bible," *Bible Study Tools*, July 11, 2023. https://www.biblestudytools.com/topical-verses/the-number-7-in-the-bible/.

Biblical Christianity, "The Olivet Discourse: Blueprint to the End Times." *Biblical Christianity,* November 20, 2019. https://biblical-christianity.com/the-olivet-discourse-blueprint-to-the-end-times.

Billy, Dennis J. *The Beauty of the Eucharist: Voices from the Church Fathers.* Hyde Park, NY: New City Press, 2010).
——. *Meeting Jesus on the Road to Emmaus: An Invitation to Friendship, Eucharist and Christian Community.* Eugene, OR: Wipf and Stock, 2017.

Bogner, Katie. "The Hour that made Fulton Sheen's Day," *The Catholic Post*, July 3, 2019. https://thecatholicpost.com/2019/07/03/the-hour-that-made-fulton-sheens-day/.

Bosetti, Elena. *Luke: The Song of God's Mercy*. Boston: Pauline Books and Media, 2006.
——. *Mark: The Risk of Believing*. Boston: Pauline Books and Media, 2006.
——. *Matthew: The Journey Toward Hope*. Boston: Pauline Books and Media, 2006.
——. *John: The Word of Light*. Boston: Pauline Books and Media, 2007.

Bowling, Ted E. "sermonette: Garden of Gethsemane: The Oil Press," Bible Tools, November 28, 2023. https://oliveknowledge.com/how-many-times-can-you-press-olives-when-making-olive-oil/.

Brown, Raymond E. *The Death of the Messiah Volume One*. New York: Doubleday, 1994.

Butler, Trent C., Chad Brand, Charles Draper, and Archie England, editors. *Holman Illustrated Bible Dictionary*. Nashville, TN: Holman Reference, 2003.

Cantalamessa, Raniero. "Meditation on the Passion," Sec 5, *Franciscan Penance Library*, n.d. https://www.franciscanpenancelibrary.com/meditation-on-the-passion/.

Catholic Online, "St. Thomas More", *Catholic Online*, n.d. https://www.catholic.org/saints/saint.php?saint_id=324.

Cedergren, Bénédicte. "Keeping Eucharistic Vigil at Rome's Altars of Repose," *National Catholic Register*, March 29, 2024. https://www.ncregister.com/features/keeping-eucharistic-vigil-at-rome-s-altars-of-repose.

Cintorino, Maria. "What Happens on Holy Thursday?" *National Catholic Register*, April 6, 2023. https://www.ncregister.com/blog/what-happens-on-holy-thursday.

Clifford, Karen. "Oils of Chrism—a sign of God's mercy", *Today's Catholic*, April 13, 2011. https://todayscatholic.org/oils-of-chrism-a-sign-of-gods-mercy/.

Compelling Truth, "What does it mean that God is the 'LORD of hosts'?" *Compelling Truth*, n.d. https://www.compellingtruth.org/Lord-of-hosts.html.

Cox, Jimmy. "The Psalm Sang at the Last Supper", *AOK Music and Arts*, April 9, 2020. https://aokmusicandarts.com/news/2020/4/9/the-psalm-sang-at-the-last-supper.

Crawley-Boevey, Mateo. *Holy Hour for Night Adoration in the Home.* Fairhaven, MA: National Center of the Enthronement, 2000.

Custodia Terrae Sanctae. "Harvesting of the Olives at the Hermitage in Gethsemane," *Custodia Terrae Sanctae: Franciscans serving the Holy Land,* October 17, 2012. https://www.custodia.org/en/news/harvesting-olives-hermitage-gethsemane/.

Dalessio, Chiara. "Light, Worship, and Finding the Right Direction," *L'Italo Americano*, May 15, 2023. https://italoamericano.org/why-old-churches-face-east/.

Davis, H. Grady, Frederick Fyvie Bruce. "The Synoptic Problem", Encyclopaedia Britannica, February 9, 2023. www.britannica.com/topic/biblical-literature/The-Synoptic-problem.

Dermody, Tom. "Catholic Doctor gives Medical View of Christ's Passion, Crucifixion," *The Catholic Telegraph*, April 10, 2019.

https://www.thecatholictelegraph.com/catholic-doctor-gives-medical-view-of-christs-passion-crucifixion/57186.

Domínguez, Joseángel. "The Mother in Heaven," *St. Josemaria Institute*, August 11, 2023. https://stjosemaria.org/the-mother-in-heaven/.

Donahue, John R. and Daniel J Harrington, eds., *Sacra Pagina: The Gospel of Matthew*. Collegeville, MN: The Liturgical Press, 1991.
——. *Sacra Pagina: The Gospel of Mark*. Collegeville, MN: The Liturgical Press, 2002.

Donnelly, Francis P. *The Our Father in Gethsemane*. New York: 1935, TAN Books.
——. *The Holy Hour in Gethsemane*. North Haven, CT: CreateSpace/public domain, 2023.

Dz, Petar. "How Many Times Can You Press Olives When Making Olive Oil?", Olive Knowledge, November 28, 2023. https://oliveknowledge.com/how-many-times-can-you-press-olives-when-making-olive-oil/.

Encyclopaedia Britannica, "Third Council of Constantinople", last modified April 13, 2023. www.britannica.com/event/Third-Council-of-Constantinople-680-681.

Escriva, Josemaria. "The Eucharist, Mystery of Faith and Love," *St. Josemaria Institute*, April 5, 2023. https://stjosemaria.org/the-eucharist-holy-thursday/.

Eymard, Peter Julian. *The Real Presence (Vol 1)*. Cleveland, OH: Emmanuel Publications, 1938.
——.*Holy Communion (Vol 2)*. Cleveland, OH: Emmanuel Publications, 1940.
——.*A Eucharistic Handbook (Vol 6)*. Cleveland, OH: Emmanuel Publications, 1948.
——. *In the Light of the Monstrance (Vol 9)*. Cleveland, OH: Emmanuel Publications, 1947.

Flanagan, Neal M. *The Gospel According to John and the Johnannine Epistles.* Collegeville, MN: The Liturgical Press, 1983.

Freedman, David Noel. *The Anchor Bible Dictionary, Vol. 2.* New York: Doubleday, 1992.

Frye, Peggy. "Water Added to the Wine During Mass." *Catholic Answers*, September 20, 2017. https://www.catholic.com/qa/water-added-to-the-wine-during-mass.

García, Manuel González, translated by Victoria Schneider, *The Bishop of the Abandoned Tabernacle.* New York: Scepter Publishers, 2018.

Glutton Life. "The Olive Harvest and Making Greek Olive Oil,' *The Glutton Life*, December 12, 2018. https://www.thegluttonlife.com/2018/12/04/the-olive-harvest-and-making-greek-olive-oil/.

Godfryd, Kurt. "The Church Militant, Suffering, and Triumphant", *St Clement of Rome Catholic Church*, September 3,2023. https://www.stclementromeo.org/the-church-militant-suffering-and-triumphant/.

Got Questions Ministries. "What are the watchmen in the Bible?" *Got Questions Ministries,* October 18, 2018. https://www.gotquestions.org/watchmen-in-the-Bible.html.
——. "What are the seven I AM statements in the Gospel of John?" *Got Questions Ministries*, 2022. https://www.gotquestions.org/seven-I-AM-statements.html.

Green, Joel B., and McKnight, Scot. *Dictionary of Jesus and the Gospels.* Illinois: InterVarsity Press, 2013.

Grondelski, John. "Holy Thursday: The Washing of the Disciples' Feet," *National Catholic Register*, April 6, 2023.

https://www.ncregister.com/blog/scriptures-and-art-holy-thursday-washing-of-the-feet.

Gustin, Marilyn. *How to Read and Pray the Passion Story.* Liguori, MO, Liguori; 1993.

Hahn, Scott. *The Fourth Cup: Unveiling the Mystery of the Last Supper and the Cross.* New York: Image, 2018.

Hardon, John A. *Modern Catholic Library.* Garden City, New York: Doubleday & Company, 1980.

Haynes, Clarence L. Jr. "What Happened to Judas after He Betrayed Jesus?" *Bible Study Tools*, August 30, 2023. https://www.biblestudytools.com/bible-study/topical-studies/what-happened-to-judas-after-he-betrayed-jesus.html.

Hearthcake and a Jug of Water, "Sunday, March 13th," n.d. http://hearthcake.com/sunday-march-13th/.

Heinlein, Michael R. "A Closer Look at the Holy Oils," *Simply Catholic*, March 25, 2024. https://www.simplycatholic.com/a-closer-look-at-the-holy-oils/.

Holy Land Site. "Bethany, Tomb of Lazarus," Holy Land Site, n.d. https://www.holylandsite.com/bethany-tomb-of-lazarus.

Ibreviary. "A.9.a. Preface of Sundays in Ordinary Time I", iBreviary, n.d. https://www.ibreviary.com/m2/messale.php?s=prefazio&id=469.

Jordan, James B. "Christ in the Holy of Holies: The Meaning of the Mount of Olives." *Theopolis Institute*, April 28, 1996. https://theopolisinstitute.com/the-meaning-of-the-mount-of-olives-2/.

Kodell, Jerome. *The Gospel According to Luke.* Collegeville, MN; The Liturgical Press; 1991.

Kosloski, Philip. "Yes, a form of the word 'eucharist' is in the original Greek New Testament, and is used by Jesus at the Last Supper.", *Aleteia*, June 15 2022, aleteia.org/2022/06/15/is-the-word-eucharist-in-the-bible.

Lewis, Charlton T., and Charles Short. *A Latin Dictionary.* Oxford: Clarendon Press. 1879.

Licursi, Arthur J. "Gethsemane and the Kidron Valley," n.d. https://artlicursi.com/articles/gethsemane-and-kidron-valley.

Malaspina, Giovanni. "Gethsemane: the Most Precious Blood of Jesus." *Custodia Terrae Sanctae: Franciscans serving the Holy Land*, July 1, 2019. https://www.custodia.org/en/news/gethsemane-most-precious-blood-jesus/.

Mar Julios, Abraham, 2017. "Confession of Faith, Eucharist and Martyrdom." *Homilitic & Pastoral Review*, September 27, 2017. https://www.hprweb.com/2017/09/confession-of-faith-eucharist-and-martyrdom/.

Marie, André. "Saint Maximus the Confessor, Saint Thomas Aquinas, and Christ's Two Wills", Catholicism.org, November 14, 2007. catholicism.org/saint-maximus-the-confessor-saint-thomas-aquinas-and-christs-two-wills.html.

Mason, Mike. "The Rock of the Agony," May 23, 2016. https://www.mikemasonbooks.com/the-rock-of-the-agony-chapter-51-of-jesus-his-story-in-stone/.

McBrien, Robert P. *The Harpercollins Encyclopedia of Catholicism.* San Francisco, CA: HarperSanFrancisco, 1995.

Miller, Dave. "Hematidrosis: Did Jesus Sweat Blood?", *Apologetics Press*, July 2017. apologeticspress.org/hematidrosis-did-jesus-sweat-blood-5436/.

Miska, Rhonda. "What is chrism?" *U.S. Catholic*, June 29, 2016. https://uscatholic.org/articles/201606/what-is-chrism/.

More, Thomas. 'The Valencia Manuscript", in *Complete Works of St. Thomas More, Volume 14, Part I, De Tristitia Christi.* Edited by Clarence H. Miller. Connecticut: Yale University Press, 1976.
——.*The Sadness of Christ.* Oxford: Benediction Classics, 2008.

Moseley, Annabelle. *Sacred Braille: The Rosary as Masterpiece through Art, Poetry, and Reflections.* St. Louis, MO: En Route Media and Books, 2020.
——. "This classic devotion will bring Holy Thursday to your home", *Aleteia*, April 6, 2023. https://aleteia.org/2023/04/06/this-classic-devotion-will-bring-holy-thursday-to-your-home.

Most, William G. "The Sacrifice of the Mass," *Eternal Word Television Network*, n.d. https://www.ewtn.com/catholicism/teachings/sacrifice-of-the-mass-234.

My Olive Tree. "Guide to the History of the Kidron Valley." November 28, 2017. https://www.myolivetree.com/kidron-valley-guide/.

Murphy-O'Connor, Jerome. "What Really Happened at Gethsemane?", April 1998, *Bible Review.* https://library.biblicalarchaeology.org/article/what-really-happened-at-gethsemane/.

O'Dea, Frank. "Eucharistic Prayer II," *Eucharist: The Basic Spirituality*, n.d. https://theeucharist.wordpress.com/index/appendix-of-eucharistic-prayers/eucharistic-prayer-ii/.

Our Catholic Faith. "Mass – Eucharistic Prayers," *Our Catholic Faith.* https://ourcatholicfaith.org/mass/eucharisticprayers.html.

Pio, Padre. *The Agony of Jesus*. North Carolina: Tan Books, 1992.

Piper, John. "The Greatest Prayer in the World: Maundy Thursday," *Desiring God,* April 17, 2014. https://www.desiringgod.org/articles/the-greatest-prayer-in-the-world/.

Pitre, Brant. *Jesus and the Jewish Roots of the Eucharist.* New York: Doubleday, 2011.

Quinn, Jon W. "Peter, James, and John," *The Front Page,* August 2016. https://bible.ca/ef/topical-peter-james-john.htm.

Rodriguez, Placido. "Homily Bishop Rodriguez Garden of Gethsemane 01 22 2018." *USCCB*, January 22, 2018. https://www.usccb.org/resources/homily-bishop-rodriguez-garden-gethsemane-01-22-2018/.

Rudd, Steve."East orientation of Jewish temples and altars." https://bible.ca/archeology/bible-archeology-jerusalem-temple-mount-east-orientation-jewish-temples-altars.htm.

Saunders, William. "The Use of Sacramental Oils," *Catholic Education Resource Center*, n.d. https://www.catholiceducation.org/en/culture/catholic-contributions/the-use-of-sacramental-oils.html.
——."The Symbolism of the Pelican," *Catholic Education Resource Center*, n.d. https://www.catholiceducation.org/en/culture/catholic-contributions/the-symbolism-of-the-pelican.html/.

Shonk, Charles. excerpt from "A Pale Light", *Dominican Friars Foundation*, n.d. https://dominicanfriars.org/bl-john-fiesole-fra-angelico/.

Siri, Joseph. *Gethsemane: Reflections on the Contemporary Theological Movement.* Chicago, IL: Franciscan Herald Press, 1981.

Smith, Gregory A. "Just one-third of U.S. Catholics agree with their church that Eucharist is body, blood of Christ," *Pew Research Center*, August 5, 2019. https://www.pewresearch.org/short-reads/2019/08/05/transubstantiation-eucharist-u-s-catholics/.

Socratic Method, "Samuel Taylor Coleridge: 'Friendship is a sheltering tree.'" *Socratic Method*, November 2023. https://www.socratic-method.com/quote-meanings/samuel-taylor-coleridge-friendship-is-a-sheltering-tree.

Southern, Randy, Christopher D. Hudson, and Selena Sarns. *Sacred Places of the Bible.* New York: Time Home Entertainment, 2013.

Sri, Edward. "The Supper of the Lamb," *Catholic Education Resource Center*, October 28, 2011. https://www.catholiceducation.org/en/culture/catholic-contributions/the-supper-of-the-lamb.html.

Stanley, David M. *Jesus in Gethsemane: The Early Church Reflects on the Suffering of Jesus.* New York: Paulist Press, 1980.

Staudinger, Josef. *Holiness of the Priesthood*, translated by John J. Coyne. Westminster, MD: 1960, The Newman Press.

Stein, Jacob. "The Historical Origins of Veronica's Veil: Inside the Cloth Relic of Jesus' Holy Face Wiped on Calvary," *EWTN Vatican*, March 25, 2024. https://www.ewtnvatican.com/articles/historical-origins-of-veronicas-veil-inside-the-cloth-relic-of-jesus-holy-face-wiped-on-calvary-2357.

Taylor, Chris, and Jennifer Taylor. "Jesus Crosses the Kidron Valley", *The Bible Journey*, n.d., https://thebiblejourney.org/biblejourney1/6-jesuss-last-journey-to-jerusalem/jesus-crosses-the-kidron-valley/

Tesniere, Albert. *The Eucharistic Heart of Jesus: Readings for the Month of June.* New York: Fathers of the Blessed Sacrament, 1908.

Thomas, John Paul. *Lessons from St. Therese: The Wisdom of God's Little Flower.* 2017, My Catholic Life!. https://mycatholic.life/books/lessons-saint-therese-wisdom-gods-little-flower/chapter-four-first-communion-confirmation/.

Tofari, Louis J. "St. Francis of Assisi and the Roman Liturgy," *Catholic Family News*, November 8, 2018. https://catholicfamilynews.com/blog/2018/11/08/2018-11-8-st-francis-of-assisi-and-the-roman-liturgy/.

de Vaan, Michiel. *Etymological Dictionary of Latin and the other Italic Languages.* Leiden, Boston: Brill, 2016.

Van Linden, Philip. *The Gospel According to Mark.* Collegesville, MN: The Liturgical Press, 1991.

Vasile Mihoc, "The Messianic Prophecies of the Old Testament", in *Das Alte Testament als christliche Bibel in orthodoxer und westlicher Sicht,* edited by Dmitrov, Ivan, Niebuhr, Karl-Wilhelm, and Dunn, James D. G., Tübingen: Mohr Siebeck,2004.

Winters, Jaimie Julia. "Priests revive traditional gifts of cloth to mothers," *Jersey Catholic,* June 23, 2023. https://jerseycatholic.org/priests-revive-traditional-gifts-of-cloth-to-mothers-1.

Wordnik, "Eucharistic", *Wordnik*, n.d., www.wordnik.com/words/eucharistic.

ALSO BY ANNABELLE MOSELEY

Sacred Braille: The Rosary as Masterpiece through Art, Poetry, and Reflections – This book has the Imprimatur and Nihil Obstat.

"Not unlike De Montford's The Secrets of the Rosary, Moseley's book seems destined to become a classic, and is an essential addition to every public and private Catholic library." –Jayson Brunelle

Our House of the Sacred Heart: A Litany of Stories with Art, Prayers, Poetry, and Reflections toward Consecration to the Sacred Heart – Winner of a 2022 Catholic Media Association Award

"Annabelle Moseley's Our House of the Sacred Heart is not simply good Catholic theology of the Sacred Heart but a work of art that raises the reader into the summum bonum of truth, beauty, and goodness." — Matt Fradd

Awake with Christ: Living the Catholic Holy Hour in Your Home – Winner of two 2024 Catholic Media Association Awards.

"What a moving and delightful book! Annabelle Moseley shows us how to stay awake with Jesus in the Garden of Gethsemane, to console Him, to give him our own loneliness and abandonment, to be replaced by lasting peace and joy. Awake with Christ is replete with powerful insights from Scripture, from well-known and lesser-known saints, with beautiful poetic prayers to Christ, and explicit guidance for adults and for children on how to make Holy Hours within our own homes. Abounding in beautiful garden metaphors that should make spiritual (if not literal) gardeners of us all, as we grow in our love for the Master Gardener." —Kevin Vost, Psy.D.

About the Author

Dr. Annabelle Moseley is a Third Order Carmelite, Professor of Theology, and Catholic author. Her award-winning books include **Awake with Christ: Living the Catholic Holy Hour in Your Home**, which has received First Place at the 2024 Catholic Media Awards; **Sacred Braille: The Rosary as Masterpiece**, which received the Imprimatur; and **Our House of the Sacred Heart**, which won a 2022 Catholic Media Award. She is the founder of CatholicHolyHour which sends guided at-home Holy Hours to thousands of members worldwide, helping them watch and pray with Jesus of Gethsemane. She is an acclaimed and widely-published poet, the inventor of the mirror sonnet, and the 2014 Long Island Poet of the Year. Annabelle's greatest blessing is her family. She lives on Long Island with her husband and children in the domestic church they hone together.

Visit **www.catholicholyhour.com** and sign up for free for the First Thursday of the Month club to receive monthly guided at-home Holy Hours dedicated to Jesus of Gethsemane.

www.ingramcontent.com/pod-product-compliance
Lightning Source LLC
Chambersburg PA
CBHW060003100426
42740CB00010B/1379